The Politics of Citizenship in Immigrant Democracies

I0084470

This book brings together scholars from various disciplines to explore current issues and trends in the rethinking of migration and citizenship from the perspective of three major immigrant democracies – Australia, Canada, and the United States. These countries share a history of pronounced immigration and emigration, extensive experience with diasporic and mobile communities, and with integrating culturally diverse populations. They also share an approach to automatic citizenship based on the principle of *jus soli* (as opposed to the traditionally common *jus sanguinis* of continental Europe), and a comparatively open attitude towards naturalization. Some of these characteristics are now under pressure due to the 'restrictive turn' in citizenship and migration worldwide.

This volume explores the significance of political structures, political agents and political culture in shaping processes of inclusion and exclusion in these diverse societies. This book was originally published as a special issue of *Citizenship Studies*.

Geoffrey Brahm Levey is an Australian Research Council Future Fellow and Associate Professor in Political Science at the University of New South Wales, Sydney, Australia.

Ayelet Shacher is Professor of Law and Political Science at the University of Toronto, Canada, where she holds the Canada Research Chair in Citizenship and Multiculturalism.

The Politics of Citizenship in Immigrant Democracies

The Experience of the United States, Canada and Australia

Edited by
**Geoffrey Brahm Leyey and
Ayelet Shachar**

Routledge
Taylor & Francis Group

LONDON AND NEW YORK

First published 2015
by Routledge
2 Park Square, Milton Park, Abingdon, Oxfordshire OX14 4RN

and by Routledge
711 Third Avenue, New York, NY 10017, USA

First issued in paperback 2017

Routledge is an imprint of the Taylor & Francis Group, an informa business

© 2015 Taylor & Francis

All rights reserved. No part of this book may be reprinted or reproduced
or utilised in any form or by any electronic, mechanical, or other means,
now known or hereafter invented, including photocopying and recording,
or in any information storage or retrieval system, without permission in
writing from the publishers.

Trademark notice: Product or corporate names may be trademarks or
registered trademarks, and are used only for identification and
explanation without intent to infringe.

British Library Cataloguing in Publication Data
A catalogue record for this book is available from the British Library

ISBN 13: 978-1-138-05798-2 (pbk)
ISBN 13: 978-1-138-88624-7 (hbk)

Typeset in Times New Roman
by RefineCatch Limited, Bungay, Suffolk

Publisher's Note
The publisher accepts responsibility for any inconsistencies that may have
arisen during the conversion of this book from journal articles to book chapters,
namely the possible inclusion of journal terminology.

Disclaimer
Every effort has been made to contact copyright holders for their permission to
reprint material in this book. The publishers would be grateful to hear from any
copyright holder who is not here acknowledged and will undertake to rectify
any errors or omissions in future editions of this book.

Contents

Citation Information

The chapters in this book were originally published in *Citizenship Studies*, volume 18, issue 2 (April 2014). When citing this material, please use the original page numbering for each article, as follows:

Chapter 1: Introduction
Citizenship and the 'right to have rights'
Ayelet Shachar
Citizenship Studies, volume 18, issue 2 (April 2014) pp. 114–124

Chapter 2
Political incorporation in America: immigrant partisans
Nancy L. Rosenblum and Andrea Tivig
Citizenship Studies, volume 18, issue 2 (April 2014) pp. 125–140

Chapter 3
Less than the sum of its parts: institutional realities and legal aspirations in early twenty-first century American immigration
Mariano-Florentino Cuéllar
Citizenship Studies, volume 18, issue 2 (April 2014) pp. 141–159

Chapter 4
Laissez-faire and its discontents: US naturalization and integration policy in comparative perspective
Noah Pickus
Citizenship Studies, volume 18, issue 2 (April 2014) pp. 160–174

Chapter 5
Liberal nationalism and the Australian citizenship tests
Geoffrey Brahm Levey
Citizenship Studies, volume 18, issue 2 (April 2014) pp. 175–189

Chapter 6
International migration at a crossroads
Stephen Castles
Citizenship Studies, volume 18, issue 2 (April 2014) pp. 190–207

Chapter 7

Faces of globalization and the borders of states: from asylum seekers to citizens
Paul James
Citizenship Studies, volume 18, issue 2 (April 2014) pp. 208–223

Chapter 8

The ideology of temporary labour migration in the post-global era
Catherine Dauvergne and Sarah Marsden
Citizenship Studies, volume 18, issue 2 (April 2014) pp. 224–242

Please direct any queries you may have about the citations to
clsuk.permissions@cengage.com

Notes on Contributors

Stephen Castles is Research Chair in Sociology at the University of Sydney, Australia. He is a sociologist and political economist, and works on international migration dynamics, global governance, multiculturalism, transnationalism, migration and development, and regional migration trends in Africa, Asia and Europe. His research and publications have made an influential contribution to the development of interdisciplinary migration research for many years.

Mariano-Florentino Cuéllar is Stanley Morrison Professor of Law and Director of the Freeman Spogli Institute for International Studies at Stanford University, California, USA. He teaches and writes primarily about administrative, criminal, and international law, and has additional interests in public organizations, legislation, public health law, and immigration and citizenship.

Catherine Dauvergne is a Professor in the Faculty of Law at the University of British Columbia, Vancouver, Canada. She works in the area of immigration and refugee law in Canada and around the world. Her research is grounded in a belief that how we define and police the boundaries of our societies determines the terrain of our political engagements and says much about our national identity. She believes that border laws are a space of unabashed discrimination, where aspirations of nationhood are writ large.

Paul James is Professor in the Institute for Culture and Society at the University of Western Sydney, Australia, Honorary Professor of Globalization and Cultural Diversity in RMIT's Globalism's Research Centre in Melbourne, Australia, Honorary Professor at King's College London, on the Council of the Institute of Postcolonial Studies, and a Fellow of the Royal Society of the Arts (London). He is author or editor of 31 books including most importantly, *Nation Formation* (Sage, 1996) and *Globalism, Nationalism, Tribalism* (Sage, 2006). His other recent books include *Sustainable Development, Sustainable Communities* (University of Hawaii Press, 2012) and 16 volumes mapping the field of globalization (Sage, 2006–2014).

Geoffrey Brahm Levey is an Australian Research Council Future Fellow and Associate Professor in Political Science at the University of New South Wales, Sydney, Australia. His recent publications include, as editor, *Authenticity, Autonomy and Multiculturalism* (2015), *Political Theory and Australian Multiculturalism* (2012, 2008), and *Secularism, Religion and Multicultural Citizenship* (with Tariq Modood, 2008).

Sarah Marsden recently completed her Ph.D. in Law at the University of British Columbia, Vancouver, Canada. Her studies focused on temporary and undocumented labour migration, in Canada and as a global phenomenon, drawing on scholarship in law, sociology, geography, and history. She is interested in documenting the impact of governance and regulatory structures on migrant workers, particularly with regard to rights and membership in the host state.

Noah Pickus is Director of the Kenan Institute for Ethics and Associate Research Professor of Public Policy Studies at Duke University, Durham, NC, USA. He co-directs the Brookings-Duke Immigration Policy Roundtable and is the author of *True Faith and Allegiance: Immigration and American Civic Nationalism, Becoming American/America Becoming*, and *Immigration and Citizenship in the 21st Century*.

Nancy L. Rosenblum is the Senator Joseph Clark Professor of Ethics in Politics and Government at Harvard University, Cambridge, MA, USA. Her field of research is political theory, both historical and contemporary political thought. Her book, *On the Side of the Angels: An Appreciation of Parties and Partisanship*, was published in 2008.

Ayelet Shachar is Canada Research Chair in Citizenship and Multiculturalism, and Professor of Law, Political Science, and Global Affairs at the University of Toronto, Canada. She is the author of *Multicultural Jurisdictions: Cultural Differences and Women's Rights*, and *The Birthright Lottery: Citizenship and Global Inequality*. She is currently completing a new book, *Olympic Citizenship: Migration and the Global Race for Talent*.

Andrea Tivig recently received her PhD in Political Theory at Harvard University, Cambridge, MA, USA, completing a dissertation on the freedom of movement within and across state borders. She is presently a Lecturer on Social Studies at Harvard. Her research interests lie in contemporary political theory, especially democratic theory and cosmopolitanism.

Preface

This book brings together scholars from various disciplines to explore current issues and trends in the rethinking of migration and citizenship from the perspective of major immigrant democracies – Australia, Canada, and the United States. These countries share, among other things, a history of pronounced immigration and emigration, extensive experience with diasporic and mobile communities and with integrating culturally diverse populations, an approach to automatic citizenship based on the principle of *jus soli* (as against *jus sanguinis*, as is traditionally common in continental Europe), and a comparatively open attitude toward naturalization. As such, they stand, in some ways, as harbingers of how globalization may reshape citizenship and migration elsewhere.

The initial spur for these essays was a conference sponsored by Harvard University's Committee on Australian Studies held in Sydney at the University of New South Wales. We are grateful to the Committee for its generous support. Other sponsors of the conference included the Australian Government's Department of Immigration and Citizenship, the Canada Research Chair in Citizenship and Multiculturalism, UNSW's Faculty of Arts and Social Sciences, and the UNSW Law School's Centre for Interdisciplinary Studies of Law. We record our sincere thanks to these bodies as well for enabling the event. Many people contributed to the success of the conference in both a scholarly and support capacity. As it would be invidious to single out names here, we offer a collective note of appreciation. Thanks are due also to our anonymous referees.

Geoffrey Brahm Levey
Ayelet Shachar

Introduction: Citizenship and the 'right to have rights'

Ayelet Shachar

Faculty of Law, Department of Political Science & Munk School of Global Affairs, University of Toronto, Canada

With all the talk about the growing ease of human mobility across borders, if Martians landed on Earth, they might believe that immigration is unrestricted and open to all. Alas, the harsh reality is that not everyone who wishes to leave his or her country of origin will be able to lawfully enter a desired destination country. Barriers to human mobility are still significant and multifaceted. That is not to say, however, that these barriers are equally distributed globally. Passport holders of the European countries that comprise the border-free Schengen Area, and authorized international visitors enjoy freedom of mobility within the free-zone area, which covers more than 4 million square kilometers and has a population of more than 400 million people. Citizens of other countries that benefit from various bilateral and multilateral visa-waiver programs can also anticipate welcome mats awaiting them in many destinations. Things look quite different, however, for the vast majority of the world's population, in particular the countless people locked – by chance, and not choice – in the world's poorer or less stable regions, who face significant, sometimes insurmountable, obstacles to lawful entry into the promised lands of immigration (Castles and Miller 2009; Gamlen and Marsh 2011; Milanovic 2011; Neumayer 2006; Shachar 2009).

A crucial task for contemporary scholars of migration and citizenship is to identify the political, institutional, and ideological conditions that define, reify, or unsettle the boundary between inclusion and exclusion, a boundary that bears dramatic consequences for individuals and political communities everywhere (including the classic immigrant democracies – Australia, Canada, and the USA), and that forms the focus of this special issue of *Citizenship Studies*. Writing in the aftermath of the human rights atrocities visited on millions in the interwar period and during the Second World War, Hannah Arendt came to see citizenship, the right to belong to some kind of an organized community, as foundational, as the 'right to have rights' – the bedrock for fulfilling and protecting our otherwise abstracted human rights (Arendt 1968 [1951], 177; Benhabib 2011).[1] For this reason, observed Arendt, sovereignty 'is nowhere more absolute than in matters of "emigration, naturalization, nationality, and expulsion"'(Arendt 1968 [1951], 278). How to address the potential contradiction between the sovereign power to exclude and the human need for inclusion in a political community that treats us as equal and worthy of respect and dignity is a perennial dilemma.

Although impressive progress has been made in the development of human rights both globally and regionally since the Second World War, our basic right to have rights remains deeply fragile and insecure so long as we can be deprived of membership in an organized political community. The emergence of fragmented and transnational variants of political membership raises additional questions, as yet unresolved, including the question of *which* political community ought to be responsible for ensuring that our basic right to have rights is fulfilled. Should this responsibility lie with the country of origin, or does the destination society implicitly take on an obligation to its long-term-resident noncitizens, even if they were not invited? If the latter, at what point does the commitment formalize, and under what conditions? Such questions of inclusion and exclusion are vital, especially in the diverse, liberal, immigrant democracies at the heart of this special issue of *Citizenship Studies* – of which Australia, Canada, and the USA are prime exemplars.

Given that control over borders and the regulation of migration entail the exercise of power and authority (primarily but not exclusively by statist activities), in which the line between inclusion and exclusion is constantly determined by the interaction between human agency and legal categories, the essays in this special issue seek to refocus the gaze of scholars, policy-makers, and activists onto the crucial role played by political structures, institutions, and the multifaceted set of agencies that constitute the modern regulatory environment in shaping and implementing citizenship and naturalization policies.

In immigrant democracies, such policies do not arise out of thin air. They are influenced by the preferences of domestic voters and elites, by interjurisdictional pressures and international norms, and by new facts that emerge on the ground. Consider the estimated 11 million undocumented migrants residing in the USA. These migrants have already become *de facto* members of that country's society and economy. However, they will only receive a shot at *de jure* citizenship if a grand political bargain is struck that leads to legislation permitting their regularization. Nothing short of this would do to release them from the harsh reality of a life in the shadows and on the margins; nothing else would undo the democratic injustice of having people in our midst who, as Michael Walzer (1983, 59) powerfully put it in another context, 'resemble citizens in every respect that counts in the host society, but are nevertheless barred from citizenship'.

In today's world, one of the most significant developments is that membership has become multifaceted, in that people consider themselves members of several different communities – local, national, and supranational. Despite this, it is not time to bid citizenship farewell. Millions of people are now on the move, but many of them will experience firsthand the effects of increasingly complex international migration trends – the 'new mobility'—in which cross-border 'traffic [flows] in more directions than one for different purposes, subject to different rules and regulations and affecting more and more people' (Aldana et al. 2013, 3). Many will not fit in the traditional image of an immigrant as a citizen-in-the-making (Motomura 2006). Instead, while seeking to attract the new breed of 'desired' international migrants – the highly skilled – as part of a dynamic global race for talent, destination countries (along with some sending countries) have pointed to economic and development-based rationales to justify temporary migration programs. These programs are designed to attract labor migrants who fit the (often pejorative) definition of 'low-skilled workers', including those providing services in agriculture, construction, care work, and the like. As the name indicates, *temporary* migration programs give migrant workers an invitation to the recipient country on the condition that they return to their country of origin at the end of a specified visa period. So long as the regulation of human mobility across borders essentially remains a sovereign prerogative, people who cross borders without authorization, some out of sheer desperation, as a result of human rights violations, forced migration, or a desire to make a better life for themselves and their families, act in breach of states' sovereign authority to regulate and control borders and admission priorities. Even if they make it into the interior of desired destination countries, they fall outside the standard incorporation regime for newcomers.

These developments are significantly reshaping our understanding of membership and its shifting boundaries. While it still operates as one of the foundational governing norms of the current interstate system, both the concept and practice of citizenship are being rethought and undergoing significant change. The extent of globalization processes remains contested, but it is undoubted that internationalized markets, multidirectional migration flows, the emergence of instantaneous communication across borders, and the impact of remittances, transnational investments, and cross-border security threats all underscore the economic, social, and political interconnectedness of today's world. These factors are now influencing people's ideas and expectations of human rights, mobility, and citizenship.

Reemerging and conflicting dynamics of globalization and protectionism in the developed countries of Europe, North America, and the Antipodes reveal yet another variant of the friction between inclusion and exclusion, here manifesting itself as a tension between universal liberal and democratic values, on the one hand, and commitment to particular national cultures and political communities on the other. As a result, notions of postnational, global, and cosmopolitan citizenship – which would seem to lend weight to the importance of international human rights institutions – sit uneasily alongside national citizenship and language tests for new immigrants and other statist measures designed to protect 'shared values' and cohesion in the wake of globalizing pressures and (real or imagined) loss of control over borders. Fierce debates about 'who belongs' to the political community and according to what criteria have erupted in recent years not only in the traditional nation-states of Europe but also in the heartland of the classic immigrant democracies – including Australia, Canada, and the USA – revealing multifaceted and at times contradictory trends.

These complex developments raise a number of pressing questions, which in turn form the focus of this special issue. Our goal is to broaden the analysis beyond the now well-traveled terrain of exploring cultural and religious diversity within immigrant democracies. We do so by canvassing contemporary challenges that broadly fall into two clusters. The first is *The Politics of Immigration in the Domestic Arena*. Here we ask: How might political partisanship contribute to the incorporation of immigrants? What role do public agencies and regulators play in shaping the boundaries of membership, and how do they interact with the variety of constituents at the intersection of law, politics, and organization? How demanding should naturalization procedures be in immigrant-receiving societies, and do they reveal distinctive national political cultures or convergence to more universalized standards? The second cluster is *The (In)Security of Migrants in Today's Volatile Global Environment.* Questions considered here include: What are the effects of the global economic crisis on cross-border mobility, remittances and the human security of migrants? What is the impact of the increased global migration of women on the (in)security of migrants and concerns about inbuilt inequalities and structural vulnerability? The securitization of citizenship has led to a mushrooming of enforcement and homeland security measures, and to the introduction and routine use of highly sophisticated techniques of extraterritorial immigration regulation designed to manage global flows of people – all of which raises significant human rights concerns (Nyers 2009; Ryan and Mitsilegas 2010; Shachar 2007). Can this new and more amorphous frontier of a 'shifting border' of immigration control and regulation be brought under check, and, if so, how, and by whom? What are the implications for citizenship and membership of the revival of temporary labor migration programs? Such programs effect a conceptual shift from the traditional emphasis on membership ties toward short-term market relations; the long-term implications of this for citizenship may be dramatic and erosive. These changing techniques and priorities of migration selection and control are only compounded by the imposition of greater restrictions and tighter naturalization requirements *post*admission, making full membership in a well-off society a pipedream for many of those who may wish for it, or need it, the most.

Like the rumors of Mark Twain's death, vogue predictions about the ultimate demise of borders and membership boundaries have been greatly exaggerated. The contributions within offer fresh perspectives and new ideas at a time when they are urgently needed.

The politics of immigration in the domestic arena

The first four essays in this special issue focus on the domestic arena of immigration politics. They examine different pathways and mechanisms for incorporating immigrants who have set down roots in a destination country but are not yet its citizens. Nancy Rosenblum and Andrea Tivig argue that while significant attention has been paid in recent years to the magnitude and importance of protest politics and grassroots migrant social movements (Cabrera 2008; Isin and Nielsen 2008; Isin, 2012; Nyers and Rygiel, 2012; Tyler and Marciniak 2013), there has been relatively little discussion of the key role that established political parties can, do, and, in their view, should play in facilitating the political inclusion of immigrants into their new home communities. Focusing on the USA, Rosenblum and Tivig argue forcefully that political participation through established and institutionalized channels bears both moral and symbolic significance. In particular, building on Judith Shklar's work, they emphasize that citizenship entails a public 'standing' and a moral register that comes with both recognition and respect. In the USA, this standing brings with it a democratic capacity to engage in the political system. While acknowledging the importance of various forms of political protest and advocacy, Rosenblum and Tivig still view participation through organized – and unabashedly partisan – channels of political membership as the 'gold standard' for immigrant incorporation, one that can lead to electoral success and the mobilization of political resources. In America's *laissez-faire* and decentralized environment, they argue, partisan political identification gains additional instrumental importance. It provides a channel for promoting immigrants' distinctive voices and interests, as well as access to positions of power at all levels of government. Partisan participation, conclude Rosenblum and Tivig, holds the promise of earning immigrants their due recognition as citizens-in-the-making.

Drawing upon his scholarly and practical experience at the White House Domestic Policy Council, where he served as Special Assistant to the President for Justice and Regulatory Policy, Mariano-Florentino Cuéllar is interested in whether the whole of America's complex multiple-agency structure for shaping and implementing immigration policy is greater than the sum of its parts. His observations paint a picture of a rather dysfunctional system, where the problems are compounded by path dependency patterns and a vested interest in the status quo. In Cuéllar's opinion, this leads to a somewhat chaotic and uncoordinated situation where the whole is *less* than the sum of its parts, causing system stagnation and an erosion of rights, which in turn makes reform and progress harder to achieve. Cuéllar's analysis is particularly valuable in that it moves beyond aspirational slogans to examine, with a critical eye, the potential for fair compromises that generate new answers to old questions, in particular the question of who will be part of the nation and according to what criteria. Resisting easy prescriptions, Cuéllar reminds us that in a complex regulatory state with strong regional and local political demands, there will always be multiple hands influencing immigration policy, even if control of immigration is formally a federal responsibility (as in the USA). These include lawmakers and executive branches, courts, various agencies with different goals and priorities, state and local authorities, and the public. Under such conditions of fragmentation, relying on party politics (echoing Rosenblum and Tivig) and accounting for demographic changes that amplify the significance of securing votes from newly minted immigrants-turned-citizens may prove important for achieving a new grand bargain on immigration after decades of polarizing and bitter stagnancy.

The tension between inclusion and exclusion of newcomers is perhaps nowhere more detectable than in the recurrent debates about citizenship tests and naturalization requirements. These tests have gained momentum across Europe as part of a retreat from multiculturalism and the advance in its stead of concepts such as 'shared values' and 'civic integration', however elusive these terms remain (Etzioni 2007; Hansen 2010; Orgad 2010). Those not born as members who wish to obtain the security and dignity associated with the basic right to have rights must seek naturalization (from *nasci*, Latin, the etymological root of 'to be born'); they must prove their 'worthiness' of the ultimate prize of membership. Declarations that multiculturalism has failed and anxieties about immigrants and immigration are not at all uncommon, especially in Europe, where they have revealed a dark underbelly characterized by renewed fear of the 'Other'. As Christian Joppke observes, the new citizenship tests in Europe are characterized not just by restrictiveness, which remains paramount, and also by the 'fusion of immigration control with immigration integration concerns' (2013, 3). In the Netherlands, to provide an extreme example, civic integration tests are now given to potential visa applicants in their country of origin, *before* they even set foot on the Dutch soil. Germany requires 600–800 h of language instruction and civic integration classes, and has been criticized for earlier *Land*-based variants of the citizenship test that sought to 'pierce' the inner belief system of the applicant to determine whether she is a fitting new citizen, an approach condemned as illiberal and coercive, as well as designed to 'weed out the undeserving' (Joppke 2013; Orgad 2010). France, which takes great pride in its civic-republican tradition, has seen its *Conseil d'État* uphold a denial of naturalization to a *niqab*-wearing Muslim woman who spoke French, was married to a French citizen, and had three French children, because her cultural and religious 'differences' made her, in the eyes of the state, 'unassimilable' to the French society. These differences were evidenced by her limited knowledge of the semisacred principle of *laïcité* (public secularism), as well as by her reclusive and domestic-centered family life, which was seen by the *Conseil* as a sign of both submission to the male figures in her family and a lack of assimilation with the French *communauté*. This is an ironic reversal of the feminist emancipatory slogan 'personal is political' – here providing excuse for a state heavy handedly to determine whether a woman ought to qualify as a citizen. This decision ultimately left the (immigrant) wife in a dependent position vis-à-vis her (citizen) husband and without the empowerment associated with a direct and independent bond between the state and the individual. This is a position of vulnerability all too familiar to generations of women and racial minorities who have been excluded from full and equal inclusion in the ranks of citizenship.

Against this backdrop, Noah Pickus considers the oldest and most established variant of citizenship tests and naturalization requirements – those practiced in the USA. Citizenship and literacy tests were introduced there by federal legislation in the early twentieth century in response to populist demands to curb 'unwanted' migration.

Counter-intuitively, Pickus argues that because the USA has long been conducting (and debating) citizenship tests as part of its naturalization process, there is relatively little appetite to stiffen these tests, as is the current trend in Europe, or to revive programs that 'Americanize' new immigrants. In Pickus' view, courts in America, having already addressed and revisited the issues currently prompting a soul searching in Europe, have concluded that they cannot assess an applicant's interior state of mind, and therefore that any contemporary attempt to create a 'confessional state' apparatus at naturalization will fail. All that can be asked is that the applicant recognizes the admitting society's constitutional values as a proxy for his or her attachment to that society. Attempts to stiffen the requirements have been met with opposition and assailed as discriminatory and exclusionary. Pickus also observes that standardized citizenship tests are inevitably limited vehicles for capturing processes of transformation and attachment to a new country that are inescapably nuanced, multilayered, and individualized, and that occur over time and through interaction with others. This is a crucial point, and one that often gets lost in the current high-stakes debates about migration, incorporation, and naturalization. As a Canadian judge once observed, shared citizenship is experienced as a *practice* of 'rubbing elbows' with others in everyday locations, such as 'shopping malls, corner stores, libraries, concert halls, auto repair shops, pubs, cabarets, elevators, churches, synagogues, mosques and temples – in a word wherever one can meet and converse with [other citizens]'. Not everyone will go to a pub or enter a temple, but the gist of the argument is unambiguous and the direction inclusive. The mutually constitutive experience of membership, for both newcomers and established populations, cannot be fully captured by a top-down governmental policy that tries to squeeze its essentials into a fixed formula as if placing a jinn into a bottle.

Ultimately, however, Pickus laments the overtly *laissez-faire* philosophy adopted by the USA, according to which the country admits large numbers of immigrants without much attention to skills or linguistic ability and then expects these newcomers to integrate quickly without significant government assistance.[2] The gaps and uncertainties created by this system, he argues, are partly to blame for the vitriolic conflicts over immigration that are now waged at the local, state, and federal levels. Much as Cuéllar and Rosenblum and Tivig search for political agents that can help transform immigrants into equal members, Pickus believes this can be done in part by clarifying the 'bargain' of mutual expectations between newcomers and citizens.

Similar pressures are also present in Canada and Australia. In Canada, the revised 2010 version of the citizenship test places greater emphasis on nation building and reiterates the country's vision of diversity (which it aims to promote along multiple lines: linguistic, regional, ethnic, national, religious, and so on) while simultaneously making explicit its commitment to other constitutional values such as gender equality. A brewing legal controversy, which may test the balance between diversity and inclusion in the months and years to come, stems from a little-known executive order by Canada's Minister of Citizenship and Immigration to prohibit face-covering women from taking the citizenship oath without revealing their face; a decision that has yet to be challenged before the courts (Shachar, 2013). Australia, which in 2007 became the last English-speaking 'new world' society to introduce such a citizenship test, now emphasizes in its test that access to full membership and equal citizenship is a privilege, not a right. In Australia, citizens-to-be are required to take a pledge as part of their citizenship ceremony, in which applicants must declare not only that they respect democratic institutions but also that they share democratic beliefs. This blurs the line between action and belief, and informs Geoffrey Brahm Levey's analysis of the multiple tensions reflected in Australia's citizenship test. Levey argues that binary categorizations that sharply distinguish between 'civic' and 'national-cultural' conceptions of membership do not capture the subtlety of political arrangements in an immigrant democracy like Australia, and arguably, Canada as well, in which questions of collective identity remain prevalent but take on a unique amalgam of civic, liberal, *and* cultural-national ingredients through a type of political architecture. He thus challenges the notion of a 'flatting world' of citizenship tests, arguing instead that there are still distinctive features of each country's own political balance of civic, liberal, and national commitments in generating and sustaining social cohesion, a sense of belonging, and a commitment to the commonweal.

Like Pickus, Levey holds that citizenship tests are legitimate, so long as they avoid inquiring into the 'inner disposition' or personal beliefs of applicants. As public rites of passage into a new political community, he accepts that citizenship tests provide an opportunity to foster shared aspects of membership, such as language competency, knowledge of civic norms and governing institutions, and perhaps also something of the history of how the nation concerned became an immigrant-receiving democracy. Even more so, it is the symbolic dimension of citizenship that Levey emphasizes. Human societies, he notes, have always marked major milestones with inductions and ceremony, and becoming a citizen, entering a new political community, is certainly a momentous milestone for both the individual involved and his or her adoptive society. The symbolism of citizenship tests and ceremonies can also resonate with those born as citizens in the nation. Levey points to the popularity of 'affirmation ceremonies' in Australia, in which born Australian citizens may, like their immigrant conationals, publicly affirm their loyalty and commitment to the country and its people.

The (in)security of migrants in today's volatile global environment

The second set of papers extends the focus to examine migration in a broader international context. In today's world, the level of connection between sending and receiving countries is increasing. The significance of temporary and circular migration is on the rise, and interdependence among peoples and regions is becoming paramount. These more dynamic and multidirectional processes arguably challenge the still-dominant, domestic-centered view of immigration manifested in the law and policy of the immigrant democracies under review here, according to which immigrants-becoming-citizens represents the ultimate success story.

Stephen Castles eloquently maps out these trends. He argues that the forces generating international migration are more powerful than ever before – but that the challenges are as well. Castles reminds us that while trade and other key aspects of cross-border flows are now subject to extensive international cooperation and global institutions such as the World Trade Organization, in the field of international migration global governance is 'conspicuous mainly for its absence'. Emphasizing a migrant-centered human security perspective, Castles reexamines the tension between inclusion and exclusion, highlighting the contradictions embedded in the current situation. Whereas globalization forces have led to greater international migration possibilities for many people, states have responded by attempting to maintain a tight grip over who may enter. They are directing tremendous resources to fortifying external border control measures (including the unprecedented use of new technologies such as unmanned drones and state-of-the-art surveillance equipment, as well as the creation of supranational 'border management' agencies, such as Frontex in Europe), while internally creating less hospitable conditions for those who have entered without permission or overstayed their visas.

In this new mobility era, some newcomers, especially the highly skilled, remain wanted and welcome, and are offered permanent settlement and eventually citizenship; for many other entrants, however, ranging from temporary to irregular migrants, from extended family members to asylum seekers, such opportunities are rare. The desire to 'manage' migration in the face of globalization, coupled with a preference for flexible migration programs, erodes the immigrant-to-citizen narrative, leading instead to the creation of many in-between categories, the members of which face risks to their human security and dignity. Castles laments the failure to place migrants' human rights at the center of states' migration policies, and does not believe that the clock can be turned back. If anything, he sees a potential for greater mobility of greater numbers of individuals from diverse backgrounds and source countries, including an increased number of female migrant workers who support their families back home and now constitute half the international migrant population (UN Population Fund 2010).

Ultimately, Castles calls for closer cooperation between governments in origin and destination countries, and for the establishment of regional and possibly global migration governance bodies and institutions. How to get from here to there is, alas, a major challenge. At present, immigration remains a preserve of national sovereignty: states, acting alone or in concert, continue to regulate borders in order to determine who may enter and who may not, just as they continue to define which noncitizen residents may stay only temporarily, which may be granted a permanent right to stay, and which may be forced to leave.

Paul James focuses his analysis on a particular category of migrants at risk – internationally displaced persons – in order to reveal an ethical predicament in which immigrant democracies are caught. On the one hand, countries such as Australia, Canada, and the USA pride themselves on playing a humanitarian role in the world and preach the importance of liberal democratic norms, human rights and the rule of law. At the same time, each of these countries has over the last few years hardened its border control and protection measures, creating complex rules to keep out uninvited migrants. In their massive effort to 'regain control', immigrant democracies threaten to breach their international and humanitarian obligations by failing to protect refugee and asylum seekers. Focusing on Australia, James seeks to uncover the maneuvers undertaken by a country that projects to its own population and the rest of the world the image of a 'good international citizen' while at the same time adopting practices that limit the ability of asylum seekers to reach its shores, even taking the extreme measure of erasing (through 'excision' legislation) some of its territory from the map for the purpose of preventing the legal entry into Australia of so-called boat people. Such developments, in Australia and elsewhere, make it close to impossible for most refugee and asylum seekers even to have the option to file protection claims in what were once the promised lands of migration; the latest United Nations High Commission for Refugees data show that approximately 80% of the world's refugees are now hosted by developing, not developed, countries. This abandonment of responsibility in the name of responding to domestic pressures or preventing the creation of incentives to 'draw in' opportunistic or unworthy protection seekers is the latest manifestation of how a legitimate power to draw boundaries can go terribly wrong.

James investigates how states make invisible the humanity, the fragility, and the very faces of those who seek refuge. This 'effacing' strategy curtails our compassion toward these strangers-in-need, engendering conditions that allow law-and-order agencies and politicians to describe refugees and asylum seekers as objects of risk that must be managed, contained and, increasingly, detained. To overcome this, James, like Castles, advocates delegating responsibility from states to regional and global institutions, although lessons from the common European asylum system and the breed of 'push back' dynamics and human rights dilemmas generated by bilateral and multilateral cooperation agreements may advise caution; switching the scale and level of authority by itself offers no panacea.

The contribution by Catherine Dauvergne and Sarah Mardsen concludes this special issue by offering an in-depth and critical analysis of the premises underlying the recent revival of temporary labor migration programs. Such temporary programs have become the *bonton* of migration policy-makers worldwide, and have been hailed as creating a 'win-win-win' matrix for migrants, the receiving countries' economies, and the sending countries' development goals. Dauvergne and Mardsen seek to expose the cracks in this framework, bringing back into the analysis the writings of Arendt, specifically her seminal *Human Condition*. They, too, adopt a migrant-centered approach, but they go a step further by challenging the ideological underpinning of the representation of labor markets within new migration discourses. They contemplate the opportunities for empowering temporary migrant workers through rights-based litigation while also identifying the limitations of such advocacy, which, as they see it, is caught by the same trap that Arendt enunciated so powerfully, namely, the difficulty in balancing the value of citizenship against the political community's right to exclude nonmembers as part of its sovereign prerogative. For vulnerable migrants of all kinds, fair access to rights protections holds the promise of emancipation and empowerment for the voiceless and powerless, and for this reason it remains an invaluable tool for change that lawyers and social activists will surely pursue in local, national and supranational *fora* – just as scholars of political power will emphasize political participation, scholars of the regulatory state will recommend administrative streamlining, and ethicists will advocate increased dialogue and clarification of the mutual expectations of migrant and settled populations.

None of these responses claims to be a cure-all. Each makes clear that much vigilance is required to address the deep tensions inherent in a system of sovereign self-governance and citizenship that still treats membership in some form of organized political community as a precondition for the basic 'right to have rights', and each acknowledges that citizenship itself – its scope, location, reach, and multiplicity – is constantly changing. The main lessons to be drawn from the current state of affairs in immigrant democracies is that people who are out of place remain extremely vulnerable, and that the proliferating 'in-between' categories must be closely monitored. These in-between categories undeniably offer new opportunities for mobility across borders in a world where permanent settlement leading to eventual citizenship (once the expected trajectory in immigrant democracies) is increasingly hard to secure for many in search of a better life. At present, those who fall into the precarious patterns of temporary migration are not yet offered adequate protections by their home countries, the receiving societies, or the international community (via its various human rights organs), all because of their intersectionist position as transnational workers and temporary residents in their host societies. Even under the most ideal conditions, their provisional and partial inclusion does not offer them anything comparable to the freedom and security that comes with full membership.

If the current immigration reform in the USA aligns with this complex map of global migration, we may witness the introduction of still more provisional membership categories. On the one hand, this would give more of the undocumented population already in the country, and more prospective temporary migrant workers, a conditional right to remain there and to move out of the shadows, which would be an improvement of great magnitude. At the same time, the possibility of entering the temple of participatory, democratic and equal citizenship would slip even further away, as it would become conditional upon the fulfillment of certain 'triggers', almost all of them representing, both legally and conceptually, the power of the state to exercise its sovereign control over its territory and membership boundaries. In the American example, this power is manifested in the surge in border patrol agents (adding 20,000 boots on the ground, nearly doubling the size of the force), the investment of billions of dollars in advanced surveillance technology and equipment, the erection of border fences, and the creation of an entry/exit registry system. These new measures, along with the proposed 'registered provisional immigrant' category, which is designed to resolve the inconsistent status of those already in the country while preventing unauthorized entry in the future, represent the most recent manifestations of the ongoing clash between logics of inclusion and exclusion, bringing back to center stage the search for new mechanisms to protect and promote our basic 'right to have rights'. Gaining provisional membership is certainly better than no membership at all, but it falls short of equal membership. For these reasons, it is too early to bid citizenship farewell as a foundational category of political organization in our globalizing world.

Notes

1. Chief Justice Earl Warren of the United States Supreme Court has famously incorporated this phrase into contemporary jurisprudence: 'citizenship is man's [and woman's – AS] basic right for it is nothing less than the right to have rights' (Perez *v.* Bromwell [1958], 356 US 44, 46).
2. Pickus and others also emphasize the significance of public schools as the core, nonpartisan institutional location for 'creating citizens', a vision that dates back to the French post-Revolutionary introduction of the public school (along with, at the time, the military) as a bedrock for fostering democratic political values and civic virtues, and in some cases imposing a collective national identity. On citizenship and education, see Callan (1997).

References

Aldana, R. E., W. Kidane, B. Lyon, and K. M. McKanders, eds. 2013. *Global Issues in Immigration Law*. Eagan, MN: West Academic.

Arendt, H. 1968 [1951]. *The Origins of Totalitarianism*. New York: Harcourt.

Benhabib, S. 2011. *Dignity in Adversity: Human Rights in Troubled Times*. Cambridge: Polity Press.

Cabrera, L. 2008. *The Practice of Global Citizenship*. Cambridge: Cambridge University Press.

Callan, E. 1997. *Creating Citizens: Political Education and Liberal Democracy*. Oxford: Clarendon Press.

Castles, S., and M. J. Miller, eds. 2009. *The Age of Migration: International Population Movements in the Modern World*. New York: Guildford Press.

Etzioni, A. 2007. "Citizenship Tests: A Comparative, Communitarian Perspective." *Political Quarterly* 78: 353–363.

Gamlen, A., and K. Marsh, eds. 2011. *Migration and Global Governance*. Cheltenham: Edward Elgar.

Hansen, R. 2010. "Citizenship Tests: An Unapologetic Defense." In *How Liberal Are Citizenship Tests?* edited by R. Bauböck, and C. Joppke, 25–27. Florence: Robert Schuman Centre for Advanced Studies.

Isin, E. F. 2012. *Citizens Without Frontiers*. London: Bloomsbury.

Isin, E. F., and G. M. Nielsen. 2008. "Introduction: Acts of Citizenship." In *Acts of Citizenship*, edited by E. F. Isin, and G. M. Nielsen, 1–12. London: Zed Books.

Joppke, C. 2013. "Through the European Looking Glass: Citizenship in the USA, Australia, and Canada." *Citizenship Studies* 17: 1–15.

Milanovic, B. 2011. *The Haves and the Have-Nots: A Brief and Idiosyncratic History of Global Inequality*. New York: Basic Books.

Motomura, H. 2006. *Americans in Waiting: The Lost Story of Immigration and Citizenship in the United States*. Oxford: Oxford University Press.

Neumayer, E. 2006. "Unequal Access to Foreign Spaces: How States Use Visa Restrictions to Regulate Mobility in a Globalized World." *Transactions of the Institute of British Geographers* 31: 72–84.

Nyers, P., ed. 2009. *Securitizations of Citizenship*. London: Routledge.

Nyers, P., and K. Rygiel, eds. 2012. *Citizenship, Migrant Activism and the Politics of Movement*. London: Routledge.

Orgad, L. 2010. "Illiberal Liberalism." *American Journal of Comparative Law* 58: 53–105.

Ryan, B., and V. Mitsilegas, eds. 2010. *Extraterritorial Immigration Control: Legal Challenges*. Leiden: Martinus Nijhoff.

Shachar, A. 2007. "The Shifting Border of Immigration Regulation." *Stanford Journal of Civil Rights and Civil Liberties* 3: 165–193.

Shachar, A. 2009. *The Birthright Lottery: Citizenship and Global Inequality*. Cambridge, MA: Harvard University Press.

Shachar, A. 2013. "Interpretation Sections of the Canadian Charter." In *The Canadian Charter of Rights and Freedoms*, edited by S. Beaulac, and E. Mendes, 147–190. 5th ed. Canada: LexisNexis.

Tyler, I., and K. Marciniak. 2013. "Immigrant Protest: An Introduction." *Citizenship Studies* 17: 143–156.

UN Population Fund. 2010. *Migration: A World on the Move*. New York: UN Population Fund. http://www.unfpa.org/pds/migration.html

Walzer, M. 1983. *Spheres of Justice: A Defence of Pluralism and Equality*. New York: Basic Books.

Political incorporation in America: immigrant partisans

Nancy L. Rosenblum and Andrea Tivig

Department of Government, Harvard University, Cambridge, MA, USA

Demographic changes and the stakes for both democracy and immigrants themselves make the political incorporation of immigrants a key political issue in the USA today. Two structural features of American politics help with political incorporation by providing multiple opportunities for political activity: federalism with its enormous number of state and local government elections and offices, and the permeable character of political parties. Naturalization, voter registration, and political participation are central to the political incorporation of immigrants, and we argue that historically and still today, political parties are the key institutions charged with political incorporation in the USA. Parties' goal in the political incorporation of immigrants should be to create long-term partisans, not just to naturalize immigrants and create voters in the next election. Partisanship has noninstrumental significance as well. As political identity and practice, partisanship has a good claim to earning immigrants' recognition as citizens, and a distinctive claim to achieving incorporation in a moral register. We conclude that partisanship stands out from movement and protest politics, advocacy, and even voting per se as a form of political incorporation.

1. Introduction

Our essay addresses the comparatively neglected topic of immigrant political incorporation. Demographics and the stakes for both democracy and for immigrants themselves give the subject timeliness and drama. We argue for the unparalleled significance of naturalization, voter registration, and participation, and we suggest that historically and still today, political parties are the key institutions charged with political incorporation in the USA. Two structural features of American politics enable incorporation by providing multiple opportunities for political activity: federalism with its enormous number of state and local government elections and offices, and the permeable character of political parties. We argue that partisanship stands out from movement and protest politics, advocacy, and even voting per se as a form of political incorporation. Partisanship as political identity and practice has a good claim to earning immigrants recognition as citizens, and a distinctive claim to achieving incorporation in a moral register. Recognition and self-identification as an American citizen depend on more than citizenship status, we argue; it entails democratic capacity as well.

We use the designation 'immigrants' to include the native-born, the already naturalized and those currently or even potentially eligible for naturalization. What this admittedly diverse group has in common is the salient fact that many are not politically mobilized, organized, registered voters, voters, or partisans. Even native-born descendants of immigrants remain on the margins of political life similar to newly arrived immigrants. We take up, then, the significance of political incorporation and the role that parties can and should play.

2. Political incorporation in a moral register

Contrary to Oliver Wendell Holmes' assertion that Americans are 'the Romans of the modern world – the great assimilating people' (quoted in Higham 2001, 88), a more apt characterization has it that the USA comprises 'a singular citizenship and a radically pluralist civil society' (Gordon 1964; Walzer 1992, 17). The contours of 'singular citizenship' as a regulative ideal and as a practice reasonably faithful to that ideal are familiar. It directs attention to legal status and enfranchisement – the right to vote and petition government, as well as civil and social rights and benefits. 'Singular citizenship' prohibits barriers to entry and naturalization based on race or national origin. It would protect naturalized citizens and native-born descendants from discriminatory treatment associated with 'second-class citizenship' or caste, and it would ensure a path to naturalization for legal residents and arguably for de facto long-term residents at the risk of becoming an 'underclass' (Massey and Sanchez 2010, 247). 'Singular citizenship' does not, however, signal that differences of ethnicity and national origin are eliminated in politics and relegated to private, social life. Immigrant diversity is not cabined in pluralist civil society. Immigrants enter politics initially at least with their origins and affiliations intact and in view, and the term 'incorporation' retains, as 'assimilation' or 'integration' does not, the notion of voting blocs and group identity as one of the elements of political organization and representation. It acknowledges that in politics many immigrants, for better or worse, remain identified as such for several generations – 'people whose status and behavior reflect a consciousness that they or their antecedents joined a preexisting society by a voluntary act of migration' – until the moment when they are 'lost, as it were, in a wider America' (Higham cited in Walzer 1992, 48).

Denial of citizenship is a categorical boundary that at present excludes men and women from formal electoral processes in the USA – despite the fact that 'the current blanket exclusion of noncitizens from the ballot is neither constitutionally required nor historically normal' (Raskin 1993, 1394). In any case, citizenship is just the beginning of the story. We know that not all eligible residents become naturalized citizens; roughly 60% of long-term permanent residents have acquired citizenship (Mollenkopf and Hochschild 2009, 9). And important as citizenship is, by itself naturalization does not lead to political incorporation. Political detachment and passivity are widespread among all democratic citizens today, but it has a special onus for immigrants. If refugee and undocumented status amount to 'civil death,' de facto disenfranchisement – the result of eligible residents not pursuing citizenship or of naturalized citizens not engaging in political participation – amounts to political powerlessness. Without political organization and representation, they lack influence over national immigration policy, over state and local implementation of policy, and over the routine decisions by government that affect every aspect of citizens' lives, from security to education.

In addition to the instrumental importance of political incorporation, we argue, is its moral and symbolic significance for immigrants. Citizenship entails public 'standing,' which is a moral status that carries public recognition and respect (Shklar 1991), and in the USA, citizenship as public standing turns on demonstrating and gaining recognition for democratic capacity, character, and intent. Those unable to mobilize political resources in defense of material interests, cultural values, and ideas about justice live not only with a sense of deprivation but also disrespect. It is true that the legitimacy of the democratic system depends on the representation of different interest groups. It is less often noted that the perceived legitimacy of immigrants as citizens depends on political incorporation: that their public standing turns on the perception of their democratic capacity and commitment. Democratic disposition is seen as the appropriate tribute that immigrants pay to the USA – more even than the 'functional citizenship' associated with hard work or neighborliness (Pickus and Skerry 2007). Residents' determination not to naturalize or the decision by naturalized immigrants or native-born descendants not to engage in democratic politics is taken as evidence that immigrants treat residence instrumentally with a sole view to employment or social services. It is taken as an affront at best, a sign of hostile self-segregation at worst.

In political philosophy, political incorporation is comparatively neglected and is only touched on indirectly. Democratic theorists focus on rights to participation not actual political incorporation. In social science, political participation takes a backseat to other indicators of immigrant socialization and acculturation. Research focuses on socio-economic mobility and on the forces that inhibit or facilitate social integration and generational change – education, employment, residential segregation, family formation, intermarriage, language practices, and religion. Indeed, social scientists note a semantic shift from citizen to earner and taxpayer as the defining characteristic of 'belonging' (Jacobson 2008, 73). Comparatively little attention is paid to the independent significance of political incorporation (notable exceptions are Andersen 2010; Bloemraad 2006; DeSipio 2011; Hajnal and Lee 2011; Hochschild and Mollenkopf 2009; Jones-Correa 1998; McCann, Connaughton, and Nisikawa 2009; Pantoja and Gershon 2006).

What does political incorporation entail? Commitment to the framework of constitutional democracy and following the democratic 'rules of the game,' for one thing. It requires that the face of immigrant political organization is democratic and populist rather than sternly autocratic, and overt rather than covert and conspiratorial. It is incompatible with 'third world' style politics, as Didion (1987, 13) describes Cuban Miami in the 1980s:

> In the continuing opera still called, even by Cubans who have now lived the largest part of their lives in this country, el exilio, the exile, meetings at private houses in Miami Beach are seen to have consequences … Revolutions and counter-revolutions are framed in the private sector, and the state security apparatus exists exclusively to be enlisted by one or another private player.

Immigrant politics normally conforms to the familiar political repertoire: movement and protest politics, demonstrations and litigation strategy on the model of black civil rights activists; organized interest and advocacy groups; voter registration and mobilization around local, state, and national elections and referenda.

Beyond such patterns of participation, political incorporation takes place in a moral register. Most important, it means that as a matter of conviction as well as strategy, immigrants are politically inclusive. One reflection of inclusiveness is the standard claim that immigrants' interests and opinions redound to the benefit of all Americans. Groups cast their values and programs as the property of the nation rather than their exclusive inheritance. (An example of parallelism is 'family values,' asserted by immigrants and mirrored in America's continued policy priority of family reunification.) True, activists' aims include public funding and support for their ethnically or religiously defined cultural institutions, social service organizations, and schools. True, too, bloc voting whether by country of origin or immigrant groups more generally 'is very useful in the politics of resource transfer and therefore in the politics of equality' (Walzer 2004, 58). That said, the dynamic of US immigrant politics presses for inclusion. When immigrant groups charge that they are deprived of some right or benefit, they represent themselves as a politically powerless minority suffering unfairly at the hands of the majority. The status of *political minority* is the compelling claim, rather than being a particular ethnic or national origin minority. In this way, immigrants evoke the unjust historical exclusion of other minorities, and direct attention to powerlessness and to diminished standing as 'second-class citizens.'

In the same spirit of inclusiveness, immigrant groups in the USA rarely assert the sort of claims for incorporation that are often standard in other democracies – guaranteed political representation, differential group rights for distinct ethnic and religious communities, official recognition and support for 'multiculturalism,' or what might be called 'corporate pluralism.' Immigrant politics has not (yet) produced 'Latino' or 'Asian' or 'Muslim' identity as an 'oppositional identity' or a tool of resistance. Rather, ordinary interest-based, group-based politics goes hand in hand with forming coalitions, constructing majorities, and stating aims and demands in terms that apply to immigrants generally and by extension to all citizens (C. Wong 2006, 3).

Inclusiveness is more than strategy, then. Transcending particular claims to rights and benefits is the aspiration to retrieve for immigrants what mythology says existed before the escalation of language wars and 'borderline madness' (Massey 2007, 129): the status that comes with public recognition of the value of immigrants for America. This includes recognition that immigration is not wholly 'exogenous'; that America by ideology and policy is an actively receiving country (Sassen 1999, 136); that immigrants are pulled toward the USA as well as pushed from their countries of origin by personal need and aspiration. If at present 'we view immigrants with rose-colored glasses turned backwards' (Rosa Simon cited in Schuck 2009, 162), the overarching goal of political incorporation is to secure the generous, hospitable environment immigrants *are owed* in appreciation not for any one group's exceptionalism or cultural superiority (liberal pluralism does not permit that claim) but for their contributions to the economic and political life of the USA.

The dynamic of inclusiveness helps account for why the abstraction 'immigrant' is commonplace in US politics. The parallel to religion may be helpful here. Nothing is more curious historically or more characteristic of religious politics in the USA today than references to 'faith' rather than to one or another denomination. Religious activists themselves commonly speak of 'religion' abstracted from theology, authority, and sectarianism. We have passed beyond Protestant versus Protestant and Protestant versus Catholic, and beyond generic Christianity and 'Judeo-Christian,' to generic 'faith.' Instead of religious pluralism producing appeals to creedal specificity, appeals are made by and on behalf of 'religion' in general. Similarly, the point is not that immigrants in the USA are undifferentiated. Fearful hostility toward Muslim immigrants and undocumented immigrants from Mexico makes this clear. So does political scientists' focus on specific immigrant groups in specific electoral arenas. That said, in many states and cities no single origin group is a majority among immigrants, and this is a force for inclusiveness that operates at several levels (Minnite 2009, 54). 'Latino' identity (Mexicans, Cubans, Puerto Ricans, Central Americans), which is widely adhered to as a common identity (Massey and Sanchez 2010, 211), is an invented category that serves the purposes of democratic political organization. The belief among Asian immigrants that they constitute a pan-ethnic group that shares a common culture turns out to fuel political activity (Wong and Pantoja 2009, 275). The dynamic at work in political incorporation requires that a group must first organize and close ranks, but at the same time selectively suppress diversity. The common umbrella designation 'immigrant' disclaims insistence that politics is rooted in the particulars of one group; it disavows the permanent political significance of origin, denomination, or ethnicity, and it demonstrates democratic inclusiveness. If overall 'immigrant identity is actively "made in the USA,"' political identity qua immigrant is clearly so (Massey and Sanchez 2010, 240–241).

The salience of inclusiveness for political incorporation in a moral register also helps explain the primacy of political parties in this process. Walzer describes a three-step dynamic to the 'politics of difference': articulation of difference; negotiation, coexistence, and coalition with other groups; and finally incorporation into more inclusive associations, among them political parties. The stronger the expressions of difference in civil society, the stronger inclusive political ties must be to demonstrate 'singular citizenship' beyond the politics of difference (Walzer 1992, 4–8, 64–66).

All this goes some way toward setting the contours of political incorporation in a moral register. In the next section, we suggest that political incorporation is the heart of citizenship in the USA because immigrants' public standing (not *de jure* status) as citizen has turned historically on the judgment whether they are (or are not) capable and disposed to be participants in democracy.

3. Citizenship and democratic disposition

Successive social struggles were required to include people regardless of race, gender, or national origin in the franchise and then to achieve the equal standing of 'singular citizenship.' But these struggles for inclusion do not owe to the fact that 'American' was an exclusive racial or ethnic category or that America was a homeland (Walzer 1992, 23–24). They arise from the fact that the defining characteristic of 'American citizen' has been the disposition and capacity for democracy, and from the presumption that a certain group does not have the required moral or intellectual credentials. The unifying sentiment behind opposition to immigrant political incorporation has been presumed incapacity for democracy or outright antidemocratic dispositions and intent. We point to the distinctively political content of national identity in the USA, a central feature of American political ideology.

Dangerous and alien political ideologies and character traits have been projected onto a variety of immigrant groups over time. Very briefly, four historical moments underscore our claim that successful democratic incorporation is the heart of American citizenship.

One is the best organized nativist movement in the USA, the mid-nineteenth century anti-Catholic crusade. The Know-Nothing party before the Civil War did not identify 'true' Americanism with any particular place of birth or ethnic origin (Higham 2001, 103–104): 'It was above all republican, more concerned about the civic virtue of the new immigrants than about their ethnic lineages.' Its main line of attack was their unsuitability for democracy, specifically the connection between Catholicism and hierarchy and political deference (Walzer 1992, 47).

The Progressive era too posed immigrant incompatibility with citizenship in explicitly political terms. Progressive criticism took aim at moral vices and above all at the 'slavish character' of immigrants. In Francis Parkman's words, universal male suffrage meant 'an invasion of peasants … an ignorant proletariat' and 'a nightmare of domination by Irish, black, and Chinese immigrants' (cited in McGerr 1986, 46). Whole constituencies were described as a 'political slum' (Parsons 1901, 276). As one historian observes: 'compelling evidence of their unfitness was the support that poor, foreign-born voters gave to political machines' (Keyssar 2000, 121). The Progressive goal was to keep these voters from the polls by effectively tightening naturalization laws, imposing onerous voter registration requirements, poll taxes, and literacy tests (Ginsberg and Shefter 1999, 185ff.; McGerr

1986, 45ff.; Mink 1986, 153; Zeidel 2004, 145). In effect, reformers redefined the electorate.

In the same spirit but a different vein, we see that from the early twentieth-century on immigrants were associated with imported political radicalism of the left and right. They were seen as carriers of communism, anarchism, nihilism, or as vicious reactionaries, as bomb-throwers and terrorists aiming at subversion or plotting to use the USA as a launching site for revolutionary or counter-revolutionary coups at home (Zeidel 2004, 10). This is a recurrent theme. Today, the Minutemen border patrol focuses its fear on the 'Reconquista movement' – 'Hezbollah Invading U.S. from Mexico' (Jacobson 2008, 132, 145). Immigrants are tied to the threat of separatism: California or Texas seceding or being annexed by Mexico (Huntington 2004; Wroe 2008, 29). Resistance to immigrant political incorporation owes to the fear that the invasion could come through ordinary politics: taking over 'by the vote if possible' (Jacobson 2008, 132).

Finally, since the 1980 Mariel boatlift brought criminals and the mentally ill as well as political refugees from Cuba to Miami, unauthorized immigration has dominated public discussion in the USA. President Clinton's 1995 State of Union assertion, which began with a piety – 'We are a nation of immigrants' – went on to intone 'But we are also a nation of laws' (cited in Wroe 2008, 125). Undocumented immigration into the USA has long had a political dimension unknown until recently in Europe, Canada, or Australia that cannot be explained by numbers alone, since most of the pragmatic objections to illegal immigration hold for legal immigrants as well (Pickus and Skerry 2007, 100). Undocumented status, which used to be a civil misdemeanor, has been criminalized. Moreover, instead of a discrete violation of the law, 'illegal aliens' are associated with 'a culture of crime,' wholly impervious to social control (Jacobson 2008, 55). Since 9/11, this connection has been concretized in the reorganization of government agencies. The 2002 Enhanced Border Security and Visa Entry Reform Act and the Homeland Security Act rolled the Immigration and Naturalization Service into the Department of Homeland Security. It structured immigration along security lines, militarized it, and put in place a system of detention and deportation that sometimes lacks even notional due process. The result is that the ethos of government vis-à-vis immigrants is enforcement, not assistance in settlement or active naturalization, and clearly not political incorporation.

From early on, in short, alliances were formed among nativists, moral reformers, and leaders of political reform movements who cast immigrants as unqualified for political incorporation and defended democracy against their presumptive antidemocratic character – slavishly deferential, vulnerable to political bosses, subversive, criminal. This unifying feature of opposition to immigrants on democratic grounds, often but not always linked to nativism or racism, underscores political incorporation as the symbolic heart of citizenship. Everywhere political participation and influence are important instrumentally, but in the USA, democratic identity is aligned with 'American,' and active citizenship earns public standing.

4. Structural opportunities for political incorporation

In practice, however, despite the standard focus on public opinion and political behavior, the political incorporation of immigrants does not turn solely on the political reception of immigrants or on the characteristics and incentives of individual immigrants themselves. Government policy matters, too, and it is worth noting that political incorporation is not the active goal of American government. Except for providing the legal apparatus of naturalization (and with the exception of assistance to refugees), government policy is laissez-faire. The USA provides information about the path to citizenship but leaves the business of assisting in settlement, naturalization, voter registration, and political organization to the voluntary associations of civil society (Bloemraad 2006, 2). That said, political incorporation *is* significantly affected by the institutional structure of US politics. Two distinctive features of American political life are positive forces that enable immigrant political incorporation, or should: political decentralization and the permeability of political parties.

Because federalism and localism result in variations in policy and implementation, decentralization ensures that immigration is not only a national issue but also a state and local issue, thus multiplying the sites of political incorporation. The federal government sets immigration policy and nominally controls the borders (states and citizen patrols do as well), but state and local governments provide social services, including health care and schooling. Multiplicity created by layers of government and variation in policies and implementation is enhanced by immigrant dispersion. The USA stands out for the number of recruitment networks to gateway cities, white suburbs, rural communities, and towns across every state. The result of federalism, decentralization, and immigrant dispersion is a wide disparity in social provision and legal enforcement. States and localities differ when it comes to freedom of movement, social benefits, work rights, and legal protection. Federalism produces variation in benefits and services to all citizens, which is why 'singular citizenship' is compatible with different levels of provision, but the variations are greater and policy implementation more sporadic for immigrants. With the cost of public services to immigrants falling on the states, both immigration politics and immigrant political activity span a wide spectrum. We see the salience of state politics at work in Arizona's 2008 law against 'knowingly hiring, recruiting, or referring for a fee an unauthorized immigrant.' The US Supreme Court recently upheld a controversial stop and search provision in Arizona's infamous 2010 SB1070 anti-immigrant law, while striking down other provisions (Liptak 2012). Not just Dade County in Florida but also small towns across the country with little experience with immigrants pass referenda requiring English-only in business. There are counterexamples, too, of sanctuary cities – state and local ordinances protective of immigrants, including the undocumented. New York State restored benefits withdrawn by Congress, and public hospitals and agencies in New York City are forbidden to inquire about or disclose individuals' immigrant status. Hospitable city governments issue photo identification cards to all residents.

Because political decentralization and dispersion make the experience of immigration variable even for men and women similarly situated with regard to language or employment, the likelihood and timing of naturalization, political involvement, and second generation participation differ too. Variations in state rules for voter registration have an impact as well (Jones-Correa 2001). For all American citizens, political participation requires positive steps – voter registration and turning-out, and partisan identification. It is not surprising that immigrants take longer to take each of these steps and may have fewer social pushes and pulls on them to engage. That said, federalism and localism at least multiply the sites, incentives, and occasions for political incorporation.

This points to the second distinctive feature of American political life that enables political incorporation: the permeability of political parties for voters-turned-partisans and for would-be candidates and office-holders. The two major parties in the USA are large enterprises; a fully staffed party system for *national* elections alone 'is a vast, vast undertaking' (Cohen et al. 2001, 15). Moreover, political party organizations mirror the tiers of government, offering stepping-stone local parties and offices. Immigrant political incorporation often begins there, where decisions about education, employment, enforcement, property taxes, and many basic services are made. State-level politics, too, determine a host of policies that directly affect immigrant lives. National politics is not the only site of partisan activity, in short. Federalism and the sheer number of elected and appointed offices multiply not just arenas of advocacy and electoral mobilization but also opportunities for organizing local political groups and partisan associations and for office-holding. 'On one election day a voter in California may cast more votes than a voter in the U.K. casts in a lifetime' (Ansolabehere 2001, 23).

We should add that political parties in the USA are also diffuse: there are no party lists selected by leadership. Party officials do not control most candidacies, even at the national level; they often have trouble recruiting candidates at all at state and local levels; and self-starter individual candidacies are common, if not the norm. In local and state elections the legal and financial barriers are low, and it is not difficult to gather the resources to run as a partisan. Comparative permeability marks the institution of American parties. This is crucial because, as we argue, parties are the chief institutional resources for political incorporation.

The significance of these structural features for immigrant political incorporation is plain: beyond the standard positive incentives and negative provocations for political incorporation, there are many sites for electoral mobilization and access to political office. Brief sketches of immigrant political incorporation point up the singular role of political parties and set the stage for our claim that partisanship is a distinctive form of political incorporation.

5. The responsibility of parties

Machine politics was a form of partisan organization in American cities, in which 'bosses' and a network of patronage brought inactive citizens, in particular new immigrants, into politics. It was one of the targets of Progressive reform in the early twentieth century. Progressives characterized immigrants as lackeys and dupes, and reformers 'unabashedly welcomed the prospect of weeding such voters out of the electorate' (Keyssar 2000, 159). Revisionist history has given Progressive reform, once lauded as 'clean government' reform, a 'sour reputation' (McCormick 1986, 254) especially with regard to immigrant political incorporation. This revised assessment turns in part on recognition that local party organizations 'represented a kind of primitive social welfare state' (Bridges 1984, 20).

> It [the machine] could fix your taxes, jury summonses, fire or sanitary inspections, get you out of jail or provide a clubhouse lawyer for whatever legal problems you might have ... It would pay a bill for you if you were strapped for cash, deliver coal and food ... It would be your entrée to city hall and the wheels of government, and could get you a job if you needed one ... The neighborhood politician knew you personally by name ... He often seemed the only man in the great impersonal metropolis genuinely concerned about you and your welfare. (Robinson 1977, 3)

So that 'long before many [immigrants] fully understood what it was to be an American, they knew quite well what it meant to be a Democrat or Republican' (Schier 2002, 16). Note too that partisanship promised immigrants not only material assistance but also a degree of respect – public standing.

We must also qualify the now standard view that since the 1970s, the provision of public welfare and social services by government has eviscerated the need for this aspect of party politics, and that civil service reforms have reduced the 'spoils' of election. In fact, as government expands in complexity and policies proliferate, there is need for assistance in navigating bureaucracies and programs. This is especially true for immigrants vis-à-vis immigration authorities, the thicket of eligibility for social services, and for receipt of local public services from repairing roads to issuing zoning permits and business licenses. Assistance in dealing with government agencies is the constituent service business of local political representatives (Wolfinger 1972). The claim that the welfare function of parties has been taken over by the state, eliminating the need for local party organization is misleading in a second respect. In the USA, by means of subsidy, contracts, direct funding and vouchers, the welfare system operates through a myriad of social groups and organizations, including ethnic and immigrant voluntary associations, that funnel state and local services to their own. These associations cannot function without public funding and inclusion in government-supported programs. Their lifeline is local, state, and federal governments; they depend on clientele relations and public–private partnerships. Finally, local and state political networks remain a source of employment through patronage. Think of the many jobs in every school system parceled out by political officials – teachers' aids, lunch monitors, and so on.

This focus on political connection and partisan support as a route to public services, jobs, and funding highlights the material incentives for political incorporation and on immigrants as beneficiaries (Mink 1986, 153). Party organization has another face as a route to political office and power. 'Urban ethnic politics has a long-standing legitimacy ... the efforts of today's Latino and Asian politicians to gain local office by wooing the ethnic vote are generally viewed as a natural ethnic succession' (Alba and Foner 2009, 292). The taint of corruption and irregularity historically attached to party machines should not spillover onto the counterpart organizations today: strong local and state parties are essential institutions for political incorporation. Machine politics 'must be judged a veritable school of politics for working-class and minority voters, compared to big city reform' (Bridges 1997, 216). Clean elections are desirable, nonpartisanship is not.

So it is helpful to contrast political incorporation via parties with the exclusion of immigrants that has marked reform cities. Newer cities in the American southwest have been described as entrepreneurial regimes promising a middle-class Anglo electorate sustained prosperity and development. These cities rejected strong party organizations from the start. Their reform charters, offshoots of Progressive anti-partyism, dictated nonpartisan city-manager government and a professional administrative apparatus of city planners and independent commissions. Reform cities hold at-large citywide elections with candidates sponsored by nonpartisan slating groups and ballots that do not specify the party affiliation of candidates. These political arrangements loosen ties between politicians and constituents. They inhibit the representation of neighborhoods, and therefore immigrant groups, and low participation and little competition at the polls are common. 'The first condition for big-city reform government was exclusion,' and the targets of political exclusion were Native Americans, African-Americans, and immigrants (Bridges 1997, 11, 18–19, 25–26; Fraga 1988, 528). Without party organizations to defend and mobilize those who are effectively excluded, reform governments are insulated from the discontent of communities they serve less well. Beginning in the 1960s, working-class voters, African-Americans and Mexican-Americans challenged the rules of local politics, taking particular aim at at-large elections in favor of fairly drawn district representation (Bridges 1997, 191, 220). Put succinctly, the demand was for government by politicians rather than 'civic statesmen.' Not surprisingly, advocates of nonpartisan 'reform' politics raised the Progressive specter of 'Eastern style' boss politics and a 'Brown Mafia' of entrenched, dishonest Mexican-American politicians (197–198).

Immigrant political incorporation depends on local and state politics, as we have seen, but elections to national office draw the most attention and resources for mobilization.

Lying behind electoral competition for immigrant voters is the fact that current immigrants and their children account for about a quarter of the US population, and 'the 1.5 and second generations move into the political arena at about the pace as native-born U.S. youth with native-born parents' (Mollenkopf and Hochschild 2009, 10). By 2050, the majority of the US population will be 'minorities.' Demographic change will have consequences for national politics and the major parties – that much is clear – but the exact electoral calculus remains murky. Even in districts with large concentrations of naturalized citizens, where immigrant voters are potentially decisive, parties do not dependably mobilize eligible candidates for naturalization, or offer support in voter registration (Andersen 2010, 64). One reason is that both major political parties are subject to cross-pressures for and against appealing to immigrant voters and recruiting them into electoral politics. Adherents of immigrant expansionism cut across party lines, and neither party presents a uniform populist, anti-immigrant face. Another explanation lies in the fact that parties consider not only the group's share of the total electorate but also the rate of participation, with past participation taken as the indication of likelihood of someone turning out at the polls. Uncertainty causes parties to back off from the business of political incorporation or to resort to discrete targeting of potential voters.

The results from the last three national elections show that, so far, the Democrats have made more efforts and have been more successful in attracting minority votes. Exit poll data are collected on the basis of race and ethnicity, and not immigrant origin, and only in less than half of the states, does it give a good indication of the political allegiances and voting patterns of immigrants (DeSipio 2011, 1200). In 2008, Obama won 95% of the black vote, 67% of the Hispanic vote, and 62% of the Asian-American vote. In the 2010 Congressional election, 91% of the black vote, 66% of the Hispanic vote, and 59% of the Asian-American vote went to the Democrats. And in 2012, 93% of the black vote, 71% of Hispanics, and 73% of Asian-Americans went to Obama (*New York Times* (2012) reporting National Election Pool Exit Poll Data). DeSipio highlights that the 2008 election involved 1.3 million more naturalized registered voters than previously, meaning that 6.3% of the electorate consisted of naturalized citizens and they were concentrated in key states (DeSipio 2011, 1190, 1201). The gap between the naturalized citizens and naturalized voters remains, however, and has even been increasing between 2000 and 2008 (DeSipio 2011, 1191).

The electoral results are often taken as an indication that immigrants are or are highly likely to become partisans for the Democrats if they were mobilized. Two notes of caution: First, voter turnout and voting for a party candidate is only part of what partisanship and political incorporation entails. It does not add up to sustained participation or partisanship absent from sustained efforts by parties to ensure registration and partisan identification. More importantly, Hajnal and Lee find that the majority of immigrants does not identify as Democrat, but rather as 'nonidentifiers.' Fifty-six percent of Latinos and 57% of Asian-Americans identify as Independent or as nonidentifiers (Hajnal and Lee 2011, 288). They do not think of themselves as Independent (which is a distinct political identity today), and either refuse to answer the question or consider partisan and nonpartisan labels to be inapplicable. It is not surprising that immigrants and their descendants exhibit less partisanship than those whose immigration to the USA occurred many generations ago. The degree of non-identification is troubling, but also shows the untapped political potential.

Outside national elections, moments of immigrant mobilization remain sporadic and rarely result in ongoing organization or incorporation of immigrants into the parties. One episode of political mobilization is the electoral dynamic of California's 1994 Proposition

187, which would have denied undocumented immigrants access to public services including health care and education, and set up a rigorous screening process requiring all state and local government employees to report suspected illegal immigrants to the Attorney General's office. Proposition 187 was a catalyst for anti-immigrant activism and received the support of three-fifths of California voters. At the same time, the referendum provoked a dramatic rise in immigrant naturalization as well as voting (a voting bloc representing 14% of registered voters and a third of the state population), though it is unclear how much owed to increased voter registration and how much to increased turnout (Wroe 2008, 107, 165). Federal courts blocked most elements of the referendum. This was a benchmark moment in immigrant politics, but it has not resulted in sustained efforts by either party to register and mobilize immigrants.

The second episode is the 2006 mobilization of 5 million immigrants protesting nationwide against legislation that would criminalize undocumented residence of immigrants as a felony (with the effect of precluding eligibility for legal immigrant status). The immigrant voice was heard in Washington (the legislation failed to pass) (Voss and Bloemraad 2011), but as DeSipio notes, there has been no repetition of this organizational feat (DeSipio 2011, 1195). Although social movements are often the starting point for political activity by immigrants, especially the undocumented, sustained political incorporation requires more: naturalization, participation, voting, and partisanship.

Our rough sketches of immigrant political incorporation – machine politics, reform governments, and ambivalent efforts by state and national parties to mobilize immigrants – were designed to underscore the importance of parties and partisanship for political incorporation. These sketches suggest the inhibitions on incorporation when politics is nonpartisan or when parties are uncertain or divided about the value of mobilizing immigrant voters or simply anemic.

Parties are not functioning today in any regular, sustained way to abet immigrant political incorporation at the level of naturalization, registration, voter mobilization, or above all, creating partisan-identified citizens. National party organizations spend few resources on immigrant voter registration and turnout except contingently in specific races, and they do little to cultivate sustained partisanship. This results in part from the uncertainty of electoral calculation, but more fundamentally to the chronically short-term, election cycle focus of party officials and candidates (Jones-Correa 2005; J.S. Wong 2006). Local party organizations are typically nonexistent between elections and lack organizational support from the national party organization (Andersen 2010, 53). Party leaders are not taking the longer view and are encouraging eligible residents to apply for citizenship as a first step toward political incorporation. Historically, as we saw, parties 'subsidized the naturalization/voting sequence – through providing advice, personal assistance, and material incentives for naturalization and participation to foreign-born residents' (Vallenly cited in Andersen 2008, 86). Today, links between naturalization and voter registration have been broken in the USA; where they exist, it owes to the efforts of community-level voluntary organizations. Today, political parties 'simply do not see encouraging naturalization as part of their responsibility, nor (apparently) as providing a potential electoral advantage' (Andersen 2008, 87).

6.   The moral distinctiveness of partisanship

The abdication of parties as agents of political incorporation is a democratic failing. For not just voting but partisanship is key to the long-term strength and representativeness of parties and therefore government (Rosenblum 2008). There are, of course, other forms of political engagement, but partisanship is distinctive – and troublingly underappreciated. The failure of parties to take on responsibility for mobilizing voters and creating partisans leaves immigration politics and other concerns to non-electoral political forces, without the countervailing power of organized citizens. And incorporation into party politics is the key to sustained public recognition of the democratic disposition and intent of immigrants we spoke of earlier.

Partisanship stands out from other forms of political activity, if for no other reason than the well-established proposition that partisanship is related to high levels of participation. We might expect that when the percentage (and demographic) of nonvoters especially among immigrants raises the alarm of democratic failing, partisanship would have strong defenders rather than being depreciated. Two additional considerations follow from our sketches of political incorporation and underscore our claim that political incorporation of immigrants into parties is central to political incorporation in a moral register.

First, political partisans are 'citizens in the second degree.' No other political identity is shared by so many segments of the population as measured by socioeconomic statuses, religion, or national origin, and partisans are not clumped tightly together on an ideological spectrum. Thinking back to the start of this essay on immigrant political incorporation in a moral register, partisanship is inclusive. Participants in party politics are more likely than those associated with interest and advocacy groups to see themselves acting as citizens in the general interest and not solely as advocates for their particular interest (Michelson 2005). Persuading a majority of the people over a broad swath of socioeconomic statuses and regions, sustaining it over more than the electoral moment is consonant with consolidating a refined and enlarged public view.

As partisans, immigrants enact not only inclusiveness but also comprehensiveness. Parties are charged with telling a comprehensive public story about the economic, social, and moral changes of the time, and about national security. Partisans share a complex of concerns and connect particular interests and opinions to a more general conception of the public interest – what Madison called a 'fixed' public opinion about the 'permanent aggregate interests of the community.' That is the transformative character of partisanship: it shapes views and commitment to others on a comprehensive range of issues that are meant to appeal to citizens generally. If 'the crucial problem of the politics of difference is to encompass the actually existing differences within some overarching political structure,' the key democratic structure is the political party (Walzer 1992, 4–8, 64–66).

From a democratic perspective, it is worrisome if more people say that interest groups and advocacy groups represent them than political parties because the two forms of political organization are not fungible. Interest and advocacy groups are typically 'single-issue' pressure groups. They agitate on specific issues and have particular beneficiaries in mind; they are not obliged to make general arguments about public interests. Most advocacy groups are professionally staffed organizations, and there are few standards for assessing the claims of self-selected leadership to represent particular people, interests, and opinions. The criteria governing authorization and accountability in formal representative institutions, loose though they may be, have not been accommodated to 'lay citizens' speaking on behalf of others. Observe, too, that the civic universe itself is 'remarkably oligarchical'; its political leadership a 'cartel of elites' (Skocpol 1999, 499).

Congress' general, if ambivalent and inadequate, support for immigration is explained by representatives' responsiveness to lobbying by ethnic advocacy groups, business groups including agricultural growers, religious coalitions of Catholic and evangelical churches seeking to reinvigorate their congregations, and unions like the Service Employees International that promote immigration as a way to replenish the ranks of unionized workers. The effectiveness of lobbying groups does not depend solely on the enfranchisement or the electoral weight of immigrants. These associations demand to be heard, pursue access to officials, and seek influence both publicly and in the chambers of power. They do not aim at political incorporation. Schattschneider's classic contrast in *Party Government* has purchase: 'The distinguishing mark of pressure tactics is not merely that it does not seek to win elections, but that in addition it does not attempt to persuade a majority' (Schattschneider 2004, 189, 203–204).

This is not to depreciate the significance of immigrant interest and advocacy groups. Voluntary association is a political resource and an element of any empowerment model of political incorporation. A central fact of a 'radically pluralist society' is the disadvantage of those who are chronically unorganized and disassociated. Political education through advocacy can be effective, and recruitment into the leadership of even nonpolitical civil society groups spills over to electoral representation and appointed offices. Moreover, given the current abdication of parties, it matters that some organizations attempt to provide a bridge from naturalization to registration to participation, and to connect immigrants to local, state, and national politics (Andersen 2008). Only a few assume this work, however. 'For the most part their [immigrant organization] environment does not provide strong incentives to mobilize immigrants electorally;' they may be 'vectors for integration' but not for long-term political incorporation (Andersen 2008, 90–92, 95–96, 100–101).

Beyond inclusiveness and comprehensiveness, the importance of partisanship for political incorporation is that it is a potentially lasting form of empowerment. For immigrants, the salient contrast is to protest and movement politics. These political forms may create a sense of solidarity, at least at the moment. They may help set political agendas. They may be catalysts for wider political 'agency,' though this is a contested claim. We do not mean to diminish the historic work of social movements, but in the case of immigrant political incorporation today, demonstration and protest are ephemeral. We are repeating here the standard charge against facilely assigning moral and political purity and priority to social movements. Admittedly, there is a particular reason for encouraging movement politics since demonstrations and protests can engage immigrants who have incentives to participate but are not citizens. They can excite undocumented immigrants to 'come out' and offer themselves as models of meritorious, would-be citizens (Jones 2010). (On the other hand, reasonable reluctance by noncitizens to take part can set a pattern for nonparticipation after naturalization.) Moreover, demonstrations may activate immigrants and, at the same time, arouse hostility in observers. This is not to say that they contribute to the view that immigrants are undemocratic; after all, the tradition of protest is entrenched in the USA. It is simply to say that this form of political incorporation, unlike partisanship, is not obviously inclusive. Organized rallies in 2006 boasted participation by both legal and undocumented immigrants, and may have provided a sense of solidarity, but they also focused attention on law and enforcement and the financial burdens immigrants impose on states. The national boycott, 'A Day Without Immigrants,' had minimal economic impact but maximum media coverage of angry protestors (Wroe 2008, 87–89).

In any case, this form of politics has the defect of 'leaving behind no organizational residue, no basis for an ongoing participatory politics' (Walzer 1992, 94). This is why 'electoral success by immigrant minorities should still be regarded as the gold standard against which other forms of political participation should be measured' (Alba and Foner 2009, 282). Of course, these modes of political engagement need not be in conflict. But it is not clear that advocacy or protest are dependable routes to either voting or partisanship, and we know that voting and partisanship have sources independent of these other forms of political activity.

We know less about the acquisition of partisan political identification by immigrant groups than the sources of 'party id' generally, however. It does not appear to be based on language dominance or economic status. Length of residence matters, but that may simply be a proxy for naturalization and political exposure. The key is active recruitment, which is most effective when new immigrants are mobilized by ethnically similar partisans and officials through the usual door-to-door canvassing and recruitment (J.S. Wong 2006, 355); the 'migration of partisanship' – partisan experience in the country of origin – may be a positive factor as well (McCann and Leal 2010). Once voters turn out, they enter the ranks of 'likely voters' (Michelson 2005, 91), more so if they identify as partisans. Again, the responsibility of political parties is to do more than mobilize voters for this or that election, though that is vital; it is to create partisans.

This responsibility for political incorporation falls on parties for reasons that have to do with the structure of American political life. It does not appear to hold for democracies generally. In some countries, Canada for example, government agencies are active in supporting and funding naturalization and incorporation, with much higher naturalization rates than the USA (Bloemraad 2006). In some democracies, a system of multiple parties and proportional representation dilutes the likelihood that partisanship will have the inclusive and comprehensive character it does in the USA. The instrumental importance of political incorporation for immigrant representation and the possibility of influencing policies that serve their interests is crucial in America, given the absence of public policies supporting immigrants and guaranteed group representation. Without political incorporation into parties and actual positions of power at all levels of government, immigrants remain passive beneficiaries or victims of political decisions over which they have no influence. 'Before these leaders can decide on important matters, they have to come to power; they have to organize a following, constitute a party, work out a program, campaign for wider support against other parties and programs, and win state office' (Walzer 2004, 128). Immigrant political engagement and participation through protest politics or advocacy, or simply voting can have constructive consequences for policy and immigrant welfare. But empowerment and political incorporation in a moral register are achieved through the sustained, inclusive, and comprehensive character of partisanship. Partisanship is where a 'radically pluralist civil society' translates into 'singular citizenship.'

References

Alba, R., and N. Foner. 2009. "Entering the Precincts of Power." In *Bringing Outsiders In*, edited by J. Hochschild, and J. Mollenkopf, 277–294. Ithaca, NY: Cornell University Press.

Andersen, K. 2008. "Parties, Organizations, and Political Incorporation: Immigrants in Six U.S. Cities." In *Civic Hopes and Political Realities*, edited by S. K. Ramakrishnan, and I. Bloemraad, 77–106. New York: Russell Sage Foundation.

Andersen, K. 2010. *New Immigrant Communities: Finding a Place in Local Politics*. Boulder, CO: Lynne Rienner.

Ansolabehere, S. 2001. "The Search for New Voting Technology." *Boston Review*, October. http://bostonreview.net/BR26.5/contents.html

Bloemraad, I. 2006. *Becoming a Citizen*. Berkeley: University of California Press.

Bridges, A. 1984. *A City in the Republic: Antebellum New York and the Origins of Machine Politics*. New York: Cambridge University Press.

Bridges, A. 1997. *Morning Glories: Municipal Reform in the Southwest*. Princeton, NJ: Princeton University Press.

Cohen, M., D. Karl, H. Noel, and J. Zaller. 2001 "Beating Reform: The Resurgence of Parties in Presidential Nominations, 1980–2000." Paper presented at the American Political Science Association Meeting, San Francisco, CA, August 30–September 2. https://www.princeton.edu/csdp/events/Zaller021102/Zaller.pdf

DeSipio, L. 2011. "Immigrant Incorporation in an Era of Weak Civic Institutions Immigrant Civic and Political Participation in the United States." *American Behavioral Scientist* 55 (9): 1189–1213.

Didion, J. 1987. *Miami.* New York: Vintage Books.

Fraga, L. R. 1988. "Domination Through Democratic Means: Nonpartisan Slating Groups in City Electoral Politics." *Urban Affairs Quarterly* 23 (4): 528–555.

Ginsberg, B., and M. Shefter. 1999. *Politics by Other Means.* New York: W.W. Norton.

Gordon, M. 1964. *Assimilation in American Life.* New York: Oxford University Press.

Hajnal, Z. L., and T. Lee. 2011. *Why Americans Don't Join the Party: Race, Immigration, and the Failure (of Political Parties) to Engage the Electorate.* Princeton, NJ: Princeton University Press.

Higham, J. 2001. *Hanging Together: Unity and Diversity in American Culture.* New Haven, CT: Yale University Press.

Hochschild, J., and J. Mollenkopf, eds. 2009. *Bringing Outsiders In: Transatlantic Perspectives on Immigrant Political Incorporation.* Ithaca, NY: Cornell University Press.

Huntington, S. P. 2004. "The Hispanic Challenge." *Foreign Policy* 141 (2): 30–45.

Jacobson, R. D. 2008. *The New Nativism: Proposition 187 and the Debate Over Immigration.* Minneapolis: University of Minnesota Press.

Jones, M. 2010. "Coming Out Illegal." *New York Times*, October 21. http://www.nytimes.com/2010/10/24/magazine/24DreamTeam-t.html?smid=pl-share

Jones-Correa, M. 1998. *Between Two Nations: The Political Predicament of Latinos in New York City.* Ithaca, NY: Cornell University Press.

Jones-Correa, M. 2001. "Institutional and Contextual Factors in Immigrant Naturalization and Voting." *Citizenship Studies* 5 (1): 41–56.

Jones-Correa, M. 2005. "Bringing Outsiders In." In *The Politics of Democratic Inclusion*, edited by C. Wolbrecht, and R. E. Hero, 75–102. Philadelphia, PA: Temple University Press.

Keyssar, A. 2000. *The Right to Vote.* New York: Basic Books.

Liptak, A. 2012. "Blocking Parts of Arizona Law, Justices Allow Its Centerpiece." *The New York Times*, June 25. http://www.nytimes.com/2012/06/26/us/supreme-court-rejects-part-of-arizona-immigration-law.html

Massey, D. 2007. "Borderline Madness: America's Counterproductive Immigrant Policy." In *Debating Immigration*, edited by C. Swaine, 129–138. Cambridge: Cambridge University Press.

Massey, D. S., and R. M. Sanchez. 2010. *Broken Boundaries: Creating Immigrant Identity in Anti-Immigrant Times.* New York: Russell Sage.

McCann, J. A., S. Connaughton, and K. Nisikawa. 2009. "Candidate-Centered Campaigning and the Incorporation of Immigrants into the U.S. Party System." Paper presented at the American Political Science Association Meeting, Toronto, ON, 3–6 September.

McCann, J. A., and D. L. Leal. 2010. "The Migration of Partisanship: How Do Enduring *Panista*, *Priísta*, and *Perredista* Identifications Shape the Partisan Socialization of Mexican Immigrants in the United States?" Paper presented at the Midwest Political Science Association Meeting, Chicago, IL, 22–25 April.

McCormick, R. L. 1986. *The Party Period and Public Policy.* New York: Oxford University Press.

McGerr, M. 1986. *The Decline of Popular Politics: The American North, 1865–1928.* New York: Oxford University Press.

Michelson, M. R. 2005. "Meeting the Challenge of Latino Voter Mobilization." *Annals of the American Academy of Political and Social Science* 601: 85–101.

Mink, G. 1986. *Old Labor and New Immigrants in American Political Development: Union, Party, and State 1875–1920.* Ithaca, NY: Cornell University Press.

Minnite, L. C. 2009. "Lost in Translation? A Critical Appraisal of the Concept of Political Incorporation." In *Bringing Outsiders In*, edited by J. Hochschild, and J. Mollenkopf, 48–60. Ithaca, NY: Cornell University Press.

Mollenkopf, J., and J. Hochschild, eds. 2009. "Setting Up the Context." In *Bringing Outsiders In*, 3–14. Ithaca, NY: Cornell University Press.

New York Times. 2012. "Election 2012 – President Exit Polls." National Election Pool Data. http://elections.nytimes.com/2012/results/president/exit-polls

Pantoja, A. D., and S. A. Gershon. 2006. "Political Orientation and Naturalization Among Latino and Latina Immigrants." *Social Science Quarterly* 87 (5): 1171–1187.

Parsons, F. 1901. *The City for the People: Or the Municipalization of the City Government and of Local Franchises*. Philadelphia, PA: Taylor.

Pickus, N., and P. Skerry. 2007. "Good Neighbors and Good Citizens: Beyond the Legal-Illegal Immigration Debate." In *Debating Immigration*, edited by C. Swaine, 95–113. Cambridge: Cambridge University Press.

Raskin, J. B. 1993. "Legal Aliens, Local Citizens: The Historical, Constitutional and Theoretical Meanings of Alien Suffrage." *University of Pennsylvania Law Review* 141 (4): 1391–1470.

Robinson, F. S. 1977. *Machine Politics: A Study of Albany's O'Connells*. New Brunswick, NJ: Transaction Books.

Rosenblum, N. 2008. *On the Side of the Angels: An Appreciation of Parties and Partisanship*. Princeton, NJ: Princeton University Press.

Sassen, S. 1999. *Guests and Aliens*. New York: New Press.

Schattschneider, E. E. 2004. *Party Government: American Government in Action*. New Brunswick, NJ: Transaction Publishers.

Schier, S. E. 2002. "From Melting Pot to Centrifuge: Immigrants and American Politics." *Brookings Review* 20 (1): 16–19.

Schuck, P. 2009. "Immigrants' Incorporation in the United States after 9/11." In *Bringing Outsiders In*, edited by J. Hochschild, and J. Mollenkopf, 158–175. Ithaca, NY: Cornell University Press.

Shklar, J. N. 1991. *American Citizenship: The Quest for Inclusion*. Cambridge, MA: Harvard University Press.

Skocpol, T. 1999. "Advocates Without Members: The Recent Transformation of American Civic Life." In *Civic Engagement in American Democracy*, edited by T. Skocpol, and M. P. Fiorina, 461–510. Washington, DC: Brookings Institution Press and Russell Sage Foundation.

Voss, K., and I. Bloemraad, eds. 2011. *Rallying for Immigrant Rights: The Fight for Inclusion in 21st Century America*. Berkeley: University of California Press.

Walzer, M. 1992. *What It Means to be an American: Essays on the American Experience*. New York: Marsilio.

Walzer, M. 2004. *Politics and Passion: Toward a More Egalitarian Liberalism*. New Haven, CT: Yale University Press.

Wolfinger, R. E. 1972. "Why Political Machines Have Not Withered Away and Other Revisionist Thoughts." *Journal of Politics* 34 (2): 365–398.

Wong, C. 2006. *Lobbying for Inclusion: Rights Politics and the Making of Immigrant Policy*. Stanford, CA: Stanford University Press.

Wong, J. S. 2006. *Democracy's Promise: Immigrants and American Civic Institutions*. Ann Arbor: University of Michigan Press.

Wong, J., and A. Pantoja. 2009. "In Pursuit of Inclusion: Citizenship Acquisition Among Asian Immigrants." In *Bringing Outsiders In: Transatlantic Perceptions on Immigrant Incorporation*, edited by J. Hochschild, and J. Mollenkopf, 260–276. Ithaca, NY: Cornell University Press.

Wroe, A. 2008. *The Republican Party and Immigration Politics: From Proposition 187 to George W. Bush*. New York: Palgrave.

Zeidel, R. F. 2004. *Immigrants, Progressives, and Exclusion Politics: The Dillingham Commission, 1900–1927*. De Kalb: Northern Illinois University Press.

Less than the sum of its parts: institutional realities and legal aspirations in early twenty-first century American immigration

Mariano-Florentino Cuéllar

Stanford Law School, Stanford University, Stanford, CA, USA; Freeman Spogli Institute for International Studies, Stanford University, Stanford, CA, USA

This essay considers the implications of some of the legal and institutional forces shaping immigration in the early twenty-first century, and explores what the character of the American system implies for citizenship and migration in an advanced industrial democracy with a complex regulatory state. The essay argues, first, that immigration law must be understood not as a raw reflection of mass public attitudes or a carefully reasoned prescriptive scheme, but instead as a politically generated, fractured system allocating benefits and burdens among a variety of constituents and public agencies. This allocation plainly affects more than just actual or potential migrants. It also shapes the lives of employers, law enforcers, politicians, and the larger public of American citizens. These interactions showcase how much the future of the nation-state may depend not only on seemingly inexorable forces reshaping the international system, but on how law is understood by the public, adjudicated by courts, and enforced by public organizations. Put differently, how much even powerful nation-states are able to shape their context heavily depends on often-tenuous compromises at the intersection between law, politics, and organization.

1. Introduction

The sun rises each morning over a world that purports to be organized along lines of national sovereignty. Yet cross-border migration patterns inevitably impact social organization across those lines. So too do migrants, whether legal or not, affect economic activity, labor markets, and political competition in sovereign nations across the planet. The Korean shopkeepers in South Central Los Angeles, the Mexican and Filipino farmworkers in California's Imperial Valley, and the Somali refugees in Washington, DC, are living examples of how national communities are never entirely static. Migration thus impacts the very character of a nation-state in a global legal scheme that takes the state as its basic unit of analysis, simultaneously showcasing both the nation-state's fluid nature and its enduring power to shape our conception of the world. Accordingly, few domains of regulation in advanced industrialized countries have effects on society as powerful and far-reaching as immigration policy.[1]

In the USA, however, the early twenty-first century legal architecture of migration has produced a mixed system – a resilient capacity to integrate newcomers into American citizenship, alongside a system with many self-defeating features eliciting near-universal derision (Archibold and Thee-Brenan 2010). In that system, some putatively eligible migrants wait decades for immigration opportunities that never materialize (MPI Task Force 2006, Chap. 40). Millions of unauthorized immigrants live at the law's margins, with their mass removal all but impossible in practical terms even as their presence remains a divisive issue across the country (Passel and Cohn 2009). Billions of dollars are spent on border controls that fail to satisfy public expectations.[2] And employers are subject to harsh laws that are only sporadically enforced (Wishnie 2007, 209–211). These realities suggest a harsh and troubling legacy for a national immigration system that has had its share of success over time – most notably its capacity to absorb by far the highest number of immigrants anywhere in the last century or so – as well as, more recently, stark failures. In part because of these limitations, the existing system gives rise to recurring questions about the evolution of a framework governing the responsibilities and rights of aliens and immigrants in the American polity (Archibold and Thee-Brenan 2010).

This article describes the major features of the institutional arrangement implementing American immigration law in the early years of the twenty-first century. It explores some of the consequences of existing arrangements for particular groups and for the country's evolving national community. The intricate structure of the American immigration system is interesting in its own right as an example of how competing pressures can produce a legal arrangement replete with contradictions yet capable of accommodating millions of immigrants over the years. But the structure is also revealing for what it illustrates about the forces shaping a domain profoundly important to the nation-state.

In particular, American immigration policy became by the mid-1990s a domain of enormous organizational complexity coupled with profound national concern in many domestic jurisdictions, forcing policy-makers, civil servants, and organized groups to grapple with a host of risks and possibilities. Broad public concern arising from the immigration status quo can fuel efforts to mitigate existing adverse consequences through legislative (or, where possible, limited executive) reforms affecting complex administrative agencies. Yet public frustration with immigration enforcement can also encourage policy changes that exacerbate problems in the implementation of immigration law and risk further eroding the legitimacy of public institutions. It is through the operation of these feedback relationships, rather than through a carefully mapped process of implementing domestic or international laws, that countries such as the USA shape the fundamental character of their national communities.

2. Immigration law as an institutional system: courts, legislatures, and executive organizations

Except for a brief period between roughly 1930 and the late 1950s, the USA has admitted at least several hundred thousand new lawful permanent residents every year since 1900 (see Figure 1; in many years, the numbers of admissions have been substantially higher). The laws that have created the framework for such relatively high levels of sustained immigration over time are sometimes described by judicial decisions and legal scholars in terms of their presumed functional aspirations. Immigration law, that is, exists for a purpose – to control the flow of people into the American sphere and ultimately into the national community in a manner consistent with the nation's interests.[3] In other cases, courts skirt the question of what immigration law is supposed to accomplish and instead underscore who is supposed to have power over it.[4] This territory, encompassing how legal power over immigration is divided plainly, generates a substantial amount of debate in judicial opinions and scholarly circles.[5]

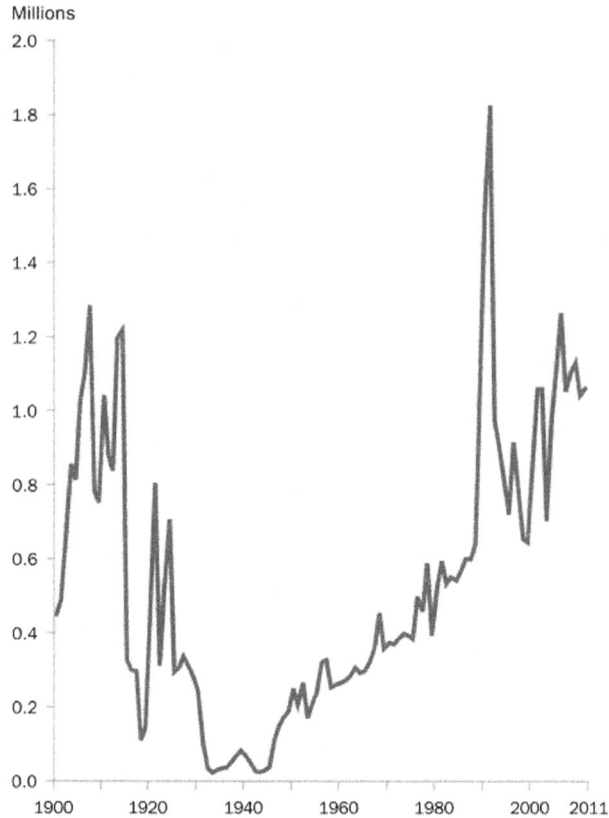

Figure 1.   Legal permanent resident flow to the USA: 1900 to 2011.
Source: Monger and Yankay (2012).

These judicial opinions and the statutes they interpret create for migrants in the USA a legal environment defined, in crucial respects, by a series of responsibilities as well as guarantees ranging from notification for foreign nationals arrested on suspicion of criminal conduct to constitutional rights of access to public education to undocumented children.[6] In the implicit structure of the American system, immigrants undertake to comply with a variety of domestic laws, including criminal laws, to pay taxes, and to obtain knowledge of English and American civic institutions when seeking citizenship. At the same time, society affords immigrants a variety of guarantees – though these are far from immune to statutory, and therefore political, developments. Statutory provisions guarantee certain process rights before immigration adjudicators and in other settings. Constitutional guarantees have historically extended to aliens in the USA.[7] Aliens in the USA also enjoy protections rooted in international law, such as *non-refoulement* rights under international refugee law and the Convention Against Torture.[8]

As accounts of how the nation actually defines the scope of its community in a system of sovereign nations, these descriptions are enormously unsatisfying. For one, they elide the temporal questions implicit in ascertaining the nation's interest when the matter under discussion is precisely about who will be part of the nation. How we evaluate the problems with our rickety immigration adjudication system depends to some degree on whether we are concerned about the interests of the people who would be members of the community if the system worked differently (or, alternatively, if it continued to work in a certain manner rather than being reformed to limit migration) or whether we are focusing only on the interests of those who are already firmly established as part of the community at a given time.

For another, judicially formulated descriptions of the nature of immigration policy tend not to dwell on the structural realties that generate the cases in the first place. Chief among those realities is the disconnect between legal aspirations and a far more chaotic reality mixing considerable discretion in some domains [such as how authorities at Department of Homeland Security (DHS) allocate investigative authorities in a world where far more people are committing immigration violations than law enforcement officials can catch] with virtually none in others (such as when immigration judges consider whether lawful permanent residents who have committed certain criminal offenses can receive discretionary relief if they believe the situation warrants it). That chaotic reality is almost certainly also a function of laws that are often easily evaded by employers with an incentive to hire unauthorized workers and by the persistence of practices fitting poorly with American aspirations of governance under law.

Plainly, courts are important actors in the American immigration system. Even when the concept of plenary power has at times proven such an important feature of the legal terrain, one can readily witness influence of the judiciary in certain pockets of immigration law. Bearing the hallmarks of judicial influence are certain open-ended legal provisions governing access to asylum, the application of pivotal statutory terms such as 'aggravated felony,' the scope of constitutional rights for unauthorized migrants, and the statutory and constitutional determinants of immigration federalism. Courts also articulate broad aspirations about the nature of sovereignty in the American context, thereby contributing to the framing of broader discussions of immigration in the polity.

Nonetheless, the questions raised in light of those aspirations are not so much about the familiar legal disputes regarding the powers of Congress and the President over immigration, but the deeper issues arising from the fact that the USA has built for itself an immigration system that almost no one likes. The widespread frustration with the existing system is all the more striking because – despite some inherent trade-offs and perhaps even contradictions in immigration law and policy in the USA and other leading advanced industrialized countries – different situations have in fact produced different outcomes. The 1965 Immigration Act, for example, exerted a major impact on law and policy for generations and – despite a variety of shortcomings that reflect and even help explain existing problems – represented a major change in the direction of expanding migration opportunities, reducing explicit racial quotas, and rationalizing an unwieldy system. In contrast, existing conditions seem to cut against major immigration policy changes, and particularly ones addressing some of the existing system's harsher and least defensible features.

Public views also are unquestionably important when explaining policy stability and change in a pluralist democracy (Alesina, Glaeser, and Sacerdote 2001; Canes-Wrone, Minozzi, and Revelry 2011). Still, as developed below, public opinion involving immigration reflects a series of odd contradictions. Today Americans appear to support, by a substantial margin, comprehensive immigration reforms including a requirement that the undocumented submit to a background check and earn legalization or face removal (Archibold and Thee-Brenan 2010). At the same time, the public also supports the recently enacted Arizona immigration law (S.B. 1070), a draconian measure allowing police to question and detain suspected unauthorized aliens that represents – for some observers – the antithesis of comprehensive reform (Pew Center for the People and the Press 2010).

These contradictions are probably best understood in light of the frustrations Americans tend to have about immigration and the ambiguous legacy of a complicated immigration scheme that few of them remotely understand.

Similarly, while the structure of American separation of powers and the organization of Congress unquestionably plays a role in gridlock on immigration and other issues (Brady and Volden 1998; Krehbiel 1998) during the early twenty-first century, American policy-makers were able to address a host of other structural problems ranging from an unwieldy tax code to health insurance while immigration continued to languish. More generally, explanations focused on gridlock in Congress make much of legislative supermajority requirements, neglecting to some extent lawmakers and the public's reaction to changing political developments – including how immigration law is organized and enforced. To better address these issues, it will be useful to step back from run of the mill and even exceptional immigration law cases to consider the forces shaping the system generating immigration law disputes.

3.   Reframing the status quo: burdens, benefits, and constituencies

Suppose an observer from Mars arrived to the USA in the early twenty-first century, having never heard of American immigration law. After clearing customs and immigration, she (it) would eventually recognize that at least six critical features define the modern American system. First, Americans have built a legal structure whose foundation rests on near-plenary legislative power over who comes and how people are treated at the border.[9] The extent of power in this domain is offset, though, by a second feature, which is a combination of domestic laws, treaty commitments, and constitutional and judicial decisions guaranteeing certain protections and privileges to migrants. These guarantees include, among others, the right to access public education for undocumented children and non-refoulement guarantees under the Refugee Convention (Aleinikoff 2002).[10] The extent of these guarantees is all the more remarkable given a third feature, which is the historically relatively high levels of absorption of immigrants from around the world achieved under American immigration law (Zolberg 2006). Under current law, the majority of immigrants are admitted through a family-based preference system (Weissbrodt and Danielson 2004), with the absolute number of employment-based immigrants still looming large relative to comparable flows in the rest of the world.

If the level of absorption of legal immigrants in American history is remarkable, though, so is a fourth feature of the American system – the size of unauthorized immigrant flows, primarily from Latin America. The flow is as high as half a million annually in recent years, adding up to a staggering 11 million or so unauthorized individuals (Passel and Cohn 2009). These workers pick and pack Americans' food, clean their homes and cut their lawns, and build the country's infrastructure. As discussed below, their presence also poses some dilemmas for law enforcement, both in terms of the need to set immigration enforcement priorities (for the federal government) and the challenge of building trust for and with the authorities.

A variety of factors contribute to this condition. The employer sanctions provisions that were supposed to align employers' incentives with the social goal if limiting unauthorized migrants' access to the domestic labor market were all but built to fail (Calavita 1990, 1041). Among other things, the current employer sanctions regime lacks meaningful civil enforcement provisions for regulators to deploy and obviously over-relies on the scruples of employers who often harbor an economic interest in avoiding compliance. The USA shares a vast border with a hemispheric region where per capita incomes are far lower than in the USA. Many potential migrants from the region (along with others from around the world who become undocumented through visa overstays) confront an administratively burdensome visa allocation scheme fashioned by wary lawmakers in the middle of the twentieth century. The scheme is replete with country-specific caps for allocating green cards and devoid of substantial ex ante administrative flexibility (Laham 2000; Zolberg 2006, 330). In addition, the current scheme provides almost no avenues for medium-term legal immigration to many individuals in some countries (such as Mexico and the Philippines) (MPI Task Force 2006, Chap. 40).

Economists would be at least partly right to describe the resulting system as one burdened by a gaping mismatch between supply and demand. Even assuming that demand could be better addressed with a greater supply of green cards, of course demand could also grow in response to greater availability of visas. The point is the evocative image of waiting at the back of the line is often a mirage, one that also elides the complex and ambivalent history. Americans have had with illicit or semi-regulated migration (Calavita 1989, 151).

A fifth feature reflects, to some degree, policy-makers' response to illicit migration as well as public concerns about threats ranging from street crime in the Southwest to powerful drug trafficking organizations – concerns which may be exacerbated for some members of the public based on the (actual or perceived) identity of the immigrants (Brader, Valentino, and Suhay 2008, 959–961, Reding 2008). To wit, the USA has sustained an unprecedented, costly, and still continuing ramp-up in border security since the Reagan Administration. During the course of about 28 years, the number of border patrol agents has increased roughly ten-fold (Bush and McClarty 2009). The number of agents doubled just between 2004 and 2009 (Pfeiffer 2010). Growth is also evident in support for law enforcement operations, detention facilities, and in a costly technological infrastructure (chronically mired in controversy because of technical problems) and physical infrastructure. These developments have coincided, meanwhile, with less discretion for judges to stop removal or to limit the use of harsh penalties.

Finally, as Americans have grown more aware of their nation-state's organizational capacity and more generally anxious about social and economic changes, they have articulated in surveys and through their elected representatives tremendously ambitious expectations of immigration enforcement – expectations that have increasingly given way to frustration (Cuéllar 2012). That frustration, in turn, has increasingly cut against the country's historic orientation toward immigrant absorption and cast in a negative light some of the statutory and constitutional guarantees for immigrants. The frustration has engendered now-infamous harsh local and state laws such as Arizona's S.B. 1070, which empowers police to detain people on suspicion of being unauthorized migrants (Chishti and Bergeron 2010). Opinion leaders often point to passage of the Immigration Reform and Control Act (IRCA) in 1986, with its expansive legalization provisions, as exacerbating the dashed expectations given its premise (if not quite its promise) of offering legalization in exchange for a putatively demanding new system to hold employers accountable and stop undocumented migration (MPI Task Force 2006, 46–52).

Available opinion surveys may be a poor guide to precisely what segment of the public wants what highly technical changes in the immigration system, but they indicate fairly widespread dissatisfaction with the status quo (Archibold and Thee-Brenan 2010; Bush and McClarty 2009). And surveys are not the only factor suggesting widespread rejection of the current system. Lawmakers with otherwise quite divergent preferences complain about it. Some of the system's institutions – such as immigration courts – are especially reviled even by those with a more sophisticated insight into the constraints faced by existing entities (Cox 2007, 1671). Employers, too, have growing frustrations with the status quo (Bush and McClarty 2009; MPI Task Force 2006, 40). Employers who want skilled labor seek an easier-to-implement temporary program (a successor to the H1B). Employers who want less-skilled labor would rather not have the risks associated with hiring undocumented workers. A few employers may prefer the benefits of lower wages associated with workers who bear the risk of deportation and lack legal status, but their particular utility profile is likely to be uncommon. Historically, organized labor has weathered internal disagreements because of immigration (Briggs 2001). But in recent years, labor organizations from the AFL-CIO to the SEIU have become increasingly concerned about a status quo that tolerates employer reliance on unlawful workers with limited labor protections.

Despite these reactions, not all of what emerges from this system is undesirable. The USA still manages to unify hundreds of thousands of families every year, settles by far the most refugees of any country in the world, and provides strong constitutional protections to aliens. Still, the existing arrangement forces Americans to shoulder some costs and chronic contradictions, such as a recognition of the value of high-skilled migration and the reality that it is poorly managed, or a simultaneous frustration with seeming toleration of undocumented migration. These contradictions help engender persistent effort at reform that have conspicuously failed in the last few years (Wasem 2010), and raise the basic question of how best to understand the forces that have wrought American immigration law.

The preceding description acknowledges that American immigration law is by and large the work of lawmakers and the executive branch – and in a democracy, unquestionably a great deal of what drives immigration outcomes begins with the public's views about the subject. Some observers might take the point a step further, however, arguing that the best way to explain Americans' immigration status quo is by the reactions of the public to an uncertain, diverse world.

It is true that the public lacks detailed views about a range of subjects ranging from military procurement to patent reform. Immigration is distinct in being saddled with the capacity to engender widespread public concern. The role of the public in immigration policy is not just a function of how pluralist democracy works, but also a reflection of a widely shared sense that the immigration issue is publicly owned: the flip side of the idea that a certain country is a 'nation of immigrants,' for example, is that the general public considers itself eminently fit to pass judgment on the issue.[11] Accordingly, public responses should be expected to play a powerful role in shaping overall immigration policy, a fact that many scholars readily acknowledge (Citrin, Green, and Wong 1997; Zolberg 2006).

Indeed, given the historical trajectory of immigration policy and its apparent consistency with evolving public attitudes, it is possible to see much of our existing immigration policy as a response to public attitudes. And indeed, one can hardly explain some critical changes in immigration policy, including among others the dramatic 1965 immigration reforms and the 1980 Refugee Act without some reference to the public's willingness to accept such changes (a willingness that helps explain why lawmakers took on the issues in the first place). By the same token, attitudes about immigration appear to track not only individuals' economic concerns, but also their attitudes about culture and globalization (Citrin, Green, and Wong 1997; Esses et al. 2002).

A closer look reveals a more complicated situation, however (Buck et al. 2003). For one, increases in immigration (and an increasingly liberalized immigration policy in America) are not always consistent with public opinion in historical perspective (Schuck

2003). For another, the practical reality is that scarce public attention focused on an enormously intricate issue is mediated through opinion leaders and political interests responding to policy outputs and perceived political opportunities. Moreover, the inability of supportive lawmakers and their allies to turn widespread interest in comprehensive reform into changes in American immigration law is almost certainly explained in part by the institutional features of American democracy (such as legislative supermajority requirements) as well as unique characteristics of the immigration context (both discussed below).

In contrast to approaches explaining the political economy of immigration law primarily in terms of raw, unmediated public attitudes, a more functionalist account of immigration law views it as primarily a domain for technocratic labor market management (Trebilcock and Sudak 2006, 234–235). Offsetting the narrative of apparent public frustration, observers might instead think about immigration policy as a compromise with a particular economic logic – one that helps explain the presence of undocumented workers (Hanson 2007) and gives some rough functional justification for the levels of immigration currently permitted. Proponents of this view may differ on whether the system is optimal, but they understand its impact primarily through the lens of the impact on small businesses, agricultural interests, industrial employers, and the labor market more generally (Borjas 1999). In a somewhat similar vein, one could attempt to describe more recent immigration policy as being largely (if not entirely) about carefully managing national security, notwithstanding the reality that large numbers of undocumented residents and high expenditures on routine immigration enforcement rather than for enforcement against high value targets may be difficult to describe as optimal security policies. Implicit in these approaches is the idea of immigration as a domain for expert analysis and management.

But it is difficult to describe existing American immigration law as an optimal response to labor market conditions, security problems, or public humanitarian concerns. It would be one thing to observe a system that falls far short of working perfectly but manages to muddle through, meeting some basic threshold of acceptability derived implicitly from the reactions of policy-makers and the public. Such a description might apply to federal tax enforcement or public health policy. The situation with immigration is starker, because the existing scheme manages to generate such an unwieldy mix of burdens and missed opportunities.

Consider first how, from an economic perspective, American immigration law and policy as it came to function by the first decade of the twenty-first century was epitomized by high costs and missed opportunities. Even as a growing chorus of observers by the turn of the twenty-first century decried the situation, American policy-makers were presiding over a system where large numbers of high-skilled immigrants eager to stay in the US were essentially forced to leave (Shachar 2006). Even if one does not adopt a vision of the world where countries are best understood as locked in a zero-sum struggle for economic advantage, it is difficult to tell a story where this arrangement is broadly desirable. Americans lose out on some of the spillover benefits arising from the work of foreign engineers and entrepreneurs who have trained at American companies. Potential long-term migrants with proven skills and a likely capacity to build longer-term links between the USA and the rest of the world are denied a permanent place in American society even as American businesses then vigorously recruit a new round of skilled but ostensibly temporary workers.[12]

The scarcity of lawful permanent resident visas and other limitations of the existing system also have downstream effects on prospective migrants. At least some high-skilled immigrants who could add value to the economy thus appear to be increasingly reluctant to come to the USA because of the difficulty in finding a longer-term place in American society. At the same time, the existing framework has also created a sub-optimal system for semiskilled workforce, impacting the economics of employment for sectors heavily relying on semiskilled workers. Note, for example, that sectors such as construction and domestic services shoulder a huge proportion of unauthorized workers, and millions of middle-and upper-income American families are in employment-related arrangements for household work with the undocumented. These effects are coupled with the economic consequences – the fiscal impact of spending large resources to maintain a status quo that most Americans dislike.[13]

Immigration and border security policy can prove especially divisive in certain regions. States near the border, or receiving large numbers of immigrants, unquestionably draw some benefits from their status: immigrants make substantial contributions to the regional economy (for example), and proximity to the border can create trade-related economic opportunities. Yet the political reactions regarding immigration and border security in certain regions are also exacerbated by the structure of federal policy-making. States facing high actual or perceived costs from immigration have little direct leverage over federal policy. Political players with power over budgets and resources in the federal government have only limited incentives to internalize costs, helping to exacerbate regional concerns. Greater federal support for receiving large numbers of immigrants could help assuage widespread local concerns about immigration (Bush and McClarty 2009). Still, such support (a tough sell particularly in the present budget climate) would be unlikely to change the long-term political logic making immigration a major issue in certain states and galvanizing state and local politicians toward ratcheting up state-level responses to immigration.

Given strong regional political demands, and the relatively weak incentives for anyone to think systematically about the downstream resource implications of building up border security, policy-makers and the public in some local areas have sought to regulate immigration directly. The US Constitution identifies the control of immigration as a major domain of federal responsibility.[14] Although some statutes and federal administrative decisions contemplate some local role for local police in coordination with the federal government, that role is quite circumscribed given the nature of existing statutes and constitutional provisions, as well as the consequences of unconstrained state or local policy-making in immigration enforcement.[15] Nonetheless, even recent Supreme Court interpretations reaffirming the primacy of the federal role in immigration leave some room for local jurisdictions to make certain policy choices relevant to immigration enforcement. Given continued concern about unlawful migration and border security in some regions, some local jurisdictions will likely continue to experiment with measures that press the limits of their authority to engage local police in certain aspects of immigration enforcement.

Concern for stricter enforcement is also evident in another crucial trend: the staggering flow of federal resources toward expanded border security – particularly border patrol agents – without sufficiently nuanced attention to the underlying goals and consequences. Lawmakers and other policy-makers have rarely focused sustained attention on building the full measure of downstream capacity to address, for example, the consequences of greater CBP apprehensions that result from building up the Border Patrol (e.g., GAO 2004). Neither, as I note in other work, have they focused much attention on interior enforcement, where domestic political pressures and practical constraints on routine police activity have contributed to an enforcement system of limited effectiveness (Cuéllar 2012,

62–74). Accordingly, one untoward security consequence thus involves the risk of undermining the benefits of improved border security because of insufficient investment in complementary resources such as detention. A further security challenge involves the opportunity cost of resource increases for border-related activities that may tend to have a less significant role in addressing swelling violence in Mexico's northern border, where trafficking organizations are engaged in an increasingly aggressive spiral of violence and the Mexican government is vigorously targeting such activities (Beittel 2009).

Some regions may also be impacted by the changing nature of illicit organization reflected by major actors in illicit activity along the Mexican border. As potential migrants along the Southwest border and elsewhere in Latin America face a heightened border security presence and a system that still provides meager avenues for legal immigration, they are increasingly adopting riskier crossing patterns (GAO 2006). Because of the potential trade-off between risk and money, other migrants appear willing to enlist the services of smuggling organizations traditionally focused on drugs. As the buildup in border security has played out over the last two decades, the new realities on the border are likely to have an impact on the level of organization and sophistication deployed by individuals seeking to cross the border. In fact, the vast increase in Border Patrol deployments and related activity appears to be coinciding with drug trafficking organizations' movement into broader lines of illicit activity, including human smuggling (Archibold 2006). These developments underscore the potential for enforcement efforts involving immigration and border security to shape the context affecting transnational actors involved in illicit activity. To the extent that heightened deployments of Border Patrol resources are having an impact not only on migrants' decisions regarding where and whether to cross but also on the activities of drug-trafficking organizations, the cost– benefit trade-off involved in evaluating border needs to consider the potential risks that could emerge from such organizations' augmented role in human smuggling.

The potential impact of immigration and border security policy on the activities of major drug trafficking organizations is just one example of the broader links between security and immigration policy that the executive branch has increasingly acknowledged. In the USA's path-breaking National Security Strategy, released in May 2010, the Obama Administration recognized the more commonly appreciated relationship between immigration and security, while also underscoring the subtler (though no less important) ways in which immigrants help fulfill the nation's goals involving strong relationships with the rest of the world and a capacity for innovation and technological progress (The White House 2010, 29–30). Breaking with narrower conceptions of security, and of the society that security is meant to protect, the strategy treats immigration as a powerful ingredient of long-term economic prosperity and innovation.[16] Just as notable is the strategy's acknowledgement that the country's security is ill-served when a vast and costly immigration-enforcement scheme is consumed by difficulty of policing a vast undocumented population whose least favorite experience is likely to be any interaction with law enforcement. In fact, the longstanding status quo in American immigration law is epitomized by a system that tolerates a vast pool of undocumented immigrants with high incentives to limit contact with authorities and providing potential opportunities for individuals posing genuine threats to hide among millions living in the shadows. As a practical matter, enforcement of existing American immigration law poses an overwhelming task for authorities as they purport to police vast industrial sites, farms, construction locations, and vast distances across difficult terrain representing the longest land border between a developing country and an advanced industrialized one. The result is a chronically overburdened enforcement system, where authorities have consumed even staggering resource increases as a result of a legal framework that interferes with nearly any reasonable effort to prioritize enforcement by focusing on the most pressing security threats posed by aliens (Bush and McClarty 2009, 28–29).

It is unquestionably true that lawmakers and executive branch officials in recent years have sought to prioritize removal of serious criminal offenders among other things (Bush and McClarty 2009, 28–29). Still, even such a scheme suffers from the drain on resources spent catching routine violators. The impact of such constraints is plain in the fact that the so-called 'catch and release' policy – whereby non-Mexican unauthorized border-crossers were essentially released into the USA pending removal – persisted into 2006 because of the enormous number of overall apprehensions that needed to be managed by the authorities (Wein, Liu, and Motskin 2009).

These direct security-related opportunity costs play out alongside subtler impacts on the nation's well-being that arise from the pronounced risk of ill treatment faced by many foreign-born individuals (Bush and McClarty 2009, 30–31). By an overwhelming margin, the process of clearing security in the USA is considered the most burdensome and uncomfortable in the world (Bush and McClarty 2009, 30–31; Schuck 2003). With the current system leaving unaddressed the large unauthorized population, and offering a loosely coupled mix of institutional practices to adjudicate and enforce in difficult considerations, the risk of ill-treatment is especially acute – even affecting some US citizens (Bush and McClarty 2009). These realities take their toll in multiple ways, by affecting the USA's capacity to inspire people around the world, and its ability to attract visitors and migrants from abroad.

4. Managing immigrants and citizenship in a separated domestic system

If rational economic policy priorities, security concerns, or careful public deliberation do not explain American immigration law, how might we better understand the distinctive mix of harshness and discretion that shapes the demographic character of the American nation? The answer lies in understanding the process that has produced modern immigration statutes, including the landmark IRCA of 1986, and that shapes the responses of public organizations and the public to each other. Competing interest group pressures have built a cluster of statutory provisions that is not designed to work, and organizational fragmentation has often made the problem worse (Cuéllar 2012). In part because of lawmakers' reluctance to create a stronger domestic enforcement regime, the laws punishing companies and individuals for hiring unlawful workers are exceedingly difficult to enforce. Poorly regulated temporary worker programs, visa allocation schemes that create decades-long waits for some applicants, and employer sanctions without civil enforcement provisions or the means to be enforced – these are the legacy of a system trying to be many things to different constituents. It does not help that in creating the DHS, Congress split immigration policy-making three ways and created extensive delays and bureaucratic infighting.

Indeed, nearly everything in American immigration policy depends on the interaction of multiple agencies with different cultures and goals. The State Department's Bureau of Consular Affairs and the DHS's Bureau of Citizenship and Immigration Services (CIS), for example, share responsibility on visa allocation for green cards (Aleinikoff, Martin, and Motomura 2008, 267–287). Because of its bureaucratic position, its congressional overseers, and its relationship to domestic constituencies, CIS is likely to be more concerned with successfully providing services domestically. In contrast, State is likely to reflect greater concern with making its visa allocation process bureaucratically tractable, and probably assigns lower priority to visa-related matters save where they have major foreign policy consequences. As a practical matter, these agencies' failure to improve coordination means that some number of available visa numbers go unused, because they are not made available early enough in the year for individuals to take advantage of them. Similarly, Justice and DHS share a role on terrorism-related inadmissibility grounds. The level of trust among these agencies (or its absence) can have a major effect on the viability of effective reforms in this area that fully address security concerns while addressing humanitarian considerations. Separately, DHS administers immigration enforcement and detention, but Justice defends DHS in court. Their incentives are almost certainly likely to be different, with DHS (having different leadership, different appropriators, and distinct career tracks) insulated from the downstream costs of its policies involving detention or enforcement, for example. Security and terrorist mobility problems also implicate the challenge of fragmentation in the policy-making process (National Commission on Terrorist Attacks Upon the United States 2004).[17]

In effect, the internal organization of the federal government itself belies any notion of a unified, rational, and inherently coordinated immigration system. The border patrol agents on a dusty road in Cochise County, Arizona; the Deputy Assistant Attorney General overseeing a swelling portfolio of immigration litigation from a large office at Main Justice in Washington, DC; the Oklahoma lawmaker skeptical of comprehensive reform; and the administrator presiding over a multi-billion dollar immigration services – all share power over the system but rarely if ever want the same outcomes.

Agency fragmentation complicates immigration policy in several ways. The separation of authority across two preeminent cabinet agencies (Justice and DHS), three major agencies within DHS, and multiple other agency players tends on balance to reflect and accentuate broader political divisions on immigration policy. The Labor Department, for example, responding in part to concerns from labor constituents, might press hard for a policy change limiting the risk that immigration enforcement will interfere with investigations involving unfair labor practices or working conditions. DHS may have different priorities. Moreover, these divisions insulate some agencies from the downstream impact of policy changes. Greater investigation and apprehension, for example, has potential consequences for the agency running prisons, which reports to an entirely different cabinet official. Finally, fragmentation makes policy coordination and change slower and more costly, as interagency disagreements need to be resolved and different interests adjudicated. At the margin, those features can decrease the responsiveness of the immigration system to developments in pluralist politics (like elections) and increase perceptions of ineffectiveness as agencies disagree about federal goals on immigration policy.

These problems are occurring in an environment where a large proportion of Americans express concern about immigration – far more so than in previous generations. In contrast to the situation that lawmakers and President Johnson faced during the 1960s, immigration became by the late twentieth century a topic of routine media coverage, congressional hearings, and public debate (Cuéllar 2012). Politically significant proportions of the public, in some cases anxious about the future of the nation-state, have become concerned about the apparent chronic failure to police the territorial, political, and social limits of their national community (Brader, Valentino, and Suhay 2008, 959–961; Cohen 2001). In response, politicians can make use (though to varying degrees of success) of these public reactions. The sequence of legislative reactions includes, for example, California's Proposition 187 in 1994 (MPI Task Force 2006, 24–27), reforms included in the Antiterrorism and Effective Death Penalty Act and later the IIRIRA legislation at the federal levels in 1994 and 1996 (Weissbrodt and Danielson 2004, 40–45), and more recent enforcement-oriented efforts involving border security without the rest of comprehensive reform (Cuéllar 2012).

The laws and policies that have resulted during the latter two decades of the twentieth century and the first decade of the twenty-first have a tendency to narrowly cast the challenges of managing immigration. Rather than encouraging lawmakers to support grand bargains in immigration policy in the decades after the IRCA reforms of 1986, the extent of public frustration and polarization instead almost certainly tends to foment the view that immigration laws are unlikely to be enforced, and encourages lawmakers and policy-makers to support even more expansive enforcement laws that are difficult to enforce and further strengthen the cycle of enacting aggressive measures that are difficult to enforce. This situation is perhaps analogous to the 'policy feedback' process described by Pierson (1993), save for the fact that the consequence tends to erode the legitimacy of public organizations and the laws they are implementing rather than cementing public acceptance of a given policy regime.

That cycle has not always taken its present form. Past episodes of reform in immigration law belie the notion that immigration policy constitutes a one-way ratchet toward increasing harshness. Recent decades contrast, for instance, with passage of the Immigration and Nationality Act of 1965 – major reform, drastically increasing migration opportunities, less public attention focused on immigration policy, and no broad legislative focus on coupling enforcement and control policies with expansion in migration opportunities (and removal of explicit racial quotas).[18] Even the Immigration Act of 1990 included substantial reforms increasing migration opportunities and rationalizing the system in areas ranging from economic migration opportunities to asylum and refugee (though not nearly as sweeping as 1965 Act), but relatively soon after 1986 reforms (before their relatively blatant failure attracted major public attention). No doubt part of the change in context now fueling political divisions over immigration policy reflects the stark failure of the IRCA of 1986, which had promised to essentially erase the problem of large-scale undocumented migration through a combination of employer sanctions, visa reforms, and legalization (Andreas 2000, 85–87). The distinctions probably also reflect not only a distinct interest group context, along with the growing salience of immigration-related issues among a public confronting the complexities of economic uncertainty and globalization. Such a state of the world makes it harder for quiet, sensible changes to occur or (absent rare exceptions) for presidents to deliberately reshape immigration enforcement or for agencies to build autonomy by inspiring confidence among the public.

If anything, public confidence is the opposite of what the existing regime has produced. A system of laws that are only sporadically enforced triggers what I call a 'polarizing implementation' dynamic encouraging passage of even harsher laws (which leads to legislative and executive initiatives exacerbating, rather than ameliorating, current difficulties). The evolution of public opinion since the 1986 immigration reform bill suggests that public frustration with immigration is exacerbated by the relatively low enforcement, which in turn fuels passage of harsher laws that are difficult to enforce (Cuéllar 2012). Examples include the employer sanction provisions of IRCA, expanded removal provisions covering less-significant criminal offenses in 1994 and 1996, expansion of the 3- and 10-year bars to adjustment of status, time limits on applications for asylum, and a REAL ID law requiring drastic, immigration-related changes in driver's licenses, that has never been fully implemented. What these provisions have in common is that they tend to increase enforcement and implementation challenges (for example, by expanding the pool of people subject to removal or the steps that state governments would need to take in order to issue compliant identifications). None has been enforced especially well, and virtually all have found their way into political rhetoric as alleged examples of why we need even tougher enforcement. Easily observed instances of immigration-related lawbreaking have helped generate disproportionate attention for border security and interior enforcement, when the deeper problems are more systemic and involve the overall regulation of immigration (Cuéllar 2012). Attention to this dimension of the issue can become self-reinforcing, as politicians respond to public concerns, and politicians' responses shape public perceptions. Meanwhile, discretion allows different players in the system to avoid the full measure of consequences associated with the status quo, making them easier to avoid supporting reforms that most Americans tend to support.

The cycle of polarizing implementation in more recent American immigration policy-making also contrasts with the evolution of legal and policy change in a number of areas that also involve a great deal of complexity and high economic and political stakes. In tobacco control policy, there is no evidence of polarized opinion where lack of enforcement of existing laws galvanizes interest in more aggressive legislative measures, since legal authority for any enforcement is limited; and political context is different, with much more explicit conflict between tobacco companies and civil society groups. Food safety policy – some similarities to polarizing implementation dynamic, with costly-to-enforce existing provisions that become (in some cases) self-defeating, which in turn galvanizes greater public concern and support for major food safety legislative measures. The issue is a less high-profile one than immigration, however, and the new laws are designed (in close consultation with the FDA) to facilitate enforcement rather than making it more difficult (a reflection, to some degree perhaps, of the autonomy and influence of the FDA relative to the immigration bureaucracies, and probably the greater interest of lawmakers in what will actually work rather than what will send a message) (Carpenter 2010).

This is not to say that any change is essentially impossible. Given the high visibility of immigration as well as the fragmentation of agency authority, presidential control of enforcement is fraught with political costs and administrative burdens (Cuéllar 2012, 50–57). Still, the DHS plan to institute a mechanism to defer action for certain undocumented youth who would have qualified for the failed DREAM Act legislation shows an example of the limited avenues available for executive action (U.S. Department of Homeland Security 2012). It would be difficult to contend that officials leading enforcement agencies lack the legal authority to prioritize enforcement decisions given a world of scarce enforcement resources. It would be odd as well to suggest that officials can set priorities but lack any power to communicate such priorities to the public in a systematic fashion. Nonetheless, the genuine impact of the Obama Administration's decision to defer any enforcement action against certain childhood arrivals is as striking as the tightly limited scope of the measure. The reprieve is granted to applicants for only two years at a time, does not constitute a path to permanent lawful status, and is available to a relatively narrow group of beneficiaries (corresponding roughly to those who would have benefited from unsuccessful efforts to enact legislation known as the 'Dream Act' that had previously enjoyed bipartisan support). Such limits emphasize the relevance of legislators, organized interests, and the larger public.

Over time, demographic changes and rising costs of legislative gridlock may also reshape the terrain for more substantial reforms of immigration statutes. The context of deferred action for Dream Act-eligible young people is a system that works poorly and that makes legislative change difficult given broad frustration with immigration policy and the ease of mobilizing groups and members of the public concerned about potential reforms. Yet the possibility of thoughtful reform remains – and remains appealing – to most Americans (Cuéllar 2012, 27–32).

Perhaps another factor in the current system's staying power owes not only to the generalized difficulty in achieving policy change in the American system, or even to polarizing implementation, but to the fact that not everyone loses in the current system. Some politicians from both parties are in a position to exploit the present equilibrium precisely because it comes across as so dysfunctional to their constituents. Regardless of whether some of these lawmakers, local elected officials, and policy-makers genuinely want to achieve a more reasonable compromise on immigration policy bearing a more easily articulated relationship to the country's interests, they at least are in a position to derive some value from the present system – though this political calculus plainly depends on the willingness of their constituents to reward the 'criticizing' politicians for the positions they are taking without punishing them for failing to fix the status quo. Perhaps some law enforcement officials who have tremendous discretion in investigating and imposing sanctions (and, in some cases, growing budgets) under the current system find something of value in it – but here again, this scenario is viable only to the extent these officials do not view it as likely that they'll be held accountable for an unpopular status quo. Some employers may value (and probably exaggerate the value) of the low cost of undocumented workers and discount the probability of sanctions against them. And employers and immigrant advocates sometimes fear changing the status quo because they might lose some elements of existing law that they value.[19]

Sources acknowledging the cultural conflict often implicit in managing immigration often hedge on whether the reluctance to embrace demographic and social change is prescriptively desirable or even acceptable (Zolberg 2006, 16). Critical to understanding the present and future of American immigration law, however, is the insight that the political economy shaping this area of law and policy must include not only labor market effects or superficial public attitudes, but also the dynamic evolution of the public's views in response to immigration and to the system that administers immigration policy. Widespread skepticism about whether immigration laws will be enforced could therefore loom large in the context of a debate that includes voices with lingering ambivalence about the USA's relatively high levels of overall immigration, or reluctant to increase levels of immigration even further in a manner that could contribute to the country's economy and limit backlogs.

5. Conclusion

Enshrined in American statutes are the legal provisions that regulate membership in the world's largest immigrant democracy. For much of its recent history, the USA has exhibited not only anxiety about unlawful immigration but also a relative acceptance of high rates of legal immigration and of social and legal arrangements supporting immigrants' access to naturalization. Though such acceptance is by no means uniform across regions and individuals, the pattern is sufficiently consistent to reflect a substantial convergence between widespread prescriptive commitments of opinion leaders and more economically focused rationales favoring immigration. While the resulting architecture is remarkable because of the large numbers of immigrants legally admitted and the path made available for legal immigrants to citizenship, these laws are just as worthy of scrutiny because they forge a largely self-defeating system capable of engendering political controversy and eroding the legitimacy of the laws and agencies implementing American immigration policy.

Ambitious legal aspirations underlie the system for allocating scarce access to lawful permanent residence, for establishing reciprocal obligations between immigrants and society, and for allowing immigrants to assume the central role of citizenship within the state. Those aspirations are all the more ambitious in light of the powerful social and economic forces that encourage continued migration to a country such as the USA (Vertovec 2003). At the same time, the hot glare of politics has come to complicate the work of nearly every aspect of the American immigration system, including the historically evolving interplay of obligation and responsibility governing the position of migrants in the USA. Despite a host of costs and burdens produced by our existing arrangement, the political economy of American immigration law limits the space for and speed of change in this domain. At the same time, the system's political logic also creates some possibilities for reform – particularly when policy-makers and civil society take seriously some of the critical and often misunderstood aspects of that political economy.

One such aspect of immigration policy involves the extent to which, even in a technologically sophisticated, advanced industrialized country, state capacity at any given time in history is a finite resource. In a world of budget constraints, security problems, and policy trade-offs, efforts to achieve near-impossible goals may be almost be as damaging to a country's desire to manage transnational forces as ignoring those forces altogether. The less tailored a nation's immigration or border security policy is to its goals and circumstances, the higher the opportunity cost, and the stronger the signal sent of a state's relatively lower capacity to manage its affairs. Even the most compelling prescriptive ideals face erosion from the bureaucracy's structure and decisions, the public's perceptions, and the incentives of the politicians who represent them.

In the end, the American immigration system remains in nearly equal parts remarkable achievement and heavily burdened, nearly dysfunctional compromise. American citizenship is an achievement in no small measure because it is flexible enough to welcome into its ranks people raised in different societies with often-starkly distinct views, and empowers all Americans – naturalized and native-born – to shape the political process. But the latest chapters in the American legal regulation of immigration illustrate, too, how rights and obligations defining the scope of national communities are generated at the fertile intersection between law and institutions. As the sun sets on any given day or period of history, national aspirations reflected in legal commitments merit an important role in understanding how the USA and other immigrant democracies approach migration. But so do institutional choices about implementation and public reactions. Only through careful analysis of these factors can we hope to understand what happens, and to advance reasonable prescriptive commitments, when states use their scarce capacity to manage powerful forces impacting the trajectory of their national communities.

Acknowledgements
I am grateful to Kyle Maurer and Warner Sallman for helpful research assistance, and to Alex Aleinikoff, Dave Martin, Esther Olavarria, and John Skrentny for thoughtful perspectives. Needless to say, they are entirely absolved from all liability for what is in these pages.

Notes
1. 'The starting point for theorizing about immigration policy is an understanding of the distinctiveness of international migration itself as a social phenomenon' (Zolberg 2006, 11).

2. On immigration enforcement, see MPI (2005). Regarding public support for the Arizona law, see Pew Center for the People and the Press (2010). For a discussion of Arizona's law, see Chishti and Bergeron (2010).
3. Cf. Chae Chan Ping v. United States, 130 U.S. 581 (1889) ('The power of exclusion of foreigners being an incident of sovereignty belonging to the government of the United States, as a part of those sovereign powers delegated by the Constitution, the right to its exercise at any time [exists] when, in the judgment of the government, *the interests of the country require it*') (emphasis added).
4. See, e.g., INS v. Chadha, 462 U.S. 919 (1983).
5. See, e.g., INS v. St. Cyr, 533 U.S. 289 (2001) (reflecting disagreements about the availability of habeas corpus relief for aliens detained under immigration statutes); and (Cox and Rodriguez (2009) (addressing debates over the scope of executive power to control immigration law and policy).
6. Medellin v. Texas, 552 U.S. 491 (2008) (discussing US responsibilities under the Vienna Convention on Consular Notification); Plyler v. Doe, 457 U.S. 202 (1982) (invalidating a state law denying funding of education for undocumented students).
7. This is a complex subject, however, and one where doctrinal subtleties implicate continued legal developments. See, for example, Motomura (1990).
8. Cf. Sale v. Haitian Centers' Council, 509 U.S. 155 (1993).
9. Though note that in recent years the plenary power doctrine has arguably been subjected to a range of doctrinal refinements resulting in some significant erosion (as the courts have grown more accepting of constitutional claims). See Aleinikoff (2002, 153–165).
10. See also Plyler v. Doe, 457 U.S. 202 (1982).
11. This situation is at least somewhat evocative of broad public participation in a few other issues, such as public safety, rather than the treatment of the issue as the province of experts designing a space shuttle or an elaborate claim compensation scheme.
12. I realize there are some complexities in working through the full social welfare calculus, particularly if one considers the impact on sending as well as receiving countries. What is relevant in this context is the poor fit between plausible versions of Americans' economic interests and the day-to-day operation of its immigration system on potential skilled immigrants.
13. On the costs of border enforcement, see MPI (2005). On public frustration with the existing system, see Pew Center for the People and the Press (2007).
14. Arizona v. United States, 567 U.S. (2012).
15. Arizona v. United States, 567 U.S. (2012).
16. For an example, see Adamson (2006, 35). On innovation, a recent study, for example, shows how a 1% increase in immigrant college graduates is associated with an increase in patents per capita of about 15% – without crowding out nonimmigrant inventors (Hunt and Gautheir-Loiselle 2008).
17. Different agendas exist at the US Attorney's Office, ICE, main DHS, State, FBI, and the intelligence community; relative lack of coordination between financial intelligence and terrorist mobility; system designed to allow local and lower-level priorities to affect enforcement action (e.g., US Attorney decisions not to prioritize, in some cases, the charging of employers after workplace raids).
18. See Zolberg (2006, 329).
19. In the case of employers, the central role they play in selecting individuals for employment-based visas, and in the case of advocates, the relatively large number of family-based permanent resident visas.

References

Adamson, F. B. 2006. "International Migration in a Globalizing World: Assessing Impacts on National Security." In *Globalization and National Security*, edited by J. Kirshner, 35–73. London: Routledge.

Aleinikoff, T. A. 2002. *Semblances of Sovereignty: The Constitution, the State, and American Citizenship*. Cambridge, MA: Harvard University Press.

Aleinikoff, T. A., D. A. Martin, and H. Motomura. 2008. *Immigration and Citizenship: Process and Policy*. 6th ed. Eagan, MN: Thomson West.

Alesina, A., E. Glaeser, and B. Sacerdote. 2001. "Why Doesn't the U.S. Have a European-Style Welfare State?" *Brookings Papers on Economic Activity* 2: 1–69.

Andreas, P. 2000. *Border Games: Policing the U.S.-Mexico Divide*. Ithaca, NY: Cornel University Press.

Archibold, R. C. 2006. "Risky Measures by Smugglers Increase Toll on Immigrants." *New York Times*, August 9.

Archibold, R., and M. Thee-Brenan. 2010. "Poll Shows Most in U.S. Want Overhaul of Immigration Laws." *New York Times*, May 3.

Beittel, J. S. 2009. "Mexico's Drug-Related Violence." *Congressional Research Service Report*, May 29.

Borjas, G. J. 1999. *Heaven's Door: Immigration Policy and the American Economy*. Princeton, NJ: Princeton University Press.

Brader, T., N. A. Valentino, and E. Suhay. 2008. "What Triggers Public Opposition to Immigration? Anxiety, Group Cues, and Immigration Threat." *American Journal of Political Science* 52: 959–978.

Brady, D., and C. Volden. 1998. *Revolving Gridlock: Politics and Policy from Jimmy Carter to George W. Bush*. Boulder, CO: Westview Press.

Briggs, V. M. 2001. *Immigration and American Unionism*. Ithaca, NY: ILR Press.

Buck, B., M. Hobbs, A. Kaiser, S. Lang, D. Montero, K. Romines, and T. Scott. 2003. "Immigration and Immigrants: Trends in American Public Opinion, 1964–1999." *Journal of Ethnic & Cultural Diversity in Social Work* 12 (3): 73–90.

Bush, J., and T. F. McClarty. 2009. *U.S. Immigration Policy*. Council on Foreign Relations Independent Task Force Report No. 63. New York: Council on Foreign Relations.

Calavita, K. 1989. "The Immigration Policy Debate: Critical Analysis and Future Options." In *Mexican Migration to the United States: Origins, Consequences, and Policy Options*, edited by W. Cornelius, and J. A. Bustamante, 151–178. Berkeley: University of California Press.

Calavita, K. 1990. "Employer Sanctions Violations: Toward a Dialectical Model of White-Collar Crime." *Law and Society Review* 24 (4): 1041–1071.

Canes-Wrone, B., W. Minozzi, and J. B. Reveley. 2011. "Issue Accountability and the Mass Public." *Legislative Studies Quarterly* 36 (1): 5–35.

Carpenter, D. 2010. *Reputation and Power: Organizational Image and Pharmaceutical Regulation at the FDA*. Princeton, NJ: Princeton University Press.

Chishti, M., and C. Bergeron. 2010, May 17. *Policy Beat: New Arizona Law Engulfs Immigration Debate*. Washington, DC: Migration Policy Institute. http://www.migrationinformation.org/USFocus/display.cfm?ID=782

Citrin, J., D. P. Green, and C. Wong. 1997. "Public Opinion Toward Immigration Reform: The Role of Economic Motivations." *Journal of Politics* 59 (3): 858–881.

Cohen, E. S. 2001. *Politics of Globalization in the United States*. Washington, DC: Georgetown University Press.

Cox, A. B. 2007. "Deference, Delegation, and Immigration Law." *University of Chicago Law Review* 74: 1671–1687.

Cox, A., and C. Rodriguez. 2009. "The President and Immigration Power." *Yale Law Journal* 119: 458–547.

Cuéllar, M.-F. 2012. "The Political Economies of Immigration Law." *UC Irvine Law Review* 2 (1): 1–90.

Esses, V. M., J. F. Dovidio, L. M. Jackson, and T. L. Armstrong. 2002. "The Immigration Dilemma: The Role of Perceived Group Competition, Ethnic Prejudice, and National Identity." *Journal of Social Issues* 57: 389–412.

General Accounting Office (GAO). 2004. *Border Security: Agencies Need to Better Coordinate Their Strategies on Federal Lands*. Report to Congress. Washington, DC: GAO.

GAO. 2006. *Illegal Immigration: Border-Crossing Deaths Have Doubled since 1995; Border Patrol's Efforts to Prevent Deaths Have Not Been Fully Evaluated*. Report to the Honorable Bill Frist, Majority Leader, U.S. Senate. Washington, DC: GAO.

Hanson, G. H. 2007. *The Economic Logic of Illegal Immigration*. Council on Foreign Relations: Special Report No. 26. New York: Council on Foreign Relations.

Hunt, J., and M. Gautheir-Loiselle. 2008. *How Much Does Immigration Boost Innovation*. National Bureau of Economic Research Working Paper No. 14312.

Krehbiel, K. 1998. *Pivotal Politics: A Theory of U.S. Lawmaking*. Chicago, IL: University of Chicago Press.

Laham, N. 2000. *Ronald Reagan and the Politics of Immigration Reform*. Santa Barbara, CA: Praeger.

Migration Policy Institute (MPI). 2005. *Immigration Enforcement Spending since IRCA*. Immigration Facts, no. 10 (November) Washington, DC: Migration Policy Institute.

MPI Task Force. 2006. *Immigration and America's Future: A New Chapter – Report of the Independent Commission on Immigration and America's Future*. Washington, DC: Migration Policy Institute.

Monger, R., and J. Yankay. 2012. *U.S. Legal Permanent Residents 2011*. Annual Flow Report. Washington, DC: U.S. Department of Homeland Security.

Motomura, H. 1990. "Immigration Law after a Century of Plenary Power: Phantom Constitutional Norms and Statutory Interpretation." *Yale Law Journal* 100 (3): 545–613.

National Commission on Terrorist Attacks upon the United States. 2004. *The 9/11 Commission Report: Final Report of the National Commission on Terrorist Attacks upon the United States*. Washington, DC: National Commission on Terrorist Attacks upon the United States.

Passel, J. S., and D'V. Cohn. 2009. *A Portrait of Unauthorized Immigrants in the United States*. Pew Hispanic Center Report. Washington, DC: Pew Research Center.

Pew Center for the People and the Press. 2007, June 7. *Mixed Views on Immigration Bill*. Washington, DC: Pew Research Center. http://pewresearch.org/pubs/503/immigration-bill

Pew Center for the People and the Press. 2010, May 12. *Public Supports Arizona's Immigration Law*. Washington, DC: Pew Research Center.

Pfeiffer, D. 2010. "The President's Record on Border Security." *White House Blog*, June 21.

Pierson, P. 1993. "When Effect Becomes Cause: Policy Feedback and Political Change." *World Politics* 45: 595–628.

Reding, N. 2008. *Methland: The Death and Life of a Small American Town*. New York: Bloomsbury.

Schuck, P. 2003. *Diversity in America: Keeping Government at a Safe Distance*. Cambridge, MA: Belknap Press.

Shachar, A. 2006. "The Race for Talent: Highly-Skilled Migrants and Competitive Immigration Regimes." *New York University Law Review* 81: 148–206.

The White House. 2010. *National Security Strategy*. Washington DC: The White House.

Trebilcock, M. J., and M. Sudak. 2006. "The Political Economy of Emigration and Immigration." *New York University Law Review* 81: 234–293.

U.S. Department of Homeland Security. 2012, August 15. "USCIS Begins Accepting Requests for Consideration of Deferred Action for Childhood Arrivals." http://www.dhs.gov/news/2012/08/15/uscis-begins-accepting-requests-consideration-deferred-action-childhood-arrivals

Vertovec, S. 2003. "Migration and Other Modes of Transnationalism: Towards Conceptual Cross-Fertilization." *International Migration Review* 37 (3): 641–665.

Wasem, R. E. 2010. *Immigration Reform Issues in the 111th Congress*. Congressional Research Service Report, February 2.

Wein, L. M., Y. Liu, and A. Motskin. 2009. "Analyzing the Homeland Security of the U.S.-Mexico Border." *Risk Analysis* 29 (5): 699–713.

Weissbrodt, D., and L. Danielson. 2004. *Immigration Law and Procedure in a Nutshell*. St. Paul, MN: Westlaw.

Wishnie, M. J. 2007. "Prohibiting the Employment of Unauthorized Immigrants: The Experiment Fails." *University of Chicago Legal Forum* 2007: 193–217.

Zolberg, A. R. 2006. *A Nation by Design: Immigration Policy in the Fashioning of America*. Cambridge, MA: Harvard University Press.

Laissez-faire and its discontents: US naturalization and integration policy in comparative perspective

Noah Pickus

Kenan Institute for Ethics, Duke University, Durham, NC, USA; Sanford School of Public Policy, Duke University, Durham, NC, USA

In the 1990s and early 2000s, conflicts over citizenship and nationhood erupted in US naturalization policy, part of a recurring pattern since the eighteenth century. Since these most recent controversies, major immigrant-receiving countries in Western Europe, as well as Australia and Canada, have introduced or revised naturalization requirements, preparatory courses, and formal ceremonies for prospective citizens. The USA's approach to naturalization is, by comparison, less demanding. The US approach is undergirded by an essentially laissez-faire philosophy in which the nation admits large numbers of immigrants without much attention to skills, values, or English-language ability and who are expected to integrate without significant government assistance. While this laissez-faire philosophy represents a gain for core liberal principles, I argue that it may also reflect reduced social solidarity and contribute to the vitriolic conflicts over immigration that are now waged regularly at the local, state, and federal level. The essay concludes by considering several efforts in the USA to clarify the bargain of mutual expectations and obligations on the part of newcomers and citizens.

1. Introduction

In the 1990s and early 2000s conflicts over citizenship and nationhood erupted in US naturalization policy, part of a recurring pattern since the eighteenth century (Pickus 2005). Since these most recent controversies, major immigrant-receiving countries in Western Europe, as well as Australia and Canada, have introduced or revised naturalization requirements, preparatory courses, and formal ceremonies for prospective citizens. What had less then 10 years ago involved analyzing a single country now calls for a comparative perspective. In part one of this essay, I make two observations. First, the USA's approach to naturalization is less demanding than is found in Western Europe today. Second, this approach is undergirded by an essentially laissez-faire philosophy in which the nation admits large numbers of immigrants without much attention to skills, values, or English-language ability and who are expected to integrate without significant government assistance.

While this laissez-faire philosophy represents a gain for core liberal principles, I argue in part two that it may also reflect reduced social solidarity and contribute to the vitriolic conflicts over immigration that are now waged regularly at the local, state, and federal level. Ultimately, the US approach to naturalization and the integration of immigrants may even reflect and contribute to the rise of new political divisions based on immigrants and citizens' complicated national and global commitments. In the final part of this essay,

I consider several efforts to address both real and speculative problems that the American model produces. These efforts seek to clarify the bargain of mutual expectations and obligations on the part of newcomers and citizens.

2. Naturalization and integration in Western Europe and the USA

Dirk Jacobs and Andrea Rea identify several often overlapping goals of the new or revised language requirements, citizenship tests, civic integration courses, and naturalization ceremonies in the major immigrant-receiving countries of Western Europe: preparation for the labor market, qualification for social benefits, and assimilation to the values, culture, and practices of the host country. In some cases, notably the German states of Baden-Wurtemberg and Hesse, the new citizenship tests have been explicitly directed at Muslim immigrants and have sought to probe their 'inner dispositions' with regard to support for gender and homosexual equality, free speech, and the separation between church and state. In the Netherlands, applicants for permanent resident status from Muslim countries are required to pass an integration exam in their home country *prior* to immigrating, and non-EU foreign nationals living in the Netherlands must pass an integration exam within three and a half years in order to obtain permanent residence status (Hansen 2008; Jacobs and Rea 2007; Joppke 2010).

Despite these examples of demanding and exclusionary requirements, Christian Joppke observes that the general trend has been to define national identity as attachment to a set of abstract liberal principles rather than religion or culture. In Germany, for instance, a federally standardized naturalization test explicitly rejected the 'moral inquisition and cultural nationalism' of Baden-Wurtemberg and Hesse. And in Denmark, the core values identified as uniquely Danish – the separation of religion and politics and the equality of men and women – were little different from those identified in other countries. Exclusion in these cases is of a distinctly liberal variety (Joppke 2010, 111–114).

Most European countries also require prospective citizens to enroll in formal integration courses. The number of hours required for these courses varied; in 2008 it ranged from 400 to 900, with the most hours devoted to language instruction and less to civics or culture (8 hours in France to 45 in Germany). While at first most integration courses were free or cost little, the trend has been toward making them fee-based. There is much variation in other areas, such as whether noncompliance results in a fine or impact on social benefits or whether short- or long-term residence depends on participation in these courses (Hansen 2008; Jacobs and Rea 2007).

Among the English-speaking countries of Australia, the UK, Canada, and the USA, the required content for citizenship as well as other demands made of immigrants are significantly less than across Europe. This is especially true in the USA where language requirements are relatively minimal, the naturalization exam is not difficult (6 out of 10 questions given orally from a list of 100 questions distributed in advance with their answers), and the content of the exam has become even more universalistic than in the past. Notably, the USA neither requires nor provides civic integration courses. While English as a Second Language courses for adults exist, they are routinely oversubscribed and fall well short of meeting the demand for them (Hansen 2008; McHugh, Gelatt, and Fix 2007). And any broader strategy for integrating immigrants is largely makeshift and dependent on a patchwork of local government and nonprofit agencies.

The United States Citizenship and Immigration Services implemented a new naturalization test in 2008 that was designed to have the same (high) passing rate but to be more meaningful, transparent, and uniform. The test redesign process took five years and included consultation with a wide variety of stakeholders. While immigrant advocacy groups had long objected to various aspects of the test, the most significant driving force behind its redesign was conservatives concerned about how poorly it instructed prospective citizens in the core democratic principles of the USA.[1]

The main change in the test is to highlight concepts related to the rights and responsibilities of citizenship rather than memorization of what many regarded as relatively unimportant trivia. The test shifts from what Julian Wonjung Park calls a 'power' to a 'principled' centered view of citizenship that focuses on individual rights, the rule of law, and divided powers and reduces attention to the federal government, the executive and nationalist symbols like the flag (Park 2008). The new test also includes more questions about the contributions of women, Native Americans, and African-Americans. As Joppke observes, the revised form 'deliberately abstains from making the test more difficult. In the post 2001 climate, such moderation is astonishing.' Similarly, the USA did not increase the difficulty of its language requirement – a striking contrast with most immigrant-receiving democratic countries (Joppke 2010; McNamara and Shohamy 2008). Uniquely, the USA focuses only on knowledge and understanding of US history and civics. Even when other countries do not require in-depth assessments of prospective citizens' views on specific issues, they still ask for more than the USA does. '[T]he British require the applicants to demonstrate "sufficient knowledge" of (daily) *Life in the UK*,' notes Liav Orgad.

> [T]he Germans ask for an 'adequate knowledge' of the legal system, the society, and the German *way of life*; the Dutch request the demonstration of 'sufficient knowledge' of the Dutch *society*; and the Australians expect 'an adequate knowledge' of Australia's *responsibilities and privileges*. (Orgad 2011, 1282)

There are several reasons why the level of mastery, the preparation required, and the content of the new naturalization exam in the USA are all so relatively undemanding. Some of these reasons relate to the different purposes of the test and the different immigrant populations in Europe and the USA. In the former, some countries explicitly use the naturalization process as a selection criterion for non-EU immigrants. This contrasts with English-speaking countries where immigration policy rather than citizenship policy is the most important point at which selection of new members is made (Joppke 2007).

Most European countries are also focused on Muslims, many of whom are already in the country, and the perceived conflict between liberalism and Islam over the role of women and church/state relations. Until recently, the USA has been preoccupied with Latinos, especially Mexicans (although quite recently there has been increasing attention to issues of values and loyalty with regard to Muslims). While concerns have been raised in the USA about the ability of Mexicans to become good American citizens owing to cultural differences or divided loyalties, there has been considerably less attention to ideological differences (Huntington 2004).

The relatively undemanding and universalistic nature of the US naturalization exam and process also stems from several reasons that are specific to the USA. The USA has fought over its naturalization test for more than 100 years and many of the issues now roiling Europe have been addressed previously. For instance, in the first two decades of the last century, there was wide variation across US courts in the strategies used to determine whether prospective citizens believe in the stated values of their new country. Eventually, though, the courts concluded that they could not assess an applicant's interior state of mind and so would look for an applicant's mere recognition of American constitutional principles as a proxy for attachment to the Constitution.

Doubts about the quality of the US's naturalization and integration process were raised again in the 1990s by the US Commission on Immigration Reform (the so-called 'Jordan Commission,' after its chair, the African-American former congresswoman Barbara Jordan). Jordan's calls for reviving programs that 'Americanize' new immigrants, and for creating a more meaningful naturalization test, were assailed as discriminatory in practice and, often, as racist in intent. Her proposals failed to gain traction, in part because of opposition to them and, in part, because of the vagueness of the commission's definition of Americanization and deep disagreements over its meaning (e.g., Pickus 1997).

Equally important, Jordan's calls to stiffen naturalization requirements and improve its content, and for the nation to undertake Americanization programs, lacked identifiable constituencies to advance them. For conservatives, the commission's recommendations were too weak. They wanted the commission to clearly spell out its opposition to affirmative action and bilingual education. In contrast, proponents of immigrant rights found the commission's proposals far too strong. The commission had few direct links to average Americans, native born or naturalized, and none to immigrants, and its recommendations did not precipitate any greater involvement by any of these groups.[2]

This lackluster response has been the story of other periodic attempts to launch a broader program of assimilation and integration. In 2006, President George W. Bush created a Task Force on New Americans to energize and coordinate the immigrant integration work of federal, state, and local government agencies, the private sector, and nongovernmental organizations. After extensive discussions, site visits, and research, the Task Force called for a national effort to launch an 'Americanization movement for the 21st century.' Yet like the Jordan Commission, little changed in practice as a result. This, too, has been the fate of calls by liberal organizations and immigrant advocates for more extensive outreach efforts to facilitate the social and economic integration of newcomers (Center for Civic Innovation 2007; Little Hoover Commission 2002; Petsod, Wang, and McGarvey 2007; Task Force on New Americans 2008).

This history points to what is perhaps the broadest reason underlying the relatively undemanding formal naturalization process in the USA: an essentially laissez-faire approach to immigration and the integration of immigrants. For all Americans periodically decrying immigrants' lack of assimilation, the unstated view seems to be that to become a citizen, and, more profoundly, an American, is something newcomers must undertake on their own. When asked, Americans may say they want immigrants to learn English and to understand and support American civic values, but they have shown little appetite to make either of these into demanding requirements for citizenship or to provide instruction in English or civics. As a result, while some observers in the 1990s and 2000s worried that a new naturalization test or a revival of Americanization programs would lead to coercion and exclusion, in fact the test was not made more difficult and the broader process of integration was largely ignored.

3. Laissez-faire and its discontents

The US's laissez-faire approach to formal programs of naturalization and integration has much to recommend it. Tests are limited vehicles for acquiring the habits, knowledge, and skills of citizenship, and civic knowledge itself does not necessarily make one a good citizen. A laissez-faire approach also implicitly acknowledges that political, social, and emotional attachment develops over time and in multiple, often informal settings. 'Assimilation,' Richard Alba and Victor Nee observe, 'is something that frequently happens to people while they are making others plans' (Alba and Nee 2003).

Demanding too much of prospective citizens can also violate the very constitutional principles the process is designed to affirm. In contrast to the more inquisitorial strategies adopted in Europe, the US approach does not seek to assess the 'inner dispositions' of prospective citizens. Doing so risks coercing an individual and undermining the right to hold opinions at variance with the political order. And, as a practical matter, pressing too hard on exactly which values a prospective citizen embraces and in what ways offers no guarantee that the applicant's responses are true.

There are also drawbacks to the US approach. While civic knowledge does not in itself make one a good citizen, it does help citizens understand political events and alters and enlarges their views on specific public issues and it makes them less likely to express alienation from public life, more tolerant, and promotes political engagement (Galston 2001). And, according to Randall Hansen, the more demanding language tests in France, Germany, and the Netherlands have had a 'measurably positive impact on language acquisition' (Hansen 2008). One lesson from Europe could be that greater expectations matched with greater investment in helping prepare immigrants can combine to improve integration.

While there has been less coercion and exclusion of immigrants in the USA post-9/11 than in earlier eras, there have also been fewer calls for solidarity and sacrifice overall – and certainly not for incorporating immigrants. This dynamic raises a difficult question: to what degree does inclusion depend on a degree of coercion and exclusion? Put differently, is there an inverse relation between tolerance and solidarity? It may be some degree of exclusion is a necessary element of a more robust program of assimilation and integration and hence a perennial threat to an expansive definition of rights.

Indeed, the successful absorption of earlier waves of immigrants may have depended partly on Americans' combination of commitment to helping them and coercion in doing so. In the Progressive Era, for instance, Americanizers lobbied for legislation to protect immigrants from unscrupulous landlords and tyrannical employers. They established outreach programs to encourage and prepare immigrants to become citizens, in the process improving the naturalization system and developing the first formal program in adult education. At the same time, leadings Americanizers like Theodore Roosevelt thundered that there was no room in this country for 'hyphenated Americans.' As the historian Gary Gerstle (2001) has suggested, Theodore Roosevelt's limiting immigration and pressuring newcomers to assimilate enabled Franklin D. Roosevelt to build his New Deal on the foundation that there existed a single shared American identity. The willingness to include may well have depended on the demand that strict and sometimes illiberal expectations be met.

In modern individualist, rights- and consumer-oriented America, it seems less likely that policy-makers or citizens are willing to either set or enforce such expectations or do much to help immigrants meet them. Americans have come to prefer a 'small-scale morality' in which tolerance and respect for diversity loom large and the desire for grand projects is more muted (Wolfe 1998).[3] Such a sensibility offers little guidance for how to knit together citizens who are increasingly disconnected from one another. The issue here is neglect, not exclusion.[4]

The result of settling for a laissez-faire policy of neglect that is undergirded by a benign tolerance is a sensibility best characterized as 'invest poorly, expect little.' On the one hand, the USA will not provide sufficient or well-delivered educational and language programs for immigrants to help them quickly and efficiently gain the skills and knowledge they need to become committed citizens and economic assets. On the other hand, the USA does not expect that newcomers will learn much about the history and values of their new country or actively engage in its public life – except in times of stress, especially wartime, where immigrants' commitments are expected to be total – nor does it expect native-born citizens to help immigrants. In this model, the USA will take in lots of immigrants, and it will not be especially picky with regard to the skills, values, or English-language ability of those it admits, so long as there are few upfront costs and immigrants are seen as responsible for their own integration.[5]

This laissez-faire logic also has implications for the politics of immigration in the USA. Immigrant advocates will continue to decry demands placed on newcomers, from revised naturalization exams to social welfare exclusions, arguing that these are illiberal and ill-advised. At the same time, many citizens will balk at the notion that noncitizens should be eligible for socially consequential benefits, be able to conduct business in languages other than English, or maintain dual citizenship or any other perceived indicator that they are not putting America first. The absence of clearly stated expectations for immigrants and for citizens in the process of assimilation and integration will thus make room for multiple voices to identify their own expectations. These expectations will often be expressed in initiatives, propositions, and referendums where scorched-earth battles are waged over up or down votes cast on a single issue. At other times, they will be the subject of intensive lobbying at the federal level. The particulars of the conflicts will vary and they will often intermix concerns about illegal and legal immigration. But in each case the controversy will be less about the specific matter and more about the background conditions where the price of continued large-scale and relatively nonselective immigration is that immigrants make it on their own.[6]

Ultimately, the US approach to naturalization and the integration of immigrants could conceivably both reflect and contribute to even broader conflicts over identities, interests, and obligations. If I were to hazard a guess, I would suggest that these as yet unframed conflicts will not simply pit immigrants against citizens. Most immigrants and their children will learn English and many will become citizens who identify themselves as Americans; some not insignificant number will serve in the US military. Some immigrants and their children will also maintain ties to their home country that, owing to revolutions in communications and transportation, a global ethos of individual rights, and the policies of sending countries, may well prove more resilient than in the past. In this they will be more like some native-born US citizens who increasingly live transnational lives themselves. While place of residence will no doubt always exert considerable influence on an individual's interests and commitments, it is likely to become less dominant for certain groups. This is especially the case for professionals whose travel, tax, and employment opportunities will make the common space they inhabit increasingly different from those tied mainly to the USA. This is the dynamic that could create new divisions characterized less by immigrants versus citizens and more by immigrants *and* citizens who possess multiple connections and loyalties versus immigrants *and* citizens who regard their US citizenship and American national identity as primary.

While these new divisions are speculative, there are real and immediate problems regarding assimilation and social cohesion that the US approach to naturalization and integration does little to address. To be sure, most immigrants are becoming part of American society. High levels of labor force participation are matched by increased social and economic mobility, income, and job quality. Equally important, most children of today's immigrants are doing well compared to their parents. Yet persistent poverty among younger immigrants or the children of immigrants, elevated school dropout rates, especially among Mexican Americans, and the prevalence of drug use and gang membership all raise concerns. The decline in manufacturing and low-wage jobs, the increased importance of formal education, and the fiscal and other burdens facing states and public schools also threaten to reduce the opportunities for immigrants and their children.

Both legal and illegal immigrants have also become the face of two sweeping forces: the fraying of local community ties and the decline of national sovereignty. The title of Robert Putnam's controversial book *Bowling Alone* has become a national metaphor for the perceived decay of social bonds and traditional institutions that have helped to make a diverse democracy function. At the same time, transformations in communication and transportation have resulted in an increasingly interconnected globe that leaves Americans and immigrants unsure about who is part of their community and where they belong.

This broader confusion is exacerbated by the tensions among local, state, and national concerns and policies. Integration happens primarily at the local level, and this context varies greatly by locale in ways that matter significantly. At the same time, integration is tied to broad national considerations ranging from education and language policy to social benefits and electoral politics. Further, there is a significant disconnect between the state and local governments, which must provide most of the public services to immigrants, and the federal government, to which most of immigrants' tax contributions are paid.

Taken together, all of these trends and tensions present challenges for integration and social cohesion at a time of historically high rates of immigration and dispersed geographic settlement patterns. They mean that newcomers and the communities that receive them find themselves increasingly bewildered about how to regard the other. Immigrants often hear strong and contradictory signals – either that they do not and cannot fit in here or that they are passive subjects who need to be tended to and managed by social service bureaucracies. Neither responses signal that much should be expected of them as citizens-in-training. These conflicting messages reflect the fact that Americans themselves disagree deeply about the very meaning of what immigrants should be joining. Some Americans focus on the term 'assimilation,' including a personal identification with US history and a common civic identity defined by a commitment to shared principles. As the 2008 interagency Task Force on New Americans emphasized, 'citizenship is an identity and not simply a benefit. Feeling and being perceived as part of the political community is an important indicator of a person's integration into a society.' By contrast, others use the term 'integration,' by which they mean social inclusion, educational and economic advancement, and civic engagement. These differences leave both immigrants and Americans confused and uncertain about the bargain to be struck between them, about what Americans are willing to invest in newcomers and what expectations those newcomers must fulfill.

4. Clarifying the bargain

Is this, then, the best that can be expected? Must the USA simply leave immigrants and citizens to flounder or flourish solely by their own devices? After all, the general thinning out of social solidarity in the USA and elsewhere is the result of factors beyond naturalization and integration policy. Nor is it a process that is easily reversed by legislative means. Yet, as Geoffrey Brahm Levey points out, at least since the 1930s the USA has itself moved away from a laissez-faire approach in other areas of public life. Perhaps, he asks, core principles today mandate something more of a fair deal than a laissez-faire one?[7] Amidst all the din and clamor over immigration, it would indeed be better if immigrants, their children, and the communities into which they enter receive stronger signals about what integration means and what is expected of them.[8]

A better and more strategic effort would recognize that assimilation and integration can be linked, that the identity, commitment, and values dimensions of the former and the social, civic, and economic dimensions of the latter can reinforce each other and send clear signals to both newcomers and native-born. An emphasis on newcomers' commitment to and investment in their new country is aimed at strengthening native-born citizens' support for integration. In turn, increasing access to education, jobs, and civic life can make it easier for immigrants to believe that they are being treated fairly. Even Teddy Roosevelt understood that 'we cannot secure ... loyalty unless we make this a country where men shall feel that they have justice' (Roosevelt 1926, 402).

Strategies that link immigrants' needs and interests to American principles and peoplehood were central to social reformers like Jane Addams in her work at Hull House in Chicago a century ago. Addams regarded a robust naturalization process as central to the process of becoming part of a new country. She believed deeply that immigrants should embrace America and its ideals. But she also regarded formal citizenship and instruction in lofty principles as only part of the bargain. Genuine attention to the needs of immigrant communities, too, was critical to fostering in immigrants an understanding of American ideals and a commitment to the country and its future. She built structures like settlement houses and devised strategies focused on areas from childcare and housing to citizenship training to help newcomers negotiate the often bewildering challenges of making a new life in a new place (Pickus 2005, 76–83, 179).

What would this kind of approach look like today? A recent report by the Brookings-Duke Immigration Policy Roundtable identifies some of the components:

- For immigrants, this process involves learning English, becoming economically self-sufficient, supporting one's family, and contributing to the community. It also means understanding and sharing core civic principles and coming to see oneself as a member in full standing of a new political community.
- For communities, this process means protecting newcomers from abusive landlords and employers and improving the conditions in which they reside and work, setting high expectations and helping newcomers reach them, and ensuring equal treatment under the law and opportunities for civic participation (Brookings-Duke Immigration Policy Roundtable 2009, 18).

The report sets out mutual expectations and obligations in several areas. For instance, it emphasizes that schools, though overburdened, are still the primary arena for both conveying social norms and aspirations and providing support services and building relationships with immigrant families. Immigrant youth are often ambivalent about whether they can or want to fit in. And they receive competing signals from society and family about the relative value of work and education. In response to the former, the report emphasizes making concerted efforts to seek newcomers' buy-in to the promise of American history and a common future; in response to the latter, it urges educators to cultivate the expectation among students that they have both the potential and the obligation to remain in school and contribute to their own and the nation's welfare. At the same time, the report stresses that schools and communities must engage in significant outreach efforts to help students and their families embrace and meet such expectations, particularly by establishing tighter links with parents. It focuses on making schools hubs of parental and community engagement and as springboards for immigrants and their families to discover venues for wider public engagement.

The report also sets out goals and mechanisms for promoting English-language proficiency and citizenship. Underlying these recommendations is the view that while neither learning English nor becoming a citizen are or should be made mandatory, the evidence is clear that doing so benefits both newcomers and communities alike. The report notes that

> newcomers who become proficient in English and naturalize increase their wages and standard of living, own homes at elevated rates, and contribute more in taxes. They are also more likely to take part in mainstream civic and political events and engage more in the life of their broader communities. In doing so, they demonstrate their commitment to their new status as full and responsible US citizens. (Brookings-Duke Immigration Policy Roundtable 2009, 19)

Yet the report notes that currently youth and adult English-language preparation fail to provide real educational opportunities. It therefore charges immigrants with learning English and becoming citizens, and government agencies and host communities with facilitating these goals. It recommends an 'invest better, expect more' approach that promotes flexibility in federal support for different approaches to teaching English while making funding contingent on educational outcomes.

The report also highlights how a more robust naturalization process can encourage immigrants to make a considered commitment to their new identity and foster bonds between newcomers and citizens. It focuses on treating prospective citizens fairly by ensuring that the test is delivered in a standardized fashion and meaningful preparation is adequately provided. Rather than simply reduce or raise naturalization standards, the right approach is to balance higher expectations with greater investment in preparation. The focus should be on enhancing the aspirations and capabilities of the large number of applicants who will become citizens rather than the small number who might be excluded.[9]

The report characterizes these components as part of an overall bargain: 'a warm and helpful welcome balanced by immigrants' progress toward the goal of citizenship and commitment to America's success.' It suggests that this bargain 'presents opportunities for confidence-building measures. Immigrants benefit from knowing the "rules of the game" and the mutual trust that comes from observing them; Americans are reassured by immigrant efforts and commitments to joining the political community' (Brookings-Duke Immigration Policy Roundtable 2009, 18).

To advance this proposed bargain, the Brookings-Duke Roundtable proposed the creation of a new federal Office for New Americans (ONA). This Office would oversee a network of state and local governments, enhancing the capacity of voluntary and nonprofit organizations, and coordinating the work of federal agencies in efforts to facilitate immigrants' assimilation and integration into mainstream American society. By comparison, Canada, Australia, and many European countries devote entire government ministries to language, citizenship, housing, welfare, and health policy for immigrants, and often promote explicitly multicultural policies. The approach taken is intentional, structured, and comprehensive.[10] Yet the United States differs from these countries in not pre-selecting immigrants deemed more likely to integrate (it prioritizes family relations over skills), favors a smaller welfare state, and promotes a more prominent singular national identity. A government-mandated or multicultural approach to integrating immigrants therefore seems unlikely to make much headway in the USA. (And to the degree it does gain ground, one unintended consequence may be a reconsideration of admissions policy to prioritize immigrants' skills and education.) The Brookings-Duke Roundtable proposed a federal office that was likely to fit the US context, one focused on coordination and the bully pulpit, delivering the message that assimilation and integration are the mutual responsibilities of immigrants and citizens alike. In conjunction with the recently created Office of Citizenship, which focuses on naturalization,

ONA would reinforce but then reach beyond formal citizenship (Brookings-Duke Immigration Policy Roundtable 2009, 19).

Even this more modest federal effort may nonetheless prove unlikely to be undertaken until even more comprehensive immigration issues are addressed. Illegal immigration, less relevant in Canada and Australia, is the most pressing issue. The Brookings-Duke Report sought to address it by balancing the rule of law and the rights of immigrants. It proposed a series of carefully sequenced and monitored confidence-building measures that link workplace verification and an effective path to legalization. The report also proposed a broader immigration bargain that included reorienting immigrant admissions to better balance family and skilled visa allocation and rationalizing the temporary worker program by creating nonrenewable, five-year provisional visas that do not tie workers to a single employer and provide the option of achieving permanent status. The overall goal is to demonstrate that despite deep differences among participants, it is possible to converge on recommendations that are a significant improvement over the status quo and that better link immigration and integration policies.

The future of such recommendations remains uncertain given the competing interests and principles at stake. Indeed, the report characterizes the possibility of comprehensive reform as 'more of a threat than settling for the status quo' for many interest groups and the present context of immigration policy as 'rigid but unstable – like the tectonic plates of the earth's crust before an earthquake.' Nonetheless, new proposals advanced in early 2013 by a bipartisan group of leading Senators reflect the Roundtable's focus on linking legalization and enforcement and on establishing a more flexible system for managing future flows of legal migrants – albeit both in ways that differ from the Roundtable's approach (Plumer 2013).[11] The bipartisan Senate proposal also includes a requirement that undocumented immigrants who seek to legalize their status learn English and civics, pay back taxes, and demonstrate a history of work in the USA. These measures align with the Roundtable's dual emphasis on fostering a common civic identity and advancing social and economic integration. In contrast to the Roundtable, the Senate proposal does not propose any broader strategies to enhance assimilation and integration – perhaps because of internal disagreements or because the resources required for such strategies fly in the face of the laissez-faire expectation that immigration and naturalization services should be paid for by applicants.

Current efforts to overhaul US immigration policy may again fail. Or, as has also happened before, legalization policies may succeed, while enforcement strategies fail. In either case, a realistic perspective might expand the assimilation and integration bargain to include the ongoing presence of unauthorized immigrants. Peter Skerry and I have explored the underpinnings and components of such a bargain (Pickus and Skerry 2007). We focus on the informal, day-to-day, and ongoing relations between individuals and between individuals and local private or public institutions. These relations capture the concerns citizens often voice about illegal immigration: packed apartment houses, cluttered communities with abandoned shopping carts and cars, crowded schools and hospitals, and the profusion of languages other than English. These local relations also capture the perplexing signals that illegal immigrants receive about whether they are wanted – yes, no, sometimes, and it depends – and about how they can best fit in. The focus, in other words, is less on being good citizens than on being good neighbors.[12]

A focus on how immigrants and citizens behave may thus offer a way to clarify expectations between citizens and illegal immigrants. Are immigrants behaving in ways that convey their intention to become part of the social and political fabric of America, or are they acting as if they are here temporarily? Likewise, are communities behaving in ways that reward responsible actions or are they penalizing even those illegal immigrants who are being good neighbors? One promising example of this behavioral approach is The Resurrection Project in Chicago's southwest neighborhoods. This church-based community development program opens opportunities for home ownership and renting on the conditions that newcomers observe neighborhood obligations. Eager to avoid being merely a service provider, the Project requires that newcomers protect and improve the property (Skerry 2003/2004, 30).

Another example can be found in a proposal from the state of California's Little Hoover Commission. The Report, *We the People: Helping Newcomers Become Californians*, called for establishing 'The Golden State Residency Program' which would be guided by three principles:

(1) all persons deserve dignity and respect;
(2) all residents are obligated to be responsible community members;
(3) new Californians need the same opportunity as others to become self-reliant and responsible community members (Little Hoover Commission 2002, i).

The Residency Program would provide government resources to immigrants who demonstrate through their behavior, rather than their legal status, that they intend to become responsible members of the community. It includes a number of criteria by which to assess such behavior:

- responsibility to the local community, as indicated by a history of paying taxes, remaining in good standing with law enforcement agencies, and where appropriate, being employed or engaged in workforce development and training;
- proficiency in English, as demonstrated by actual skills or enrollment in appropriate programs;
- participation in civic affairs, for example, in public, volunteer, and community-based programs;
- responsibility for children and other family members, as demonstrated by care for dependent family members and enrollment and regular attendance of children in school and health plans;
- commitment to establish citizenship, open to undocumented immigrants until federal policies are reformed, and enforced by a time frame for establishing citizenship once a person is eligible (Little Hoover Commission 2002, vii–viii).

In return for satisfying such criteria, immigrant enrollees would become eligible for benefits that might include a driver's license, in-state tuition at public colleges and universities, eligibility for public health insurance, and even welfare support. The *We the People* report directed state policy-makers to ensure that public programs effectively address the needs of immigrants and communities from health care to education. So, for example, labor and workforce development agencies are charged with ensuring that immigrants have access to training and skill development opportunities; state and consumer services agency are instructed to assess how well they protect immigrants from discrimination in employment, housing, and public accommodation; and community colleges and adult schools are required to develop and implement plans to increase the number of students who become proficient in English. The state itself is directed to create a commission that can monitor progress by defining and measuring immigrant integration and self-reliance. The Golden State Residency Program would thus also reflect an 'invest better, expect more' philosophy, one that would offer incentives for participating and penalties for nonparticipation: 'California can make a commitment to invest in immigrants who are committed to helping improve California. Those who choose not to commit to be responsible community members receive lower priority to access public sector services' (Little Hoover Commission 2002, x–xi).

There are obviously many tensions and inconsistencies that would arise with such a program. How, for instance, would it relate to enforcement strategies? How would immigrants' commitments be assessed and would Californians be willing to provide resources in return? Is it possible to build support for a common national citizenship while offering local membership to those here illegally? We are mindful of the uphill battle that making such a bargain faces given the deep differences over how to regard and respond to the large numbers of illegal immigrants in the USA. Even the bargain we have proposed for legal immigrants will be difficult to foster in a laissez-faire society that is divided over the very meaning of its identity and at a time when the traditional obligations of citizenship have become attenuated. The USA does not, for instance, require military service – and its all-volunteer army counts permanent residents and even illegal aliens among its numbers. Still, whatever forms of political community prove most durable in the future will require answers to perennial questions about recognition and obligation. The bargains we propose at least seek to address these questions and the range of problems the USA currently faces, some of which are openly debated and some of which lay below the surface. This explicitness seems better, on balance, than accepting the stalemate of a status quo, which is also filled with contradictions. Programs like the Golden State Residency Program, structures like the Office of New Americans, and policies on assimilation and integration like those proposed by the Brookings-Duke Roundtable would make more overt the terms of the bargain struck between immigrants and Americans. This would help immigrants and Americans by turning vague assumptions into conscious choices that ask something of both sides (Pickus and Skerry 2007, 113).

5. Conclusion

Issues of identity, obligation, and mutual expectations are unavoidably caught up in debates over naturalization and integration. At the same time, tests and preparatory courses are not particularly well suited to address, let alone resolve, these debates. They are blunt instruments for getting at complex questions of understanding and commitment. Even incremental efforts to address assimilation and integration are further undermined by the general thinning out of social solidarity in a globalizing world. In eschewing precision where it does not belong, the US's laissez-faire approach thus offers clear virtues for those anxious over the demands made of prospective citizens in Western Europe. But in its unwillingness to clarify the expectations immigrants and citizens should have of one another, that approach also offers a cautionary tale complete with its own set of practical, political, and normative problems. The challenge in the USA is whether it can respond to those problems by finding sufficiently robust ways to foster a shared sense of commitment.

Notes

1. The Hudson Institute's John Fonte helped establish a new Office of Citizenship (Department of Homeland Security 2007; Laglagaron and Devani 2008).
2. For discussion of the naturalization process in the Progressive Era and of the Jordan Commission, see Pickus (2005, 90–100, 166–167).
3. Wolfe's analysis may overstate how deep and wide this tolerance runs, but he has identified a significant driving force in contemporary American politics. See Brooks (2001).

4. Myers (2007) lays out the case for older, largely white citizens to invest more in immigrants and their children, but those older citizens do not seem convinced.

5. It is interesting to consider as well the differences among US states on the costs citizens expect to bear and the treatment of immigrants (legal and illegal). To speculate, in Texas social provisions are generally lower and a rough and ready expectation seems to prevail that immigrants who find work are acceptable. Immigrants in Texas may have fewer state-provided resources to fall back on, but they have also not been subject to the more extreme exclusionary efforts of other states. By contrast, California is relatively more generous in providing social benefits and it has been a flashpoint for much of the local- and state-level conflicts over immigration that have had a national impact.

6. A different interpretation of the proliferation of various local- and state-level policies regarding immigrants is to see them as de facto experiments with integration – a kind of Brandesian 'laboratories of democracy' at work. (I thank Jennifer Hochschild for this point.) Of course, many of the most controversial policies – Proposition 187 in California and SB 1070 in Arizona – are not designed to foster integration; they are designed to reduce illegal immigration. Still, to the degree that some policies make it harder or easier for immigrants to stay in a particular state, say by limiting state benefits or by topping up federal benefits, there is a kind of integration experimentalism taking place.

7. Personal communication, 24 March 2011.

8. Peter Skerry and I articulated this perspective in a 2006 op-ed, a 2007 article, and a 2009 policy report, all of which I draw on here. See Pickus and Skerry (2006, 2007) and Brookings-Duke Immigration Policy Roundtable (2009) (William Galston served as our co-convenor of the Roundtable). See also Skerry and Fernandes (2006).

9. Liav Orgad rightfully questions the ways in which programs to bolster civic knowledge make a difference: 'Does a list of disconnected events and values really foster social cohesion or create a sense of belonging?' That, of course, is one reason why it is important to tell the story of America in ways that connect ideas and symbols and that invites newcomers to see themselves as part of a specific nation. Further, as indicated above, the evidence is clear that civic knowledge does reduce alienation and promote engagement. It is true that setting higher expectations for newcomers may not necessarily lead to greater involvement in the process on the part of citizens in a sustained way. But it does undermine the notion that newcomers do not want to belong. The risk, of course, is that requiring greater demonstrations of the desire to belong will become illiberal. In this regard, Orgad offers a suggestive proposal that the standard expected should be more than mere knowledge that may become rote memorization but less than the kind of attachment that opens the door to exclusion. Instead, he expands on language proposed by Barbara Jordan's US Commission on Immigration Reform, and suggests that the focus should be on commitment to the US form of government and values, which 'leaves room for private disagreement as long as one pledges to act or refrain from acting in a specific way ....' As the Commission put it, a pledge that 'commits[s] to serve the best interests of the United States ... [and respects] freedom of speech and religion; and ... commit[s] not to discriminate again others on the basis of nationality, race, sex, or religion.' See Orgad (2011, 1292).

10. Some analyses suggest that such integration policies increase immigrants' naturalization rates, political influence, and a general sense of inclusion in the political system. These policies have also come under intense scrutiny for promoting a separatist rather than a shared national identity and for fostering welfare state dependency rather than individual responsibility. See, for instance, Bloemraad (2006) and Malik (2011).

11. The Roundtable focused enforcement efforts at the workplace rather than the border and it rejected open-ended guest worker programs.

12. On local relations between citizens and legal and illegal immigrants, see Skerry (2006).

References

Alba, R., and V. Nee. 2003. *Remaking the American Mainstream: Assimilation and Contemporary Immigration*. Cambridge, MA: Harvard University Press.

Bloemraad, I. 2006. *Becoming a Citizen: Incorporating Immigrants and Refugees in the United States and Canada*. Berkeley: University of California Press.

Brookings-Duke Immigration Policy Roundtable. 2009. *Breaking the Immigration Stalemate: From Deep Disagreements to Constructive Proposals.* A Report from the Brookings-Duke Immigration Policy Roundtable. Washington, DC: Brookings-Duke Immigration Policy Roundtable.

Brooks, D. 2001. *Bobos in Paradise: The New Upper Class and How They Got There.* New York: Simon & Schuster.

Center for Civic Innovation. 2007. *"You Say Tomato, I Say Tomato": A Right-Left Conversation about Immigration, Integration and Assimilation.* Civic Bulletin No. 50. New York: Manhattan Institute.

Department of Homeland Security. 2007. *Fact Sheet: USCIS Naturalization Test Redesign.* The United States Citizenship and Immigration Services. Washington, DC: Department of Homeland Security.

Galston, W. 2001. "Political Knowledge, Political Engagement, and Civic Education." *Annual Review of Political Science* 4: 223–226.

Gerstle, G. 2001. *American Crucible: Race and Nation in the Twentieth Century.* Princeton, NJ: Princeton University Press.

Hansen, R. 2008. *A New Citizenship Bargain for the Age of Mobility? Citizenship Requirements in Europe and North America.* Washington, DC: Migration Policy Institute.

Huntington, S. 2004. *Who Are We? The Challenges to America's National Identity.* New York: Simon & Schuster.

Jacobs, D., and A. Rea. 2007. "The End of National Models? Integration Courses and Citizenship Trajectories in Europe." *International Journal on Multicultural Societies* 9 (2): 262–283.

Joppke, C. 2007. "Beyond National Models: Civic Integration Policies for Immigrants in Western Europe." *Western European Politics* 30 (1): 1–22.

Joppke, C. 2010. *Citizenship and Immigration.* Cambridge: Polity Press.

Laglagaron, L., and B. Devani. 2008. *High Stakes, More Meaning: An Overview of the Process of Redesigning the US Citizenship Test.* Washington, DC: Migration Policy Institute.

Commission, Little Hoover. 2002. *We the People: Helping Newcomers Become Californians.* Sacramento, CA: Little Hoover Commission.

Malik, K. 2011. "Assimilation's Failure, Terrorism's Rise." *New York Times,* July 6.

McHugh, M., J. Gelatt, and M. Fix. 2007. *Adult Language Instruction in the United States: Determining Need and Investing Wisely.* Washington, DC: Migration Policy Institute.

McNamara, T., and E. Shohamy. 2008. "Viewpoint: Language Tests and Human Rights." *International Journal of Applied Linguistics* 18 (1): 89–95.

Myers, D. 2007. *Immigrants and Boomers: Forging a New Social Contract for the Future of America.* New York: Russell Sage.

Orgad, L. 2011. "Creating New Americans: The Essence of Americanism under the Citizenship Test." *Houston Law Review* 47 (5): 1227–1297.

Park, J. W. 2008. "A More Meaningful Citizenship Test? Unmasking the Construction of a Universalist, Principle-Based Citizenship Ideology." *California Law Review* 96: 999–1047.

Petsod, D., T. Wang, and C. McGarvey. 2007. *Investing in Our Communities: Strategies for Immigrant Integration.* Baltimore, MD: Annie E. Casey Foundation.

Pickus, N. 1997. *Becoming American/America Becoming.* Durham, NC: Terry Sanford Institute of Public Policy.

Pickus, N. 2005. *True Faith and Allegiance: Immigration and American Civic Nationalism.* Princeton, NJ: Princeton University Press.

Pickus, N., and P. Skerry. 2006. "Process Must Foster Better Bonds." *South Florida Sun-Sentinel,* May 25.

Pickus, N., and P. Skerry. 2007. "Good Neighbors and Good Citizens: Beyond the Legal-Illegal Immigration Debate." In *Engaging the Opposition: Fresh Perspectives on the Politics of Immigration,* edited by C. Swain, 95–113. New York: Cambridge University Press.

Plumer, B. 2013. "READ: Senators Release Bipartisan Plan for Immigration Reform." *The Washington Post,* January 28.

Roosevelt, T. 1926. "'Americanism.' Address Delivered Before the Knights of Columbus, Carnegie Hall, New York, October 12, 1915." In *The Works of Theodore Roosevelt,* edited by H. Hagedorn, 388–405. Vol. 18. New York: Scribner.

Skerry, P. 2003/2004. "Citizenship Begins at Home: A New Approach to the Civic Integration of Immigrants." *The Responsive Community* 14 (1): 26–37.

Skerry, P. 2006. "Immigration and Social Disorder." In *Uniting America: Restoring the Vital Center to American Democracy*, edited by N. Garfinckle, and D. Yankelovich, 124–138. New Haven, CT: Yale University Press.

Skerry, P., and D. Fernandes. 2006. "Citizen Pain: Fixing the Immigration Debate." *The New Republic*, May 8.

Task Force on New Americans. 2008. *Building an Americanization Movement for the Twenty-First Century: A Report to the President of the United States from the Task Force on New Americans.* Washington, DC: Task Force on New Americans.

Wolfe, A. 1998. *One Nation After All: What Middle-Class Americans Really Think about God, Country, Family, Racism, Welfare, Immigration, Homosexuality, Work, the Right, the Left, and Each Other.* New York: Penguins.

Liberal nationalism and the Australian citizenship tests

Geoffrey Brahm Levey

School of Social Sciences, University of New South Wales, Sydney, Australia

Scholars have debated whether citizenship regimes in Western democracies are tracking a liberal universalistic path or continue to follow distinctive national traditions. This essay argues that the Australian case does both through a distinctive liberal nationalist architecture. Increasingly since the 1970s, Australian citizenship acquisition and status have largely followed a civic nationalist or liberal universalist formulation. However, this has been executed within a broader liberal nationalist approach to national identity and culture that accommodates these aspects of national life. The essay discusses the idea of liberal nationalism as a political architecture of differentiated domains, Australia's construction of this architecture, and how Australia's two recent citizenship tests illustrate this framework in action. It concludes with some thoughts on the symbolic significance of citizenship tests for liberal legitimacy and the future of the liberal nationalist project.

One of the major immigrant democracies alongside Canada and the USA, Australia nevertheless followed the lead of European countries rather than its North American cousins on the matter of citizenship tests. Such tests have been a feature of the immigration process in the USA since the early twentieth century and in Canada since 1994 (Etzioni 2007). Australia introduced its first citizenship test only in 2007 after Britain, the Netherlands, and Germany had done so or flagged their intention of doing so. As in the European cases, the immediate spur to this Australian policy innovation was a series of local and international controversies involving Muslim immigration and militancy. Australia's citizenship tests also unsurprisingly reflect its general approach to citizenship. But how best to characterize or interpret that approach?

According to Joppke (2013), Australia's citizenship regime is akin to that of Canada and the USA in primarily being civic and liberal universalistic in orientation. While it has, he says, displayed some aspects of the 'restrictive turn' taken by European countries in recent years – such as public concern about the compatibility of Muslim immigrants and introducing a 'two-step' immigration process and 'earned citizenship' in policy – its standing as a New World democracy built on 'chosen' immigration has ensured that its general universalistic and welcoming approach to immigration and citizenship remains intact (Joppke 2013). Indeed, for Joppke, the most significant story about citizenship globally is the inexorable force of universal liberal values and globalized markets. Even Old World European states now grappling with mainly 'unchosen' immigration – such as Britain, Germany, and Denmark – are subject to the 'universalist paradox'; while they might wish to impose cultural nationalist strictures, they find themselves unable to go far down that road any more (Joppke 2010, 2013).

This picture of citizenship regimes in Europe has been contested. While these scholars acknowledge a 'civic turn' in citizenship and integration in many European jurisdictions, notwithstanding some backsliding, they maintain that how this civic-ness is discussed and institutionalized continues to display the imprint of particular national political cultures and party alignments (Koopmans et al. 2005; Mouritsen 2013; cf. Howard 2009). On this view, national differences continue to matter and defy grand generalizations about citizenship.[1]

In this essay, I want to argue that something of both the 'universalist' and the 'nationalist' accounts apply in the Australian case, though in its own fashion. On the one hand, it would be hard to deny the influence of liberal universalist values on Australia's citizenship and integration regimes over the last 40 or so years. What is more, these values are clearly identified as liberal democratic values; there is no particular effort to wrap them in a nationalist idiom or formulation other than to say they are part of Australia's democratic heritage. The one possible exception is that references to equality commonly invoke the legendary Australian tradition of the 'fair go.'[2] Affirmations of loyalty are to the polity, its political institutions and norms, and to its people, and *not* to a particular national culture or the 'Australian way of life.' To this extent, it is fair to describe Australia's citizenship regime as 'civic' and liberal universalistic in character.

On the other hand, leaving the story at that is also misleading. Australia's approach to citizenship cannot be divorced from its attempt to grapple with the broader question of national identity and, in that regard, from its adoption of state multiculturalism in the 1970s. And here it is a particular form of liberal nationalism and not liberal universalism that overwhelmingly defines this attempt. Moreover, insofar as this liberal nationalist settlement is *politically* contested in Australia, the significant challenge comes from cultural nationalists. Liberal universalists or 'civic nationalists' (as they are otherwise known) in Australia are mostly confined to the academy and bookshops. As we shall see, the Australian citizenship tests replay this tussle between the cultural nationalist and liberal nationalist visions in Australian politics more generally. Exclusively focusing on the domain of citizenship (as does Joppke) misses how this 'civic' domain is itself incorporated within a liberal nationalist governing framework in Australia.

I will begin by considering how liberal nationalism may be construed as a political architecture, one that enables citizenship to be treated as a distinct domain. In the second part, I will outline the liberal nationalist architecture that Australia has fashioned for dealing with citizenship and national identity since the 1970s, including the part played by multiculturalism, on the one hand, and the continuing challenge from cultural nationalists, on the other. In the third part, I will examine how the civic nationalist, cultural nationalist, and liberal nationalist positions have variously contributed to Australia's venture in citizenship tests since 2007. I will conclude with some remarks on the liberal credentials of Australia's citizenship tests, and on the symbolic significance of such protocols for the individuals concerned, liberal legitimacy, and the future of the liberal nationalist project.

National identity and citizenship: liberal nationalism as architecture

The relation between national identity and citizenship has long been ambiguous. Formally, the distinction between the two core notions is clear: membership of the nation (nationality) as against membership of the state (citizenship). In the modern era of nation-states, however, where the two memberships were intended to be coterminous, 'nationality' and being a 'national' convey the same legal meaning as an individual's citizenship (Hammar 1996). The touchstone for the discussion of national identity and citizenship is, in many ways, still Kohn's (1965) influential distinction between ethnic nationalism and civic nationalism. Kohn differentiated an ethno-cultural form of nationalism based on primordial peoplehood, hereditary, and emotion, which he associated mainly with Central and Eastern European countries, from a political form of nationalism based on liberal and rational principles, and which he saw as characteristic of advanced 'Western' countries. The distinction's popularity and utility lie in the fact that it does help capture identifiable differences in *emphasis* among states.

The ethnic/civic nationalism distinction intersects rather than overlaps the distinction in nationality law between *jus sanguinis* and *jus soli*. The former principle of extending citizenship based on 'blood' through one's parents need not, for example, be exclusive to members of a particular ethnic group in the manner of ethnic nationalism (Joppke 2010, 19). A standard criticism of the ethnic/civic nationalism distinction is that it only works as a relative contrast (as was intended by Kohn) and not as exclusive categories, since many states combine ethno-cultural and territorial-civic nationalist elements. However, this way of putting the matter is only half-right, as there is a basic asymmetry between the two sides to the contrast.

Ethnic nationalist states, even on a strict definition, have actually existed. Germany before its 1999 reforms, Australia during the heyday of the White Australia policy, and Israel from its establishment until today are all textbook examples of ethno-nationalism in action. Each case legislated national membership or belonging on the basis of a particular ethnic heritage or bloodline. In contrast, a civic nationalist state, as such, has nowhere yet existed. In part, the problem lies with the concept itself. If a state were only 'civic' in its affairs, then it would not be nationalist; and if it is nationalist, then it cannot be fully 'civic' (Nielsen 1996–97; Kuzio 2002). The reality is that all liberal democracies, including the standard example of liberal neutrality and a 'civic nationalist' state, the USA, privilege particular cultural-national traditions and seek to inculcate nationalist sentiment among their citizenry (Yack 1999). Liberal states mandate a particular language or languages as the *lingua franca*, adopt a particular calendar to organize the year, recognize certain public holidays, prescribe what narratives are taught as history, and invoke particular cultural motifs for their official symbols, insignia, flags, and anthems. Indeed, some scholars contend that the nationalist credentials of even the USA go much farther than these aspects (Lind 1995; Kaufmann 2000).

There are, however, two ways of understanding civic nationalism. One is to see its emphasis on shared territory and civic values as a repudiation of nationalism and notions of national identity. This account of civic nationalism amounts to what others – perhaps semantically more aptly – advocate variously as liberal universalism, post-nationalism, or cosmopolitanism. These approaches attempt to answer the national or nationalist question by seeking to dissolve it. Joppke's brand of liberal universalism seems to be of this sort; as he remarks hopefully: 'The weakening of the particularistic identity-lending dimension of citizenship is tantamount to the retreat of nationalism, at least in the West' (Joppke 2010, 142). Since nationalism stubbornly persists, however, this school of civic nationalism remains aspirational (Calhoun 2007).

But civic nationalism may instead be understood as an attempt only to depoliticize matters of national identity, to withdraw government from this particular field of concern. Kohn (1965, 29) himself seemed to intend this second meaning when he described nationalism in the modern West as 'predominantly a political movement to limit governmental power and to secure civil rights.' This version of civic nationalism does not so much seek to address the nationalist quest as put it to the side, beyond the reach of government. National identity becomes the province of the citizenry and civil society, while the business of government properly concerns itself with statecraft and the political rights and obligations of citizens. Again, even this account of civic nationalism is deficient in ignoring the degree to which liberal states do engage in the promotion and reproduction of national cultures and nationalist sentiment. However, thinking of civic nationalism in this way is suggestive of how certain domains, such as citizenship, may lend themselves to this vision's focus on formal rights and obligations without denying the legitimacy or actuality of national identity in other spheres.

The form of nationalism that aims to marry cultural nationalist and civic nationalist elements both within and outside the purview of government is typically called 'liberal nationalism.' Though it has been theorized only relatively recently, and while it also has been variously formulated (e.g., Tamir 1993; Canovan 1996; Kymlicka 1995; Miller 1995; Soutphommasane 2012), liberal nationalists share at least two convictions.[3] The first is that national identity can and does play an important role in generating and sustaining social cohesion, a sense of belonging, and a commitment to the commonweal, and that these features are legitimate interests of democratic states. The second is that the notion that liberal democracies can be culturally neutral and only endorse political values is a fiction. Unlike *civic* nationalists, then, liberal nationalists recognize the inevitability in practice and the legitimacy in principle of some state endorsement of national-cultural values. But unlike *cultural* nationalists, they believe that this cultural privileging – typically, of a majority group – should be seriously limited and matched by some redress for cultural minorities who are also members of the political community.

Liberal nationalism is often described as a weak form of cultural nationalism in virtue of its limited state endorsement of a national culture. But, of course, it also incorporates and endorses decidedly civic-cum-liberal democratic values and institutions. It is more accurate, therefore, to describe liberal nationalism as a form of political architecture. Unlike ethnic, cultural, and civic nationalisms, it does not push one substantive value-set so much as structure and arrange the cultural and the civic nationalist sets (it conscientiously rejects the 'ethnic' nationalist set). Those states conventionally cited as being civic nationalist on the basis of the ethnic–civic distinction are in reality more proximate exemplars of liberal nationalism. They combine domains where government emphasizes political – typically, liberal democratic – norms and institutions almost to the exclusion of everything else, areas where government also engages in the propagation of national identity, and areas where government defers matters of national identity to civil society and may even relax the prescription of liberal democratic norms. The basic architecture of liberal nationalism thus follows what Walzer (1984) has called liberalism's 'art of separation,' an attempt to delimit which animating principles and institutions are appropriate to which spheres of state and society.

Citizenship can be understood as a domain from which many liberal-democratic governments increasingly have come to withdraw national identity prescriptions in favor of a formal legal status based on a commitment to respecting the laws and political institutions of the country. However, it is likely that this withdrawal has worked so well for this domain precisely because national identity may be pursued and expressed in other areas of state and society. Despite this success or, indeed, because of it, citizenship has become something of a battleground today. Cultural nationalists find liberal citizenship too cold and arid and seek to 'renationalize' it with all manner of warm cultural-national content and sentiment. Meanwhile civic nationalists, post-nationalists, and liberal universalists find the liberal model of citizenship so compelling that they wish to extend this civic regime into every area of societal governance and national life. Liberal nationalist architecture simultaneously provokes and checks both these inclinations.

Australia's turn to liberal nationalism

Though the term 'liberal nationalism' scarcely figures in Australian political discourse, Australians have largely lived according to its basic architecture since the 1970s. Prior to that, Australia sought to address the question of national identity in two other ways. From federation in 1901 until at least the 1940s, Australia defined itself and acted as if it were an ethnic nation. The first legislation enacted by the newly established Australian Commonwealth was the Immigration Restriction Act (1901) or 'White Australia' policy. Under the policy, Australia was to be a '(White) working man's paradise' in which democratic equality was to be realized for those of the 'British race' (Tavan 2005; Brawley 2007). Those not of British descent were deemed unassimilable and were to be excluded from Australian society; this applied as much to Aborigines inside Australia as to would-be immigrants outside it.

Officially abolished in 1973, the White Australia policy effectively began to unravel in the 1940s under pressure to populate Australia and grow the economy. As too few British immigrants could be found, the definition of acceptability was broadened first to allow Northern Europeans' entry and then Southern Europeans,' who did not look very 'white' at all (Cole 1971). In 1945, a federal Department of Immigration was established and charged with formulating a national assimilation policy (Jordens 1997). Where previously the reigning ethno-nationalist assumption was that race determines culture, henceforth and increasingly Australia entertained the notion that Anglo-conformity could be achieved through assimilation. This cultural-nationalist formula – which required cultural conformity but no longer the 'right' ethnic heritage – grew to ascendancy in the 1950s and 1960s.

Australia turned to a liberal nationalist approach to national identity in the 1970s, courtesy of several local and international developments. Already by the late1960s, the Department of Immigration had concluded that full assimilation of Australia's growing migrant population was unlikely to occur no matter what the policies or pressures to do so (Zubrzycki 1995). A reformist Labor government came to power in 1972 after decades of conservative rule. It officially buried the White Australia policy, signed international human rights protocols, and introduced antidiscrimination institutions and law. At the same time, Britain's receding imperial ambitions and sudden switch to the European community in 1973 forced Australia and Australians to reassess their sense of self (Curran and Ward 2010). In short, the Australian state and Anglo-Australian identity were cleaved apart. While Anglo-Australian culture and institutions have remained dominant, the state was no longer coterminous with this particular identity (Davidson 1997).

Australia's adoption of multiculturalism in the 1970s, following Canada, was another piece in the liberal nationalist architecture. Unlike Canadian multiculturalism, which focused on long-standing cultural minorities, Australian multiculturalism was initially intended as an integration regime for new immigrants (Jupp 1996; Lopez 2000). Also, unlike Canada's emphasis on cultural maintenance or Britain's emphasis on a 'community of communities' a decade or so later, the emphasis of Australian multiculturalism has been on access and equity or nondiscrimination, and then on the rights of individuals and not groups. Even the right to cultural identity or cultural respect, always one of the positive provisions across the now four national multiculturalism policy statements spanning the period 1989–2011, is cast as an entitlement of individual Australians. As the *National*

Agenda for a Multicultural Australia puts it, 'Fundamentally, multiculturalism is about the rights of the individual' (OMA 1989, 15). Similarly, while British Prime Minister David Cameron found it possible, in 2011, to contrast British multiculturalism and what he called 'muscular liberalism' (*BBC News* 2011), Australia's multiculturalism policies have always stressed the imperative of respecting core liberal-democratic norms and institutions: namely, reciprocity, tolerance and equality (including of the sexes), freedom of speech and religion, the rule of law, the Constitution and parliamentary democracy. English as the national language is the only 'cultural' imperative stipulated in the same list. If one were to judge Australia's multiculturalism only on this basis, it would be hard to imagine an integration policy that better illustrates Joppke's thesis of the march of liberal universalism.

However, underscoring its liberal nationalist credentials, Australian multiculturalism also allows for the expression of national identity in two related respects. First, the policy recognizes Anglo-Australian institutions and culture as foundational to the nation, even as it has sought to check and delimit this privileging and secure the rights of minorities. The first national multiculturalism policy, for example, acknowledged the importance of 'our British heritage' in helping 'to define us as Australian'; multiculturalism, it said, 'does not entail a rejection of Australian values, customs and beliefs' (OMA 1989, 50–52). Two decades later the Australian Multicultural Advisory Council, which advised the Gillard government in revamping Australia's multicultural policy, put it this way:

> Australia is very different to the Australia of the mid-20th century ... [but] much is unchanged: our political and legal institutions; our democracy; our liking for freedom, fairness and order; *our language and the way we speak it; our love of the beach, the bush and sport.* (AMAC 2010, 11; emphasis added)

Second, and at the same time, Australian multiculturalism entertains an open future in which 'our evolving national character and identity' will inevitably reflect the changing composition of the Australian people (OMA 1989, 52; NMAC 1999, 7). There is an acceptance that Australian national identity and culture are works in progress and an expectation that someday, through the culturally diverse backgrounds and everyday interactions of Australians, these things are likely to be very different from what they have been and are today. This dynamic aspect distinguishes Australia from, say, Quebec and many European democracies (and their respective integration regimes), where the dominance of their foundational cultures tends to be considered indelible (Bouchard 2011; Taylor 2012).

For almost 40 years, then, a liberal nationalist architecture as described above has governed Australia's approach to liberal democracy and national identity. It has not, however, gone unchallenged. Cultural nationalist sentiment remains strong and even dominant in some institutions. At the popular level, public opinion research consistently finds that a majority of Australians believe that migrants should adopt the Australian way of life rather than maintain their distinct customs (Markus 2011). Outbursts from conservative politicians, such as calling for bans on wearing the hijab or having migrants be instructed to use deodorant, still occur and make headlines, though their proposals typically come to nothing. More significantly, the cultural nationalist legacy continues to be felt in some Australian institutions. This occurs especially in matters involving the symbolic or actual inclusion of minorities in official activities. One example, at the center of Australian democracy, is the persisting custom of opening sessions in both houses of federal Parliament with the Lord's Prayer despite multicultural lobbying to have the ritual better reflect Australia's diversity (Cahill et al. 2004). Another example is the scheduling, in recent times, of national elections and government summits on Jewish religious festivals; such barriers to equal participation were among the very things Australian multiculturalism was supposed to remove. The liberal nationalist 'settlement' in Australia is thus not yet complete (Levey 2013). It is against this background and these tensions that the two Australian citizenship tests need to be viewed.

National identity and the Australian citizenship tests

The citizenship test introduced in 2007 seemed to reverse the thrust of how Australian citizenship had been conceived for decades. Until then, the liberal nationalist and multiculturalism era inaugurated in the 1970s had witnessed the progressive redefinition of Australian citizenship from one of a national-cultural community and emotional connection to it, to one of 'proceduralism' and the formal acceptance of rights and obligations (Betts 2002; Betts and Birrell 2007). In 1986, for example, the requirement in the Oath of Allegiance to state one's name and to renounce all other allegiances was dropped. In 1994, the Oath of Allegiance was replaced in its entirety with a Pledge of Commitment as a Citizen, in which reference to the Queen was omitted. The new pledge, which all new citizens must make, reads:

> From this time forward, under God, I pledge my loyalty to Australia and its people, whose democratic beliefs I share, whose rights and liberties I respect, and whose laws I will uphold and obey. (The phrase 'under God' is optional; quoted in Betts 1994, 49)

The shift to a procedural definition of Australian citizenship as a legal status granted on the basis of respect for the law and liberal democratic norms reached its logical conclusion in 2002. The Australian Citizenship Amendment Act 2002 (Cth.) permitted Australian citizens to acquire other nationalities without losing their Australian citizenship. Australia's diverse population (22% then being immigrants and 43% having at least one parent born overseas), the international mobility of Australians, anomalies whereby migrants to Australia might hold dual citizenship whereas 'born Australians' could not, and a claimed international trend toward recognizing dual citizenship were among the reasons cited for the reform. Betts (2002) has characterized (and criticized) these changes in the definition of Australian citizenship as a move from 'patriotism' to 'proceduralism.' This is not quite right. As the new citizen pledge indicates, there is strong civic patriotism in the affirmation of loyalty to Australia and its people, to its law and institutions (Fozdar and Spittles 2010). However, clearly the redefinition of Australian citizenship in civic terms was a far cry from the culturally normative conception of Australian citizenship proposed by the Department of Immigration in 1955, in which not only the 'responsibilities and privileges of citizenship' would be stipulated but also 'what it means by the Australian tradition or the Australian way of life' (quoted in Jordens 1995, 6–7).

The 2007 citizenship test with its questions on Anglo-Australian culture seemed to hark back to this earlier era and conception. Joppke (2013) is right that the reversal was, by European standards, modest, and aspects of it were short-lived. However, also significant is that when the reversal in direction came, few Australians were much surprised by it even though many objected to it. The test was presided over by the country's most conservative prime minister in the postwar period, in his 11th and, what proved to be, final year in power. When John Howard assumed office in 1996, he was known as a staunch, Anglo-Australian cultural nationalist. During his first years in government, he famously refused even to utter the word 'multiculturalism,' and throughout his prime ministership promoted Anglo-Australian culture as the core of Australian national identity (Johnson 2007;

Tate 2009). In a 1999 referendum, for example, he sought to have the legendary Australian tradition of 'mateship' enshrined in the preamble to the Australian Constitution (the attempt failed). In the same year, his government rebadged multiculturalism policy as 'Australian multiculturalism' to signal its Australian pedigree, and put more stress on social cohesion, community harmony, and the obligations of Australians under the policy as against their rights (Commonwealth of Australia 1999; Castles 2001, 809–811). Few doubted that Howard had lost his dislike of a policy that stood for accommodating and celebrating cultural diversity.

The fraught international environment in the wake of Islamist terrorist attacks in New York, Bali, Madrid, and London in the 2000s, and the reaction to these events by Britain, the Netherlands, Germany, and others in seeking to tighten the conditions of citizenship and debating the wisdom of 'multiculturalism' presented Howard with an opportunity to act on long held convictions. He moved swiftly. In 2006, his government flagged a raft of changes, including renaming the Department of Immigration and Multicultural Affairs the Department of Immigration and Citizenship and otherwise dropping the word 'multiculturalism' from federal government use, extending the residency eligibility period for acquiring citizenship from two to four years, and introducing an English-language proficiency and citizenship ('history and values') test for those seeking to become Australian citizens (Bennett and Tait 2008; Fozdar and Spittles 2009).

The fact that it was Howard who introduced the English and citizenship tests ensured that many Australians would view these reforms suspiciously. To many, the tests recalled the infamous language dictation tests of the White Australia policy, by which officials could exclude anyone they wanted to. Any lingering doubt among critics was removed with the announcement that the citizenship test would include questions on Australian cricket heroes and other cultural icons along with questions on Australian political institutions. These were not the kind of cultural matters that served an instrumental state purpose, such as English as a *lingua franca*, and which some liberals have defended as 'statist nationalism' (Gans 2003, 15). They were manifestly an attempt to redefine Australian citizenship in cultural nationalist terms. However modest and ultimately ineffectual was this attempt, the symbolic politics of what was at stake was obvious to Australians, supporters and critics alike. The sense that a fundamental change was being visited on Australian politics is well caught by Fozdar and Spittles' (2009, 512) account, in which Howard's citizenship test:

> functioned as part of an ideological re-imagining of Australia as a nation proudly based on Enlightenment liberal democratic values, explicitly linked to its colonial past, and having a Judeo-Christian and Anglo-Saxon/Celtic heritage ... The Howard Government explicitly used citizenship to exclude those who do not fit this anachronistic vision of Australia, and to reinforce the Anglo-privilege that policies since the 1970s had sought to challenge.

In the eyes of critics, Howard was overstepping an implicit and presumptively settled boundary. Just as he had sought to inject an Anglo-Australian trope like 'mateship' into the Constitution where it did not belong, he was now seeking to inject Anglo-Australian identity into the domain of citizenship where it does not belong. This sense of a boundary is the key to understanding the Australian case.

Joppke is right to detect the influence of liberal universalism and the 'universalist paradox' on Australian citizenship. It was the Howard government, after all, that passed the Australian Citizenship Amendment Act 2002 (Cth.) that enabled Australian citizens to hold dual and multiple citizenships. The format of the 2007 citizenship test was hardly onerous. The computer-based test, conducted at test centers around the country, comprised 20 multiple-choice questions randomly drawn from 200 questions based on material supplied in the citizenship resource booklet, *Becoming an Australian Citizen* (DIAC 2007). To pass the test, applicants needed to answer correctly 12 of the 20 questions, including 3 mandatory questions treating the 'responsibilities and privileges of Australian citizenship' (the revised 2009 test requires 15 correctly answered). Applicants could attempt the test as many times as needed to pass it. Those with a mental or physical incapacity or under the age of 18 or over 60 were exempt from the requirement to do the test (Bennett and Tait 2008).

Between 1 October 2007 and 30 June 2009, about 138,000 people sat for the Australian citizenship test, with a pass rate of almost 97%. While rates varied among different streams of applicants and different national origins, generally the pass rate remained very high after two attempts (DIAC 2009a). So even under the auspices of the most culturally conservative Australian prime minister in modern times, the test was not exactly exclusionary in its impact, and perhaps not even in its intent. Moreover, the provocative cultural questions were outweighed by the civic questions on Australia's history and institutions. Finally, within a few years, after Howard and the conservatives lost office in late 2007, a new citizenship test was enacted without the questions on sporting and cultural icons. For all that, it is my contention that the influence of liberal universalism in the Australian case registers and is incorporated within a broader *liberal nationalist* framework.

As far back as 2000, the Australian Citizenship Council, an independent body established 'to advise the Minister for Immigration and Multicultural Affairs on Australian citizenship matters that are referred to it by the Government' (DIMA 1998), recommended what was essentially a civic or post-nationalist vision for Australia. The Australian Citizenship Council (2000) suggested that a 'civic compact' setting out the ground rules by which Australians live should replace the notion of a national identity. The proposal, which sought to extend the civic ethic governing the acquisition of Australian citizenship to national life generally, went unheeded. Similarly, when the recalibration of the citizenship test came in 2009, after a governmental review, it did not reject outright the notion of Australian national culture and traditions. Rather, testable questions were restricted to historical and civic themes alluded to in the Pledge of Commitment (part of the citizenship ceremony), while material on Australian social and cultural life was supplied in a booklet, *Australian Citizenship: Our Common Bond* for background reading and which had no bearing on applicants' aspiration to become citizens (DIAC 2009b). In other words, national culture and identity are acknowledged as being significant to life in Australia, but beyond, not for, the purposes of holding citizenship – a classic liberal nationalist resolution of differentiating spheres.

There are other grounds for not viewing Australian citizenship in terms of a liberal universalist paradigm. For one thing, there is still too much discretion, non-transparency, and nonaccountability in the administration of migration law and in ministerial decisions regarding the 'good character' test (Meagher 2009; Glass 2012). For another, there is arguably a residual strain of cultural nationalism at play even today. Australian governments on both sides of the political divide have summarily disowned Australian citizens who find themselves in serious trouble abroad. The Howard government, for example, turned its back on David Hicks and Mamdouh Habib when they were incarcerated in Guantánamo Bay, the former eventually convicted, in a plea bargain, on charges of providing material support to terrorism and the latter never charged. The Gillard Labor government was similarly quick to wash its hands of Julian Assange once WikiLeaks released confidential USA diplomatic cables. On a liberal universalist conception of citizenship, one might expect the government to be concerned for the rights and welfare of its nationals even when they are in trouble with the law. Instead, Australian governments have acted as if a wayward family member has brought shame on the nation and needs to be cut loose.

These are side issues, however. The key to understanding the Australian case remains the manner in which its prevailing liberal nationalist architecture differentiates domains. Citizenship has been effectively 'denationalized' in a *cultural sense* (notwithstanding the occasional cultural reflex in regard to wayward nationals as per above). At the same time, matters of national identity and culture are acknowledged and accommodated elsewhere, both within and outside the purview of government. This arrangement is certainly challenged from the right by cultural nationalists seeking to 'renationalize' citizenship, and from the left by civic nationalists-cum-liberal universalists seeking to 'citizenship-ize' national identity. Australia's liberal nationalist settlement has to date continued to repel these conflations through its art and architecture of separation.

For this reason, there is some irony in the Australian government's symbolic replacement of 'multiculturalism' with 'citizenship' in the nomenclature of the Department of Immigration, in effect since 2007. Multiculturalism Australian-style, as we have seen, insists on the priority of core liberal democratic values while acknowledging the importance and place of both a foundational and dynamic conception of national identity. Australian citizenship, on the other hand, has been carved out as a status and a domain where discourse on national identity and culture are deemed to be inappropriate, and where a commitment to civic-ness and an abstract loyalty to people and country holds sway. In the Australian context, it is the concept and practice of 'multiculturalism' rather than the concept and practice of 'citizenship,' then, that actually provides a richer set of resources to a department charged with fostering national integration and cohesion.

Conclusion: the symbolic significance of the tests

Many liberals accept that citizenship tests are legitimate if they meet certain conditions (e.g., see the contributions by Bauböck and Joppke (2010)). In particular, they should avoid inquiring into the 'inner disposition' or personal beliefs of applicants or testing familiarity with the national or dominant culture, and should focus instead on language competency, knowledge of civic norms and governing institutions, and perhaps also something of the history of how the nation concerned became a democracy. Importance is also placed on the relative ease of the test conditions: that is, the tests should not be prohibitively expensive to prepare for or undertake, and applicants can retake the test until they pass.

On these measures, the two Australian citizenship tests do not do too badly. Both tests meet the 'relative ease of test conditions' principle. As we have seen, the 2007 test infringed the principle of not testing familiarity with the dominant culture, but this was soon rectified in the 2009 (and current) test. That said, other kinds of cultural questions might legitimately be introduced. Some cultural knowledge is simply useful for getting around the place, perhaps even surviving in it. The British citizenship test asks a multiple-choice question about what one should do if one accidently knocks over a patron's beer in a pub. Knowing that one should offer to buy him another rather than pat him dry could just be life- or face-saving. The Australian equivalent may be to know not to press one's car horn behind another vehicle unless absolutely necessary. It might be argued that the Pledge of Commitment new citizens must give at their citizenship ceremony (common to both tests) violates the principle of not inquiring into the inner disposition of applicants. The pledge requires new citizens to declare that they *share democratic beliefs*, not simply that they will respect democratic institutions. As far as inquisitions go, however, it is a slight one.

Orgad argues that 'national constitutionalism' is the appropriate protocol by which immigrants are entitled to become citizens in a liberal democracy. Under this protocol, 'immigrants would have to be familiar with, and accept, a state's essential constitutional principles before becoming citizens – as long as these principles are just considering the state's circumstances' (Orgad 2010, 98–99). One could scarcely imagine a protocol least suited to the Australian case. The Constitution of the Commonwealth of Australia, a bone-dry document, figures not at all in the public imagination and making Australian citizenship conditional on its familiarity and acceptance would only produce a mass exodus and, one imagines, little influx. It is no accident that Jürgen Habermas' constitutional patriotism has no profile in the public or even scholarly debate over Australian multiculturalism and national identity.[4] Mouritsen's (2013) point about the resilience of national traditions is especially relevant here.

National context also impinges on the concept of 'earned citizenship,' one of Joppke's markers of a 'restrictive turn' in Europe. As he puts it, 'If "earned citizenship" is what Australia now offers to, or rather expects of, its immigrants, this is demonstrably a European – more precisely: British – import' (Joppke 2013, 2). Long ago, MacIntyre (1971) warned social scientists of the folly of assuming that the same words mean the same thing in different cultural contexts. Australia may be English-speaking and a child of Britain but differences abound. When the Australian Citizenship Test Review Committee (2008) recommended that a concept of 'earned citizenship' be introduced, it was to *ease* the path to Australian citizenship for certain struggling groups by allowing other criteria and experience to be taken into account instead of having to pass the citizenship test. It was not, as in Britain, a proposed points-based system in which migrants would have to earn their citizenship by undertaking civic or community work or other tasks. Ironically (given Joppke's thesis), the earned citizenship proposal in Australia could be considered the more liberal approach, and its ultimate rejection by the government the less liberal outcome.

This raises the question of whether there is need of a citizenship test at all. Is not 'the most liberal citizenship test … none at all?' (Carens 2010). As far as fairness goes, Hansen (2010) points out that born citizens have undergone years of mandatory formal education and socialization so a limited test over a few hours for newcomers is not unreasonable. I want, however, to stress the symbolic importance of such tests. Moving to a new society with a view to full membership is a significant transition in anyone's life. It is also a significant moment for the host society. Human beings down the ages have marked such transitions with inductions and ceremony. Becoming a citizen of a new political community would seem to warrant at least as much fuss. Citizenship tests also have wider significance for the problem of liberal legitimacy. The authority of liberal institutions ostensibly derives only from the consent of those subject to them. Yet most of us cannot remember when we granted that consent. Citizenship tests and pledges today are nothing if not attempts to formally solicit the consent of newcomers to the authority of the host society's governing norms and institutions. This raises two intriguing prospects.

One follows Honig's (2001) suggestion that the inductions and ceremonies that immigrants undergo to become citizens serve as a kind of conduit for the vicarious consent of those of us born into the political community. I have suggested something similar regarding converts to Judaism (who undergo a much more rigorous induction than most would-be citizens) and the significance of their example for secular Jews in their own relation to Judaism (Levey 1994). Joppke (2013, 13) dismisses Honig's suggestion as a 'brainy, if not ludicrous construction,' but it is his dismissal that is cerebral and silly.

The spectacle of immigrants taking seriously their newfound citizenship is real and experiential (Aptekar 2012). In Australia, the ceremonies are widely reported in the media, so much so that in 1999, the federal government instituted a citizenship affirmation ceremony for born Australian citizens who also wished to 'publicly affirm their loyalty and commitment to Australia and its people.'[5] The affirmation ceremonies, which remain popular, are entirely voluntary and have no legal standing or implication whatsoever. They are purely a symbolic exercise in the appreciation and significance of citizenship.

A second intriguing prospect relates more directly to immigrants. In the case of liberal democracies, nationalism may be said to compensate for the absence of formally obtained consent at the heart of the liberal legitimacy problem. Sentiment is the tie that binds when agreement is weak or unavailable. What will happen, then, to national identity and nationalist sentiment as increasing numbers of immigrants become citizens via formal consent protocols? Will their affective ties be any less deep or abiding as a consequence? To raise such questions is to concede the possibility that the liberal nationalist quest to separate a domain of citizenship from domains of national identity may have a shelf life, and that contractualism may ultimately replace national sentiment and identity. There is a sting here also for cultural nationalists. Those who, like John Howard in Australia, embraced citizenship tests in hopes of further securing the cultural nation, may have in fact reached for a measure that works only to undercut the place of the cultural nation. Mill ([1859] 1972, 29) pondered a kindred question: whether moral community and social ties are vulnerable to the 'dissolving force of analysis' and rational deliberation. Ultimately, he thought, they are not. In the present case, we will not really know the answer until 'contracted citizens' reach a critical mass in the population, which, even in Australia, is still some generations away.

For now, Australia's liberal nationalist architecture mediates and contains civic nationalism (or liberal universalism), effectively making it the reigning regime in the single domain of citizenship acquisition and status. Elsewhere in Australian politics and society, national identity and culture are allowed to percolate in conjunction with civic norms and liberal-democratic institutions. More than any other political or cultural attribute today, it is Australia's liberal nationalist architecture that now governs how it responds to the challenges of diversity, citizenship, and national identity.

Notes

1. It should be noted that this 'nationalist' position is rather more sophisticated and nuanced than Brubaker's (1992) earlier work explaining the different approaches of France and Germany to citizenship in terms of their particular conceptions of the nation. Brubaker (1999) subsequently rejected this 'Manichean' way of construing citizenship regimes.
2. 'Mateship,' another famed Australian tradition, is a more equivocal value politically, being, among other things, highly masculine.
3. I draw here on points made by Levey (2012, 260).
4. The controversial provisions in the Australian Constitution concerning the status of Aborigines would also require an unedifying debate about whether these meet Orgad's condition of being 'just considering the state's circumstances.' In this respect, it is noteworthy that a 'national constitutional' approach is not adopted in a position paper, coauthored by Orgad, outlining a strategy for Israel's immigration policy (Avineri, Orgad, and Rubinstein 2010). The stress on Jewish historical rights and Israel as the state of the Jewish people in the constitutive Declaration of the Establishment of the State of Israel of 1948 presumably does not make for easy endorsement by all those seeking entry or acceptance into Israel today.
5. See www.citizenship.gov.au/ceremonies/affirmation/

References

AMAC (Australian Multicultural Advisory Council). 2010. *The People of Australia: The Australian Multicultural Advisory Council's Statement on Cultural Diversity and Recommendations to Government*. Canberra: AMAC.

Aptekar, S. 2012. "Naturalization Ceremonies and the Role of Immigrants in the American Nation." *Citizenship Studies* 16: 937–952.

Australian Citizenship Council. 2000. *Australian Citizenship for a New Century*. Canberra: AGPS.

Australian Citizenship Test Review Committee. 2008, August. *Moving Forward ... Improving Pathways to Citizenship* (Report), Canberra: Commonwealth of Australia.

Avineri, S., L. Orgad, and A. Rubinstein. 2010. *Managing Global Migration: A Strategy for Immigration in Israel*. Jerusalem: The Metzilah Center.

Bauböck, R., and C. Joppke, eds. 2010. *How Liberal Are Citizenship Tests?* EUI Working Papers 41. Florence: RSCAS.

BBC News. 2011. "State Multiculturalism has Failed, Says David Cameron." February 5. http://www.bbc.co.uk/news/uk-politics-12371994

Bennett, S.-J., and M. Tait. 2008. "The Australian Citizenship Test." *Queensland Law Student Review* 1: 75–87.

Betts, K. 1994. "The Issues Paper on Citizenship." *People and Place* 2 (2): 46–50.

Betts, K. 2002. "Democracy and Dual Citizenship." *People and Place* 10 (1): 57–70.

Betts, K., and B. Birrell. 2007. "Making Australian Citizenship Mean More." *People and Place* 15 (1): 45–61.

Bouchard, G. 2011. "What is Interculturalism?" *McGill Law Journal* 56: 435–468.

Brawley, S. 2007. "Mrs O'Keefe and the Battle for White Australia." *Memento* (Winter). Canberra: National Archives of Australia.

Brubaker, R. 1992. *Citizenship and Nationhood in France and Germany*. Cambridge: Harvard University Press.

Brubaker, R. 1999. "The Manichean Myth: Rethinking the Distinction Between Civic and Ethnic Nationalism." In *Nation and National Identity: The European Experience in Perspective*, edited by H. Kriesl, K. Armingeon, H. Siegrist, and A. Wimmer, 55–71. Zurich: Verlag Rüegger.

Cahill, D., G. Bouma, H. Dellal, and M. Leahy. 2004. *Religion, Cultural Diversity and Safeguarding Australia*. Melbourne: Australian Multicultural Foundation.

Calhoun, C. 2007. *Nations Matter: Culture, History and the Cosmopolitan Dream*. London: Routledge.

Canovan, M. 1996. *Nationhood and Political Theory*. Cheltenham: Edward Elgar.

Carens, J. 2010. "The Most Liberal Citizenship Test is None at All." In *How Liberal Are Citizenship Tests?* EUI Working Papers 41, edited by R. Bauböck, and C. Joppke, 19–20. Florence: RSCAS.

Castles, S. 2001. "Multiculturalism in Australia." In *The Australian People: An Encyclopedia of the Nation, Its People and Their Origins*, edited by J. Jupp, 807–811. Cambridge: Cambridge University Press.

Cole, D. 1971. "'The Crimson Thread of Kinship': Ethnic Ideas in Australia 1870–1914." *Historical Studies* 14: 511–525.

Commonwealth of Australia. 1999. *A New Agenda for Multicultural Australia*. Canberra: AGPS.

Curran, J., and S. Ward. 2010. *The Unknown Nation: Australia After Empire*. Melbourne: Melbourne University Press.

Davidson, A. 1997. *From Subject to Citizen: Australian Citizenship in the Twentieth Century*. Cambridge: Cambridge University Press.

DIAC (Department of Immigration and Citizenship). 2007. *Becoming an Australian Citizen*. Canberra: DIAC.

DIAC. 2009a July. *Australian Citizenship Test Snapshot Report*. Canberra: DIAC.

DIAC. 2009b. *Australian Citizenship: Our Common Bond*. Canberra: DIAC.

DIMA (Department of Immigration and Multicultural Affairs). 1998. "Australian Citizenship Council Announced." Media release MPS 104/98, August 7.

Etzioni, A. 2007. "Citizenship Tests: A Comparative Communitarian Perspective." *The Political Quarterly* 78 (3): 353–363.

Fozdar, F., and B. Spittles. 2009. "The Australian Citizenship Test: Process and Rhetoric." *Australian Journal of Politics and History* 55 (4): 496–512.

Fozdar, F., and B. Spittles. 2010. "Patriotic vs. Proceduralist Citizenship: Australian Representations." *Nations and Nationalism* 16 (1): 127–147.

Gans, C. 2003. *The Limits of Nationalism*. Cambridge: Cambridge University Press.

Glass, A. 2012. "Multiculturalism and Migration Law." In *Political Theory and Australian Multiculturalism*, edited by G. B. Levey, 188–205. New York: Berghahn Books.

Hammar, T. 1996. "Citizenship: Membership of a Nation and of a State." *International Migration* 24 (4): 699–788.

Hansen, R. 2010. "Citizenship Tests: An Unapologetic Defence." In *How Liberal Are Citizenship Tests?* EUI Working Papers 41. edited by R. Bauböck and C. Joppke, 25–27. Florence: RSCAS.

Honig, B. 2001. *Democracy and the Foreigner*. Princeton, NJ: Princeton University Press.

Howard, M. M. 2009. *The Politics of Citizenship in Europe*. Cambridge: Cambridge University Press.

Johnson, C. 2007. "Howard's Values and Australian Identity." *Australian Journal of Political Science* 42 (2): 195–210.

Joppke, C. 2010. *Citizenship and Immigration*. Cambridge: Polity Press.

Joppke, C. 2013. "Through the European Looking Glass: Citizenship Tests in the USA, Australia, and Canada." *Citizenship Studies* 17: 1–15.

Jordens, A. 1995. *Redefining Australians: Immigration, Citizenship and National Identity*. Sydney: Hale & Iremonger.

Jordens, A. 1997. *Alien to Citizen: Settling Migrants in Australia, 1945–1975*. Sydney: Allen & Unwin.

Jupp, J. 1996. *Understanding Australian Multiculturalism*. Canberra: AGPS.

Kaufmann, E. 2000. "Ethnic or Civic Nation? Theorizing the American Case." *Canadian Review of Studies in Nationalism* 27: 133–154.

Kohn, H. 1965. *Nationalism, Its Meaning and History*. Rev. ed. Princeton, NJ: Van Nostrand.

Koopmans, R., P. Statham, M. Giugni, and F. Passy. 2005. *Contested Citizenship: Immigration and Cultural Diversity in Europe*. Minneapolis, MN: University of Minnesota Press.

Kuzio, T. 2002. "The Myth of the Civic State: A Critical Survey of Hans Kohn's Framework for Understanding Nationalism." *Ethnic and Racial Studies* 25: 20–39.

Kymlicka, W. 1995. *Multicultural Citizenship*. Oxford: Oxford University Press.

Levey, G. B. 1994. "Jews by Choice." *Generation* 4: 42–44.

Levey, G. B., ed. 2012. "Multiculturalism and Australian National Identity." In *Political Theory and Australian Multiculturalism*, 254–276. New York: Berghahn Books.

Levey, G. B. 2013. "The Australian Multiculturalism Debate Today." In *State of the Nation: Essays for Robert Manne*, edited by G. Tavan, 176–188. Melbourne: Black.

Lind, M. 1995. *The Next American Nation*. New York: Free Press.

Lopez, M. 2000. *The Origins of Multiculturalism in Australian Politics 1945–75*. Melbourne: Melbourne University Press.

MacIntyre, A., ed. 1971. "Is a Science of Comparative Politics Possible?" *Against the Self-Images of the Age, Essays on Ideology and Philosophy*, 260–279. New York: Schocken Books.

Markus, A. 2011. "Attitudes to Multiculturalism and Cultural Diversity." In *Multiculturalism and Integration: A Harmonious Relationship*, edited by J. Jupp, and M. Clyne, 89–100. Canberra: ANU E Press.

Meagher, D. 2009. "Examining the Character of Australian Citizens." *Public Law Review* 20: 95–100.

Mill, J. S. [1859] 1972. *Utilitarianism, on Liberty, and Considerations on Representative Government*, edited by H. B. Acton. London: J.M. Dent & Sons.

Miller, D. 1995. *On Nationality*. Oxford: Clarendon Press.

Mouritsen, P. 2013. "The Resilience of Citizenship Traditions: Civic Integration in Germany, Great Britain and Denmark." *Ethnicities* 13: 86–109.

Nielsen, K. 1996–97. "Cultural Nationalism, Neither Ethnic Nor Civic." *Philosophical Forum* 28: 42–52.

NMAC (National Multicultural Advisory Council). 1999. *Australian Multiculturalism for a New Century: Towards Inclusiveness*. Canberra: AGPS.

OMA (Office of Multicultural Affairs). 1989. *National Agenda for a Multicultural Australia*. Canberra: AGPS.

Orgad, L. 2010. "Illiberal Liberalism: Cultural Restrictions on Migration and Access to Citizenship in Europe." *American Journal of Comparative Law* 58 (1): 53–105.

Soutphommasane, T. 2012. *The Virtuous Citizen: Patriotism in a Multicultural Society*. Cambridge: Cambridge University Press.

Tamir, Y. 1993. *Liberal Nationalism*. Princeton, NJ: Princeton University Press.

Tate, J. 2009. "John Howard's 'Nation' and Citizenship Test: Multiculturalism, Citizenship, and Identity." *Australian Journal of Politics and History* 55 (1): 97–120.

Tavan, G. 2005. *The Long, Slow Death of White Australia*. Melbourne: Scribe.

Taylor, C. 2012. "Interculturalism or Multiculturalism?" *Philosophy and Social Criticism* 38: 413–423.

Walzer, M. 1984. "Liberalism and the Art of Separation." *Political Theory* 12: 315–333.

Yack, B. 1999. "The Myth of the Civic Nation." In *Theorizing Nationalism*, edited by R. Beiner, 103–118. Albany: State University of New York Press.

Zubrzycki, J. 1995. "The Evolution of the Policy of Multiculturalism in Australia." In *1995 Global Cultural Diversity Conference Proceedings*. Canberra: DIAC.

International migration at a crossroads

Stephen Castles

School of Social and Political Sciences, University of Sydney, Sydney, Australia,

In the early twenty-first century, the forces generating international migration are more powerful than ever, and human mobility has become a key facet of global integration. Yet public concern about migration also remains powerful. Origin countries fear loss of skills and increased dependency on remittances from destination countries. Many people in destination countries see migration as a threat to prosperity, identity and security. The securitization of migration in the Global North since 2001 ignores the fact that South–North migration is the result of growing global inequality and lack of human security in the South. It is important to understand that migration is a crucial aspect of human development that can improve the capabilities of individuals and the innovation capacity of societies. This essay provides an overview of some of the key issues in international migration, including a discussion of the effects of the global economic crisis. In conclusion, the essay discusses the 'global governance deficit' in migration and looks at some long-term prospects.

Introduction

In the early twenty-first century, the dilemmas of human mobility across international borders are more evident than ever before. The economic, demographic and political drivers of migration remain powerful, yet the public hostility to migration in some receiving countries continues to gain in strength. International and intercontinental flows of labour at all skill levels are crucial to the global economy. Together with other cross-border flows – of commodities, capital, intellectual property and culture – human mobility is an integral part of globalization. Yet, states continue to regulate entry of foreigners as a symbol of national sovereignty. At a time when regulatory frameworks for finance, trade and many other aspects of international cooperation have been adopted, global governance of migration remains conspicuous mainly for its absence.

Yet this is a time of change. The global economic crisis (GEC) has disrupted patterns of migration and brought about declines in remittances to poor communities that had become dependent on them. However, migrant populations in rich countries have proved more resilient than many expected. At the same time, flows to new industrial areas in Asia, Latin America and Africa have grown. Developed countries and newly industrializing countries are competing for scarce skills, while even the supply of lower-skilled labour is beginning to appear finite in view of the demographic transitions taking place throughout the world. The labour-importing countries – after many years of refusal – have begun to talk to governments of migrant-origin countries through such mechanisms as the UN High

Level Dialogue on Migration and Development in 2006 and 2013, and the Global Forum on Migration and Development, which has met annually since 2007.

This is therefore a good moment to take stock of some of the key issues in international migration. This article looks first at the significance of migration for human security and human development, and links this to processes of globalization. It goes on to examine some emerging forms of migration, with special attention to women migrants and forced migrants. Issues of diversity and multiculturalism in destination societies are discussed, followed by some information on the effects of the GEC. Finally, the article discusses possible future trends and the 'global governance deficit'.

The significance of migration for human security and human development

Since the beginning of the twenty-first century, governments have increasingly portrayed migration as a threat to security. The New York terrorist attacks of 11 September 2001 followed by the Madrid bombings of 2004 and the London bombings of 2005 led to a widespread belief that Muslim migrants could constitute a danger to democratic societies. This ignores the facts that the overwhelming majority of Muslims oppose fundamentalism and that very few of those involved in these attacks were either migrants or refugees. The idea of immigrants as a potential 'enemy within' is not new (Guild 2009). Indeed, immigrants have for centuries been seen as a threat to state security and national identity. Before Muslims, a succession of other groups was cast in this role (Cohen 1994). Such attitudes have in turn been used to justify immigration restrictions and reductions in civil liberties – often not just for immigrants but for the population as a whole.

The securitization of migration and ethnic minorities is based on a perspective that emphasizes the security of rich northern states and their populations, while ignoring the reality that migration and refugee flows are often the result of the fundamental lack of human security in poorer countries in Asia, Africa and Latin America. This absence of human security – which finds its expression in poverty, hunger, violence and lack of human rights – is not a natural condition, but is a result of past practices of colonization and of more recent imbalances in economic and political power, which have created extreme inequality. For example, in less-developed countries with natural endowments of oil and other minerals, much of the wealth is often monopolized by local elites and multinational companies, leaving the majority of the population as poor or even poorer than ever (the so-called 'resource curse'). Internal conflicts about economic and political power often lead to warfare, persecution of civilian populations and mass displacement. Thus, the social transformations inherent in globalization do not just affect economic well-being, they also lead to increased violence and lack of human security. Growing numbers of people have to leave their homes in search of protection and better livelihoods.

Migration policies too can exacerbate human insecurity. Where states refuse to create legal migration systems despite strong employer demand for workers, migrants experience high levels of risk and exploitation. Smuggling, trafficking, bonded labour and lack of human and worker rights are the fate of millions of migrants. Even legal migrants may have an insecure residence status and be vulnerable to economic exploitation, discrimination and racist violence. Many governments around the world try to resolve the contradiction between strong labour needs and public hostility to migration by creating differentiated entry systems that encourage legal entry of highly skilled workers, while excluding lower-skilled workers or only admitting them on a restricted and temporary basis. Since labour market demand for the lower-skilled workers is strong, millions of migrants are pushed into irregularity.

Irregular migration affects most countries. Statistics are unreliable, due to the nature of such movements, and because estimates may be manipulated for political reasons. The most accurate data are for the USA: as of 2010, there were 10.8 million irregular migrants living in the USA, down from the peak of 11.8 million in 2007 (Hoefer, Rytina, and Baker 2011). An estimated 7.8 million irregular migrant workers make up 5.1% of the US workforce (Passel and Cohn 2009). The best estimates for the European Union (EU) range from 1.8 to 3.3 million irregular residents – less than 1% of the EU's total population (Clandestino 2009). Irregular migration is thought to be widespread in Africa, Asia, the Middle East and Latin America – but data are poor, partly because many countries do not make clear distinctions between regular and irregular migration.

A fundamental change in attitudes is a necessary step towards fairer and more effective migration policies. It is important to see migration not as threat to state security, but as a result of the human insecurity that arises through global inequality. Throughout human history, people have migrated to improve their livelihoods and to gain greater security. Migration is an important aspect of human development. This approach to migration corresponds with social philosopher and economist Amartya Sen's (2001) principle of 'development as freedom'. Mobility is a basic freedom, and has the potential to lead to greater human capabilities. Reducing migration restrictions and ensuring that people can move safely and legally helps enhance human rights, and also can lead to greater economic efficiency and social equality (United Nations Development Programme 2009).

Globalization and migration

Human mobility is an integral part of globalization. As less-developed countries are drawn into global economic linkages, powerful processes of social transformation are unleashed. Neoliberal forms of international economic integration undermine traditional ways of working and living (Stiglitz 2002). Increased agricultural productivity displaces people from the land. Environmental change compels many people to seek new livelihoods and places to live. People move to the cities, but there are not enough jobs there, and housing and social conditions are often very bad (Davis 2006). Weak states and impoverishment lead to lack of human security, and often to violence and violations of human rights. All these factors encourage emigration.

At the same time, globalization leads to social transformation in the economically developed countries of the Organization for Economic Cooperation and Development (OECD), where industrial restructuring since the late 1970s has meant de-skilling and early retirement for many workers. The new services industries need very different types of labour. But, due to declining fertility, relatively few young nationals enter the labour market. Moreover, these young people have good educational opportunities and are not willing to do low-skilled work. Even at time of high youth unemployment – like the current Eurozone crisis – young nationals are often reluctant to accept low-status jobs in construction, catering and care occupations. At the same time, population ageing leads to increased dependency rates and demand for labour in the services sector – especially for health services and aged care. Developed countries have high demand for both high- and low-skilled workers, and need migrants – whether legal or not.

Globalization also creates the cultural and technical conditions for mobility. Electronic communications provide knowledge of migration routes and work opportunities. Long-distance travel has become cheaper and more accessible. Once migratory flows are established they generate 'migration networks': previous migrants help members of their families or communities with information on work, accommodation and official rules.

Facilitating migration has become a major international business, including travel agents, bankers, lawyers and recruiters. The 'migration industry' also has an illegal side – smuggling and trafficking – which governments try to restrict. Yet, the more governments try to control borders, the greater the flows of undocumented migrants seem to be.

According to the latest UN statistics, some 214 million people were living outside their countries of origin in 2008 (UN Population Division 2009). This sounds a lot, but is just 3.1% of the world's people – most people remain in their countries of birth. However, the main determinant of economic, social and cultural effects is the level of concentration of migrants: some origin areas are profoundly affected by large-scale outflows, while other areas are affected by large-scale inflows (as will be discussed below).

From 1990 to 2010, there was little increase in international migration into countries in Asia, Africa and Latin America – the big growth in international migration was to Europe and North America, reflecting an increase in migration from the Global South to the North. In 2005, the UN provided data which divided international migrants into four geographical categories. The largest number of migrants (62 million) had moved from the less-developed countries of the South to the developed countries of the global North. These migrants were very diverse and included highly skilled specialists (doctors, IT experts, engineers and managers), as well as low-skilled workers, refugees and family members. The second largest group (61 million) had moved from one southern country to another. The third group (53 million) consisted of migrants who had moved between rich northern countries. The smallest category was of people who had gone from North to South (14 million) (United Nations Department of Economic and Social Affairs 2005).

However, focusing on international migration in isolation can give a deceptive picture. Many people in poorer areas move within their own countries. Internal migration attracts far less political attention, but its volume in population giants like China, India, Indonesia, Brazil and Nigeria is far greater than that of international movements, and the social and cultural consequences can be equally important. In China, the 'floating population' of people moving from the agricultural central and western provinces to the new industrial areas of the east coast numbers at least 100 million, and many of them experience legal disadvantage and economic marginalization similar to international migrants elsewhere (Skeldon 2006a).

Emerging forms of migration

This section discusses a few important trends in international migration. The 'classical immigration countries' like Australia, Canada and the USA still base their ideologies on permanent immigration of mainly male heads of household, leading to permanent settlement and eventually to citizenship. But the realities of migration in the twenty-first century are rather different, with strong trends to temporary and circular migration, migration of women and emergence of non-economic types of migration.

Temporary and circular migration

Governments of migrant-destination countries have often preferred temporary migration to permanent, both because it is supposed to minimize integration costs and because it is seen as more acceptable to existing populations. The European 'guestworker' policies of the 1960s and early 1970s were key examples, but, in fact, had unintended consequences, since many of the originally temporary workers became permanent settlers in the wake of the 1973 'oil crisis'. But temporary or contract labour systems have continued, especially in the Gulf oil states and in emerging Asian industrial countries. In Europe, most countries adopted 'zero immigration policies' in the 1970s and 1980s, but more recently temporary migration policies have made a comeback under the new euphemism of 'circular migration'.

Such policies were adopted by several countries, including Germany and Spain in the 1990s (Castles 2006; Plewa and Miller 2005). The idea was the same as the old guestworker policies: to recruit labour, but not to allow workers to bring in their families or to stay permanently – in other words 'to bring in workers but not people' (as the Swiss playwright Max Frisch put it). The new approaches were based on rigid limitations on duration of stay, job-changing and other worker rights. Such schemes became less significant in recent years due to both the Eurozone recession and the accession of Eastern and Central European countries to the EU, which provided new labour reserves for Western and Southern Europe. Nonetheless, the principle of circular migration has been endorsed as the best approach to managing migration by the European Commission (2007, 2011).

The desire for flexible temporary or circular migration schemes is, of course, not limited to Europe. In recent years, the US Government has expanded temporary work-related visa schemes, which now bring in far more skilled workers than the green cards (that allow permanent residence). In 2010, 1.7 million temporary workers were admitted, mainly highly skilled personnel. The intake of seasonal agricultural workers (H2A visas) also increased from 28,000 in 2000 to 139,000 in 2010 (Orrenius and Zavodny 2010). The main countries of origin for temporary workers were Canada, Mexico and India (United Nations Department of Economic and Social Affairs 2009). This is a temporary rather than a circular scheme, even though workers may be allowed to re-apply after returning home. By contrast, New Zealand's Recognized Seasonal Employer scheme is based on circularity. It allows agricultural and horticultural employers to recruit seasonal workers under agreements with the Kiribati, Tuvalu, Samoa, Tonga, Solomon Islands and Vanuatu. Workers are only allowed to stay for a limited period of under one year, but can return in subsequent years (Ministry of Business Innovation and Employment 2013). Temporary or circular migration schemes have also been adopted in Canada and Australia, and are common in newer industrial countries, like South Korea, Malaysia and Taiwan.

Women in migration

A key development is the growth of female migration (International Organization for Migration (IOM) 2005, 109–110). Although women have always played a major role in migration, their numbers have grown in recent years, and increasingly they move independently rather than as spouses of male migrants. Demand for female domestic workers surged from the 1980s in the Middle East, and, from the 1990s, within Asia. The female share among first-time migrant workers from the Philippines rose from 50% in 1992 to 72% by 2006 (International Labour Organization 2007). Although some women migrate to take up professional and executive positions, many migrant women are concentrated in jobs regarded as low-skilled and 'typically female': domestic workers, entertainers and hostesses, restaurant and hotel staff and assembly-line workers in clothing and electronics. Often, these jobs offer poor pay, conditions and status. Female migration has considerable effects on family and community dynamics in the place of origin. Married women have to leave their children in the care of others, and long absences affect relationships and gender roles.

A rapidly increasing form of female migration is for marriage. Since the 1990s, foreign brides have been sought by farmers in rural areas of Japan, South Korea and Taiwan, due to the exodus of local women to more attractive urban settings (Lee 2008). International marriages accounted for almost 14% of all marriages in South Korea in 2005, with even higher percentages in rural areas. Marriages are often arranged by agencies. This is one of the few forms of permanent immigration permitted in Asia. The young women involved (from the Philippines, Vietnam and Thailand) can experience severe social isolation. China's one-child policy has led to considerable gender imbalances, so that Chinese farmers are beginning to seek brides through agents in Vietnam, Laos and Burma. By 2003, 32% of brides in Taiwan were from the Chinese mainland or other countries, and births to immigrant mothers made up 13% of all births (Skeldon 2006b, 281). This has important cultural implications: the countryside is frequently seen as the cradle of traditional values, and the high proportion of foreign mothers is seen by some as a threat to national identity (Bélanger, Lee, and Wang 2010).

Refugees and forced migration

Forced migration of people seeking refuge from violence and persecution continues to grow. Annual figures released in June 2010 by the Office of the United Nations High Commissioner for Refugees (UNHCR) showed that some 43.3 million people were forcibly displaced worldwide at the end of 2009, the highest number of people uprooted by conflict and persecution since the mid-1990s. At the same time, the number of refugees voluntarily returning to their home countries had fallen to its lowest level in 20 years. The largest category – more than 27 million people – was of internally displaced persons: people forced from their homes, but who remained within their country of origin. More than 15 million were refugees – people who had found refuge in other countries – while about 1 million were asylum seekers – people seeking protection in other countries (UNHCR 2010). In 2008, a quarter of the world's refugees were from Afghanistan, while Pakistan was the country with the largest refugee population – some 1.8 million – followed by Syria and Iran. Eighty per cent of refugees were hosted by developing countries (UNHCR 2009).

The number of forced migrants has increased sharply over the last half century. Far from improving human security and reducing conflict, globalization has had the opposite effect. Situations of conflict, violence and mass flight developed from the 1950s, in the context of struggles over decolonization and formation of new states. Local conflicts became proxy wars in the East–West conflict. Following the end of the Cold War, Northern economic interests – such as the trade in oil, diamonds and weapons – continued to play an important part in starting or prolonging local wars. At a broader level, trade, investment and intellectual property regimes that favour the industrialized countries maintain underdevelopment in the South. Conflict and forced migration are thus an integral part of the North–South division. This reveals the ambiguity of efforts by the 'international community' (which essentially means the powerful Northern states and the intergovernmental agencies) to prevent forced migration.

As rich countries become less and less willing to admit asylum seekers, many seek refuge in new destinations like South Africa (now amongst the world's main refugee-receiving countries), Kenya, Egypt, Malaysia and Thailand. Refugees and asylum seekers are the most disadvantaged of all in the new global migration hierarchy: in the past they were seen as worthy of international protection; now entry rules have been tightened up to the point where it is virtually impossible to enter most northern countries to make a protection claim. Refugees are forced to become illegal migrants and often end up in long-term illegality.

Other emerging types of migration

Improvements in transport and communications have made it possible for people to migrate for a wider range of reasons, and often to move temporarily and repeatedly. Indeed, some analysts now prefer to use the term 'mobility' to stress the flexible nature of emerging types of movements for purposes such as:

- Education: students move internationally, especially for graduate studies, and some of them stay on in the destination country to work for a period or permanently. Many students have to work part-time during their studies, due to high student fees and living costs, providing a source of relatively cheap labour for retail, catering and similar sectors.
- Lifestyle: some people – especially younger people of middle-class background – move in search of new experiences and different lifestyles. Such mobility is mainly temporary, but it can have significant impacts on destination areas.
- Retirement: older people, often from affluent backgrounds, move upon ceasing employment in search of better climates, lower living costs and more attractive lifestyles. Examples include British people moving to Spain or Turkey, French people buying property in Morocco, North Americans moving to Latin America or the Caribbean, and Japanese going to the Philippines, Australia or New Zealand.
- Climate-change-induced displacement: where climate change leads to major shifts in conditions of production or community life, some people may seek to move to seek new opportunities. In the case of sudden and catastrophic events, this movement may be seen as forced migration, while in the case of slow-onset change, migration may be one possible response strategy among others. However, most climate-change-induced displacement takes place within national borders (EACH-FOR Programme 2009; Hugo 2008; McAdam 2010). Moreover, people are more likely to follow economic opportunities by migrating into areas of potential environmental stress – like the Asian mega-cities – than out of them (Foresight 2011).

Immigrant concentration

As pointed out above, concentration has become a major issue. Immigrants are concentrated in the most developed countries, making up between 5% and 23% of the population in the EU, North America and Australia. The USA had an estimated 43 million overseas-born residents in 2010, 14% of the total population, Russia had 12 million immigrants, followed by Germany with 11 million, and then Saudi Arabia and Canada with 7 million each. In terms of share in the total population, the small oil states (like Qatar and Kuwait) come first, with migrant workers and other expatriates accounting for more than 70% of their population. The share in Saudi Arabia is 28% and in Canada 21% (data from UN Population Division 2010). Australia had an immigrant population of 4.8 million in 2005, making up 23% of the total population. If children with at least one immigrant parent are added, about 45% of the Australian population were immigrants or their immediate descendants. But European countries, which until recently aspired to be homogeneous nations, have also changed dramatically. Germany's foreign-born residents,[1] make up 13% of the population – nearly as high as the USA. Other Western European countries host millions of immigrants, with population shares between 5% and 13% (data from OECD 2007).

The mono-cultural nation seems to be a figment of an outdated nationalist imagination – in highly developed countries at least. However, there are exceptions. Eastern European countries are in a state of economic and political transition, and experience both emigration and immigration, so immigrants are only 2–5% of their populations. In Japan foreign residents only make up 1.7% of the population, while in South Korea, they make up 2% (and numbers are growing fast) (OECD 2012).

Many new industrial countries are experiencing large-scale immigration: Malaysia, Hong Kong, Singapore, Taiwan and the Gulf oil states all rely heavily on migrant labour. The governments of such countries reject the idea of permanent settlement (as European states did back in the 1970s), and therefore refuse to allow migrants to bring in their families or become citizens. In Latin America, Argentina and Chile attract many migrant workers, while Mexico – still a major emigration country – is also a transit country for migrants from South and Central America, and increasingly also a destination for immigrants. As for Africa, although Europeans focus on migration northwards across the Mediterranean, more than 90% of African migration is actually within the continent, with both highly skilled and lower-skilled migrants moving to growth areas, for example in Libya, Gabon, Ghana and South Africa (Bakewell and de Haas 2007).

Migrants and their descendants settle mainly in large cities: for instance they make up 44% of the population of Toronto (Statistics Canada 2007) and 25% in London (Office for National Statistics 2002). Migrants go where the jobs are, and immigration can be used as a barometer of economic dynamism. Migrants also go where they can join compatriots, who help them to find jobs and accommodation – the 'network effect'. These mechanisms reinforce each other, and lead to residential clustering, especially in the early period of settlement of each group.

Concentration affects origin areas too. In some countries and regions it has become a normal part of young adulthood to spend a period working abroad – leading to a 'culture of emigration'. Currently about 10% of the populations of Mexico, Morocco and the Philippines are living abroad (Castles 2008). The Philippines has an official policy of being the 'supplier of workers for the world' – and the majority of migrants are women who work as domestic helpers, teachers, nurses and 'entertainers' in Japan, the Middle East, Europe and North America (Asis 2005, 2008). Migrants come from specific areas, where working abroad has become part of the local political economy – for India, the state of Kerala is the prime example for labour migration to the Gulf. Often it is middle-income people with property and skills who have the resources to move, so that emigration can both exacerbate skills shortages and inequality.

Diversity, integration and multiculturalism

Migration changes communities and societies in complex ways. In areas of origin, returnees may import new ideas that unsettle traditional practices and hierarchies – such influences have been called 'social remittances' (Levitt 1998), and they may be just as important as the better-known economic remittances (money sent home by migrants, usually to their families). In destination areas, migration leads to unprecedented cultural and religious diversity. Migrants are often seen as symbols of threats to jobs, livelihoods and cultural identities resulting from globalization. Campaigns against immigrants and asylum seekers have become powerful mobilizing tools for the extreme right.

Historically, nation-states have been based on ideas of common origins and culture. Most migrants moved either with the intention of permanent settlement or of a temporary sojourn in one receiving country. Today it is possible to go back and forth, or to move on to other countries. Increasingly, migrants see themselves as members of *transnational communities*: groups that live their lives across borders (Portes, Guarnizo, and Landolt

1999). Many receiving countries have changed their nationality laws to help immigrants and their descendants to become citizens (Bauböck et al. 2006a, 2006b), for instance by recognizing dual citizenship (Faist 2007). 'Classical immigration countries' like the USA, Canada and Australia built their populations and nations through immigration, but were still largely unprepared for the increased cultural diversity resulting from the globalization of migration since the 1960s. European immigration countries have found it particularly hard to cope with the unexpected emergence of multicultural societies.

This helps to explain why there has been a backlash against multiculturalism. From the 1970s to the early 1990s many countries had moved towards policies designed to recognize the cultural identities and social rights of minorities, and to reinforce the role of the state in combating discrimination and racism. In some cases there were explicit multicultural policies (e.g. Canada, Australia, the UK); in others terms such as 'immigrant policy' (Sweden) or 'minorities policy' (the Netherlands) were used; in yet others the notion of 'integration of foreign fellow citizens' (Germany) was applied. France was an apparent anomaly, with its Republican Model, which mandated rejection of ethnic monitoring and non-recognition of immigrant cultures and communities. But even here there were surrogate minority policies under the euphemistic label of 'policy of the city'. In the USA, the prevailing view was that cultural affairs should not be the concern of the Federal Government, and that integration was best left to the economy and the community. However, in the wake of the Civil Rights Movement of the 1960s, Federal and State governments did introduce measures to combat racial discrimination and to guarantee equal opportunities for all, while local authorities supported measures for minority education and participation.

Since the mid-1990s such trends has been reversed. US affirmative action measures have been removed, and there have been campaigns against use of minority languages. In Australia and Canada, multicultural policies still exist, but there is a new emphasis on citizenship and integration. In Europe, the official focus is no longer on the recognition of minority cultures, but on civic integration, social cohesion and 'national values'. In Britain, for example, critics of multiculturalism argued that it had failed to provide a unifying national identity (Solomos 2003). This was (explicitly or implicitly) linked to concerns about the integration and loyalty of Muslims, especially after the London bombings of July 2005. A citizenship test was introduced to promote knowledge of British society and values. Although government statements remained positive about the religious and cultural rights of minorities, a new pressure to confirm with mainstream cultural and behavioural patterns was evident.

Similarly, the French Government reacted to riots by ethnic minority youth in Autumn 2005, not by trying to understand the social and economic causes of the unrest, but by introducing tough new law and order measures (Body-Gendrot and Wihtol de Wenden 2007). These were seen as discriminatory by people of migrant origin, but were popular with many French voters, and helped Nicholas Sarkozy to become President in 2007. The Dutch Government also made sharp changes in policy (Vasta 2007), while Germany, Sweden and other countries moved in similar directions. However, it is important to note that multicultural *discourses* have often declined more than actual multicultural *policies*: measures to recognize the social and cultural needs of immigrants and minorities have often changed little, even as public discourse has shifted (Banting and Kymlicka 2012). The realities of diverse populations and their different lifestyles and social needs make special measures essential, especially at the local level.

The backlash against multiculturalism has been interpreted in various ways. A dominant approach in the media and politics is to acknowledge the social disadvantage and marginalization of many immigrant groups – especially those of non-European origin – but to claim that ethnic minorities are themselves to blame by clustering together and refusing to integrate. In this interpretation, recognition of cultural diversity has had the perverse effect of encouraging ethnic separatism and the development of 'parallel lives' (Cantle 2001). A model of individual integration – based if necessary on compulsory integration contracts and citizenship tests – is thus seen as a way of achieving greater equality for immigrants and their children. The problem for such views, however, is that the one country that has maintained its model of individual integration, France, is also experiencing dramatic problems, which came to a head with the youth riots of 2005 and 2007.

By contrast, proponents of multicultural policies argue that the marginalization still experienced by members of ethnic minorities reflects the unwillingness of destination societies to deal with two issues. The first is the deep-seated cultures of racism that are a legacy of colonialism and imperialism. The second issue is the trend to greater inequality resulting from globalization and economic restructuring. Increased international competition puts pressure on employment, working conditions and welfare systems. At the same time, neoliberal economic policies encourage greater pay differences and reduce the capacity of states to redistribute income to reduce poverty and social disadvantage. Taken together, these factors have led to a racialization of ethnic difference. Minorities often have poor employment situations, low incomes and high rates of impoverishment. This in turn leads to concentration in low-income neighbourhoods and growing residential segregation. The existence of separate and marginal communities is then taken as evidence of failure to integrate, and this in turn is perceived as a threat to the host society (Schierup, Hansen, and Castles 2006).

The effects of the global economic crisis on migration

Since 2008, the GEC has had important effects on migration, and on the economic and social positions of migrants. Policy-makers and employers in labour-importing countries often see the 'flexibility' of migrant labour as one of its chief advantages: it can help match labour supply and demand, because migrants are not meant to come when jobs are not available. There was therefore an expectation that the crisis would lead to: a fall in new labour migration; a decline in migrant stocks (i.e. the number of migrants present in receiving countries); and a fall in remittances by migrants to their families and communities in the homeland.

Short-term effects

The immediate impacts of the GEC were felt most strongly in the richer economies (Phillips 2011). Overall *unemployment* in the OECD grew by 55% between December 2007 and January 2012. In most OECD countries migrants have been more affected by unemployment than the native-born (OECD 2012, 63). Yet, foreign *employment* in European OECD countries actually increased by 5% from early 2008 to the third quarter of 2010, while the employment of native-born persons declined by more than 2% (OECD 2011, 74–75). In other words, foreign unemployment increased, but so did foreign employment!

To understand this apparent paradox it is important to look both at short-term changes and at longer-term structural changes in developed-country economies. Short-term declines in demand led to a sharp decline in manufacturing and construction. Yet structural changes like the shift away from manufacturing to the services and the demographic decline in the domestic labour forces of European countries continued. Migrants working in declining sectors lost their jobs, but other migrants were able to gain jobs in emerging sectors.

Migrant men were far more affected by job losses than migrant women. This is because migrant men tended to be employed in the sectors hardest hit by the downturn, especially manufacturing and construction, while migrant women were more concentrated in less-affected sectors, notably social services, care work and domestic work. In fact, 643,000 new jobs were created in OECD countries in 'residential care activities' from 2008 to 2011, and more than half were taken by foreign-born workers. Immigrants (especially women) also filled 193,000 new jobs as domestic workers (OECD 2012, 67). At the same time, the GEC has reinforced the trend towards part-time, temporary and causal employment, with women more likely to enter such employment relationships than men (OECD 2011, 78–81). Women thus often have to work long hours to make up for the loss of male migrants' earnings.

Taking a broader view, new labour migration fell globally in 2008 and 2009, but has partially recovered since, albeit unevenly. In the USA, both overall employment and migrant employment fell sharply in 2008–2009 (IOM 2011, 55), but with the hesitant return to growth in 2010–2011, migrant employment grew faster than employment of natives (Mohapatra, Ratha, and Silwal 2011, 5–6). In South America, the picture is mixed. In view of importance of migration to the USA and the relative stagnation of labour demand there, migratory flows to the North have been much reduced. Emigration to Spain from Ecuador and other Latin American countries has also fallen, and there has been significant return migration. However, the emergence of new migration poles (such as Brazil, Chile and Argentina) within Latin America has also led to a growth of migration within the continent.

In early 2009, the sharp economic downturn was causing some governments in Southeast and East Asia to close their borders to new migrant workers (Abella and Ducanes 2009). But by 2011 it was becoming clear that the effects of the GEC on Asian migration were moderate and short-lived (IOM 2011, 68). Migrant departures from Bangladesh, for example, which had fallen by 20% in 2010, grew by 37% in the first three quarters of 2011. Deployments of overseas contract workers from the Philippines grew by 20% from 2008–2010 despite the GEC, and by a further 7% in the first three quarters of 2011. This growth was due to the high demand for labour in the Gulf Cooperation Council (GCC) countries as well as in Russia, which in turn was linked to the high price of oil. Recruitment of Filipino seafarers, who sail the oceans under many flags, also increased (Mohapatra, Ratha, and Silwal 2011, 9).

Similarly, in 2008–2009 there were sharp falls in migrant labour flows from the poorer countries of the former Soviet Union in Central Asia like Tajikistan and Kazakhstan to Russia (Canagarajah and Kholmatov 2010). But in 2011, flows recovered considerably, as labour demand increased again in Russia and other destination countries. Many African economies rebounded relatively quickly from the GEC, although the Arab Spring negatively affected growth in North Africa from 2011. However, the economic outlook remains optimistic particularly for sub-Saharan Africa, and such countries as Ghana, South Africa, Mozambique and Angola continue to attract migrants, primarily from within the continent but also from China and even Southern Europe.

Other forms of migration have been less affected by the GEC than labour migration. These include *family reunion* as well as *migration for marriage, retirement, education and lifestyle reasons*. It is important to remember that the largest single entry category for immigrants, especially in OECD countries, is family reunion – spouses, children and other relatives coming to join existing primary migrants. Since family reunion generally only takes place once a migrant has been able establish himself or herself, there is generally quite a long time-lag. This is further increased by the bureaucratic procedures needed to obtain family visas. Similarly, marriage migration is generally the result of long-term demographic and social factors, and is unlikely to be affected much by short-term economic trends. On the other hand, migration for education – a growing trend in recent years – could well be reduced, if parents are unable to pay the costs of student fees and living costs in destination countries.

Another form of migration not likely to be reduced by the crisis is *forced migration* or *refugee flows*. The need of people to seek protection from violence and persecution might even increase in a crisis situation, due to increased conflict and impoverishment in the South. However, states' willingness to recognize and accept refugees – already in sharp decline since the early 1990s – might well diminish further (Zetter 2009). At present, statistical data to test these assumptions are not available.

Significantly, *migrant stocks* have generally not fallen. Migrants have been unwilling to leave richer countries, even if they become unemployed. Several destination country governments (e.g. Spain, the Czech Republic and Japan) set up schemes to give migrants financial incentives to return home. However, few have been willing to take up such schemes (Plewa 2009; Ratha, Mohapatra, and Silwal 2009). This is partly because conditions are often even worse back home, partly because migrants fear they will not be readmitted once the recession is over. However, increasing numbers of Latin Americans did return home from Spain in 2009, mostly independently of the government's voluntary return scheme (Mazza and Sohnen 2010). Interestingly, many Poles and other Eastern Europeans have left the UK and Ireland – as EU citizens, they have the right to come back once jobs become available.

The actual fall in *remittances* has also been rather small. Remittances to all developing countries declined from US$324 billion in 2008 to US$307 billion in 2009. They then recovered to US$325 billion in 2010 and an estimated US$351 billion in 2011. Remittance flows are not directly related to migration flows, but rather to the stock of migrants in a specific country (Ratha, Mohapatra, and Silwal 2009, 4). Since migrant stocks have not declined much (if at all), remittances levels have on the whole been maintained. However, some migrants have lost their jobs or experienced wage cuts, reducing their capacity to remit. Yet, this has sometimes been made up by migrants' willingness to make sacrifices in order to continue to provide support for their families and communities at home.

Possible long-term effects

To understand the potential impacts of the 2007–2010 crisis, it is useful to look at historical precedents. The World Economic Crisis of the 1930s led to massive declines in industrial production, international trade and labour migration. There was also considerable return migration (sometimes compulsory) of migrants from countries like the USA and France. However, many migrants did not return home, but settled and became members of the permanent population of receiving countries.

The recession following the 'oil crisis' of 1973 was a major turning point in the global economy and in migration. 'Guestworker migration' ended in Europe, and processes of family reunion and permanent settlement started, leading to the formation of new ethnic minorities. Large corporations developed strategies of capital export and a 'new international division of labour', which led to the emergence of new industrial centres especially in Asia, the Middle East and Latin America – and in the long run to new flows of labour migration.

The effects of the 1997–1999 Asian financial crisis were more modest. Several governments introduced policies of national labour preference and sought to expel migrants – especially undocumented workers. In some cases, migrants were blamed for unemployment and other social ills – like epidemics and criminality. However, employers (for instance in the Malaysian plantation industry) quickly discovered that many nationals were unwilling to take on 'migrant jobs', even in a recession. Such employers demanded an end to expulsion policies. In any case, the interruption to economic growth in Asia was only short-lived – after 1999 migration grew again and reached new heights.

Overall, the effects of economic downturns on migration are complex and hard to predict. It is mistaken to believe that migrants will serve as a sort of safety valve for developed economies, by providing labour in times of expansion and going away in times of recession. Migrants are not just economic actors, who follow income maximization motives. They are social beings, who put down roots and form relationships in new countries. At times of recession, the motivation to migrate may be even higher than before, and remittances may prove a resilient form of international transfer, because of migrants' obligations to their families

It will be some years before the full significance of the 2008–2011 GEC for migration becomes evident. The immediate effects appear to have been less than predicted in 2008 and 2009. One of the key findings to emerge from the many studies is the unexpected degree of resilience of migrant employment. Although migrant workers did play a 'buffering role in the labour market both during expansion and contraction phases of the business cycle' (OECD 2010, 85), they also continued to be a structural part of destination-country economies. Nonetheless, hardships have often been severe for many migrants and for their dependents. Origin countries have had to face serious financial consequences. Another consequence has been the rise of hostility to migrants in many destinations countries, giving rise to dangerous outbursts of racism and, in some cases, motivating exclusionary action by authorities.

A return to economic growth is likely to lead to new migratory flows to dynamic economic areas, just as in the past. The intriguing question is whether these dynamic economic areas will be the same as before. The GEC may be a symptom of a long-term shift in economic power away from the USA and the other older industrial economies to the emerging BRICS economies (Brazil, Russia, India, China and South Africa). All these countries (except perhaps China) are already poles of attraction for international migrants. China still mainly relies on internal migration, although it is beginning to recruit overseas professionals, while some immigration of Arab and African traders and migrants is also occurring. In 10 years' time, we may well look back at the 2007–2012 GEC as a turning point to the emergence of important new migration systems, just as we do today with regard to the post-1973 recession.

Migration and international relations: the governance deficit

Globalization had led to the establishment of institutions of global governance, such as the International Monetary Fund (IMF) and the World Bank for finance, and the World Trade Organization (WTO) for trade. Migration, by contrast, has been seen as a preserve of national sovereignty. There is a serious governance deficit: the international community has failed to build institutions to ensure orderly migration, protect the human rights of migrants and maximize development benefits (Bhagwati 2003).

Elements of an international framework already exist in International Labour Organization (ILO) Conventions No. 97 of 1949 and No. 143 of 1975, and in the 1990 United Nations Convention on the Protection of the Rights of All Migrant Workers and Members of Their Families. However, relatively few countries have ratified these instruments, and there is little effective cooperation. In fact, the most important international measure, the 1990 UN Convention, had only been ratified by 46 nations by 2012 – out of the 193 members of the UN. Emigration countries have been concerned with reducing internal labour surpluses and maximizing remittances. Immigration countries have been reluctant to take steps which might increase labour costs.

Some regional bodies seek to cooperate on migration. The EU has gone furthest by introducing free movement for citizens of member states, and common policies towards asylum and migration from non-members. Most regional bodies in Africa, Asia and Latin America claim to be moving towards free movement of their citizens within the region, but few have actually achieved this. Both such multilateral arrangements and bilateral cooperation between states could bring benefits. Migrants could gain through better protection and social security. Emigration countries could benefit from smoother transfer of remittances and through regulation of agents and recruiters. Immigration countries could gain a more stable and better-trained migrant workforce.

In 2003, a Global Commission on International Migration (GCIM) mandated by the UN Secretary General took up its work. The GCIM Report (GCIM 2005, 79) argued that migration should 'become an integral part of national, regional and global strategies for economic growth, in both the developing and the developed world'. The GCIM put forward proposals for maximizing the benefits of international migration, including measures to limit the 'brain drain', to prevent smuggling and trafficking, to encourage the flow of remittances and to enhance the role of diasporas as agents of development. Migration and development was the topic of a High Level Dialogue of ministers and senior officials at the UN General Assembly in September 2006. This led to the establishment of a Global Forum on Migration and Development, which has met annually since 2007. A further High Level Dialogue at the UN took place for 2013 (Betts 2011).

Such bodies have no decision-making powers: they fulfil a merely advisory role, and powerful states have been unwilling to implement any measures that might lead to higher costs for migrant labour. But the difficulties experienced by developed states in managing migration may in future lead to more willingness to cooperate with origin states. Perhaps this might bring about greater North–South dialogue and cooperation on migration issues. However, this will only happen if all concerned are willing to move away from prioritizing short-term interests, and look for new ways forward that will be of benefit to migrants, sending countries and receiving countries alike.

Future migration trends

The experience of the GEC makes it clear that short-term economic fluctuations do not alter the fundamental forces that bring about international flows of people in an increasingly interlinked world. Economic inequality and the demographic imbalances between the ageing populations of the North and the large cohorts of working-age persons in the South remain important factors in generating migration. At the same time, the improvements in transport and communications inherent in globalization make it easier for people to live in expanded social and cultural spaces, which have little to do with the borders of nation-states.

Yet, under the current global migration order, states still have the power to differentiate between those who allowed to be mobile under conditions of safety and dignity (especially the privileged and highly skilled), and those who are forced to risk injury and exploitation in order to seek better livelihoods elsewhere (mainly lower-skilled workers and asylum seekers). In the long run this unequal migration order may not prove sustainable. At present, policy-makers in highly developed countries seem to believe that there is an inexhaustible supply of labour available in less-developed countries. This may be so for the next few decades, but it is unlikely to be so for much longer. The demographic transition to lower mortality and fertility is taking place everywhere. By the middle of this century, many areas in Latin America, South and Southeast Asia and Africa may begin to experience their own labour shortages. They may no longer have reserves of young labour-market entrants, willing to accept high levels of risk and exploitation in order to migrate to today's highly developed economies.

Demand for migrants is likely to remain strong in the North, but states may have to work towards a new migration order based on cooperation between origin and destination states and all the social groups affected. It will become crucial to re-conceptualize migration not as a problem to be solved through strict control, but as a normal part of global change and development, in which decision-makers should aim to minimize potential negative effects and to help realize the potential benefits for the migrants as well as for the economies and the societies involved.

It is mistaken to see migration in isolation from wider issues of global power, wealth and inequality. Mobility of people is an integral part of the major transformation currently affecting all regions of the world. Increasing economic and political integration means cross-border flows of capital, commodities, ideas and people. In recent years growing environmental challenges have made us realize that we live in one world, and that national approaches on their own are inadequate. The same principle applies to migration: global cooperation is essential, especially on human rights standards for migrant, and this requires approaches that abandon short-term national interests in favour of long-term cooperation between rich and poor nations. Fairer forms of migration should be an integral part of comprehensive development strategies designed to reduce global inequality.

Note

1. About 7 million of Germany's foreign-born population are of non-German origin (the largest group being Turkish immigrants and their descendants), while about 4 million are 'ethnic Germans', most of whom came from the former Soviet Union and Eastern Europe after 1990.

References

Abella, M., and G. Ducanes. 2009. *Technical Note: The Effect of the Global Economic Crisis on Asian Migrant Workers and Governments' Responses*. Bangkok: ILO Regional Office for Asia and the Pacific. http://www.age-of-migration.com/uk/financialcrisis/updates/1d.pdf

Asis, M. M. B. 2005. "Caring for the World: Filipino Domestic Workers Gone Global." In *Asian Women as Transnational Domestic Workers*, edited by S. Huang, B. S. A. Yeoh, and N. Abdul Rahman, 21–53. Singapore: Marshall Cavendish Academic.

Asis, M. M. B. 2008. "How International Migration Can Support Development: A Challenge for the Philippines." In *Migration and Development: Perspectives from the South*, edited by S. Castles, and R. Delgado Wise, 175–201. Geneva: International Organization for Migration.

Bakewell, O., and H. de Haas. 2007. "African Migrations: Continuities, Discontinuities and Recent Transformations." In *African Alternatives*, edited by P. Chabal, U. Engel, and L. de Haan, 95–117. Leiden: Brill.

Banting, K., and W. Kymlicka. 2012. "Is There Really a Backlash against Multiculturalism Policies? New Evidence from the Multiculturalism Policy Index." GRITIM Working Papers, Universitat Pompeu Fabra, Barcelona.

Bauböck, R., E. Ershøll, K. Groenendijk, and H. Waldrauch, eds. 2006a. *Acquisition and Loss of Nationality: Policies and Trends in 15 European States, Volume I: Comparative Analyses* [IMISCOE Research]. Amsterdam: Amsterdam University Press.

Bauböck, R., E. Ershøll, K. Groenendijk, and H. Waldrauch, eds. 2006b. *Acquisition and Loss of Nationality: Policies and Trends in 15 European States, Volume II: Country Analyses* [IMISCOE Research]. Amsterdam: Amsterdam University Press.

Bélanger, D., H.-K. Lee, and H.-Z. Wang. 2010. "Ethnic Diversity and Statistics in East Asia: 'Foreign Brides' Surveys in Taiwan and South Korea." *Ethnic and Racial Studies* 33 (6): 1108–1130.

Betts, A., ed. 2011. *Global Migration Governance*. Oxford: Oxford University Press.

Bhagwati, J. 2003. "Borders beyond Control." *Foreign Affairs* 82 (1): 98–104.

Body-Gendrot, S., and C. Wihtol de Wenden. 2007. *Sortir des banlieues. Pour en finir avec la tyrannie des territoires*. Paris: Autrement.

Canagarajah, S., and M. Kholmatov. 2010. *Migration and Remittances in CIS Countries during the Global Economic Crisis*. Washington, DC: World Bank. http://www.worldbank.org/eca

Cantle, T. 2001. *Community Cohesion: A Report of the Independent Review Team*. London: Home Office.

Castles, S. 2006. "Guestworkers in Europe: A Resurrection?" *International Migration Review* 40 (4): 741–766.

Castles, S. 2008. "Comparing the Experience of Five Major Emigration Countries." In *Migration and Development: Perspectives from the South*, edited by S. Castles, and R. Delgado Wise, 255–284. Geneva: International Organization for Migration.

Clandestino. 2009. *Comparative Policy Brief – Size of Irregular Population*. Hamburg: Clandestino Research Project. http://clandestino.eliamep.gr

Cohen, R. 1994. *Frontiers of Identity: The British and the Others*. London: Longman.

Davis, M. 2006. *Planet of Slums*. London: Verso.

EACH-FOR Programme. 2009. "Environmental Change and Forced Migration Scenarios (EACH-FOR).", http://www.each-for.eu/index.php?module=main

European Commission. 2007. *Circular Migration and Mobility Partnerships between the European Union and Third Countries* [COM 248]. Brussels: European Commission.

European Commission. 2011. *The Global Approach to Migration and Mobility, Communication from the Commission* [COM 743 final]. Brussels: Commission of the European Communities.

Faist, T., ed. 2007. *Dual Citizenship in Europe*. Aldershot: Ashgate.

Foresight. 2011. *Migration and Global Environmental Change. Final Project Report*. London: The Government Office for Science.

Global Commission on International Migration. 2005. *Migration in an Interconnected World: New Directions for Action: Report of the Global Commission on International Migration*. Geneva: Global Commission on International Migration. http://www.gcim.org/en/finalreport.html

Guild, E. 2009. *Security and Migration in the 21st Century*. Cambridge: Polity.

Hoefer, M., N. Rytina, and B. Baker. 2011. *Estimates of the Unauthorized Immigrant Population Residing in the United States: January 2010*. Washington, DC: Department of Homeland Security.

Hugo, G. 2008. *Migration, Development and Environment* [Migration Research Series]. Geneva: International Organization for Migration.

International Labour Organization. 2007. *Labour and Social Trends in ASEAN 2007*. Bangkok: International Labour Office Regional Office for Asia and the Pacific.

International Organization for Migration. 2005. *World Migration 2005: Costs and Benefits of International Migration*. Geneva: International Organization for Migration.

International Organization for Migration. 2011. *World Migration Report 2011: Communicating Effectively about Migration*. Geneva: International Organization for Migration.

Lee, H.-K. 2008. "International Marriage and the State in South Korea: Focusing on Governmental Policy." *Citizenship Studies* 12 (1): 107–123.

Levitt, P. 1998. "Social Remittances: Migration Driven Local-Level Forms of Cultural Diffusion." *International Migration Review* 32 (4): 926–948.

Mazza, J., and E. Sohnen. 2010. *On the Other Side of the Fence: Changing Dynamics of Migration in the Americas*. Washington, DC: Migration Information. Accessed June 2, 2010. http://www.migrationinformation.org/Feature/display.cfm?id=784

McAdam, J., ed. 2010. *Climate Change and Displacement: Multidisciplinary Perspectives*. Oxford: Hart.

Ministry of Business Innovation and Employment. 2013. *Recognised Seasonal Employer (RSE) Policy*. Wellington: NZ Government. Accessed April 12, 2013. http://www.dol.govt.nz/initiatives/strategy/rse/

Mohapatra, S., D. Ratha, and A. Silwal. 2011. *Outlook for Remittance Flows 2012–14* [Migration and Remittances Unit Migration and Development Brief]. Washington, DC: World Bank. http://siteresources.worldbank.org/INTPROSPECTS/Resources/334934-1110315015165/MigrationandDevelopmentBrief17.pdf

Organization for Economic Cooperation and Development (OECD). 2007. *International Migration Outlook: Annual Report 2007*. Paris: OECD. http://www.oecdbookshop.org/oecd/display.asp?K=5L4RW7MZQN46&lang = EN&sf1 = RegularIdentifier&st1 = REG81011P1&sort = sort_date/d&ds = International%20Migration%20Outlook&m = 4&dc = 5&plang = en

OECD. 2010. *International Migration Outlook: SOPEMI 2010*. Paris: OECD.

OECD. 2011. *International Migration Outlook: SOPEMI 2011*. Paris: OECD.

OECD. 2012. *International Migration Outlook: 2012*. Paris: OECD.

Office for National Statistics. 2002. *Social Focus in Brief: Ethnicity 2002*. London: Office for National Statistics.

Orrenius, P., and M. Zavodny. 2010. *How Immigration Works for America* [Annual Report: Federal Reserve Bank of Dallas]. Dallas: Federal Reserve Bank of Dallas.

Passel, J. S., and D. V. Cohn. 2009. *A Portrait of Unauthorized Immigrants in the United States*. Washington, DC: Pew Hispanic Center. http://pewhispanic.org/files/reports/107.pdf

Phillips, N., ed. 2011. "Migration and the Global Economic Crisis." In *Migration in the Global Political Economy*, 259–266. Boulder, CO: Lynne Rienner.

Plewa, P. 2009. "Voluntary Return Programmes: Could They Assuage the Effects of the Economic Crisis?" Working Paper 10-75, Centre on Migration, Policy and Society, Oxford. http://www.compas.ox.ac.uk/publications/working-papers/wp-10-75/

Plewa, P., and M. J. Miller. 2005. "Post-War and Post-Cold War Generations of European Temporary Foreign Worker Policies: Implications from Spain." *Migraciones Internacionales* 3 (2): 58–83.

Portes, A., L. E. Guarnizo, and P. Landolt. 1999. "The Study of Transnationalism: Pitfalls and Promise of an Emergent Research Field." *Ethnic and Racial Studies* 22 (2): 217–237.

Ratha, D., S. Mohapatra, and A. Silwal. 2009. *Migration and Remittance Trends 2009* [Migration and Development Brief 11]. Washington, DC: World Bank. http://siteresources.worldbank.org/INTPROSPECTS/Resources/334934-1110315015165/MigrationAndDevelopmentBrief11.pdf

Schierup, C.-U., P. Hansen, and S. Castles. 2006. *Migration, Citizenship and the European Welfare State: A European Dilemma*. Oxford: Oxford University Press.

Sen, A. 2001. *Development as Freedom*. Oxford: Oxford University Press.

Skeldon, R. 2006a. "Interlinkages between Internal and International Migration and Development in the Asian region." *Population, Space and Place* 12: 15–30.

Skeldon, R. 2006b. "Recent Trends in Migration in East and Southeast Asia." *Asian and Pacific Migration Journal* 15 (2): 277–293.

Solomos, J. 2003. *Race and Racism in Britain*. 3rd ed. Basingstoke: Palgrave Macmillan.

Statistics Canada. 2007. *Immigration and Citizenship: Highlight Tables, 2001 Census*. Ottawa: Statistics Canada. http://www.census2006.ca/english/census01/

Stiglitz, J. E. 2002. *Globalization and Its Discontents*. London: Penguin.

Population Division. 2009. *International Migrant Stock: The 2008 Revision*. New York: UN Population Division. Accessed July 6, 2010. http://esa.un.org/migration/p2k0data.asp

UN Population Division. 2010. *International Migration 2009: Graphs and Maps from the 2009 Wallchart*. New York: UN Population Division. http://www.un.org/esa/population/publications/2009Migration_Chart/IttMig_maps.pdf

United Nations Department of Economic and Social Affairs. 2005. *Trends in Total Migrant Stock: The 2005 Revision*. New York: United Nations Department of Economic and Social Affairs.

United Nations Department of Economic and Social Affairs. 2009. *Trends in International Migrant Stock: The 2008 Revision*. New York: United Nations Department of Economic and Social Affairs, Population Division. http://esa.un.org/migration/

United Nations Development Programme. 2009. *Human Development Report 2009: Overcoming Barriers: Human Mobility and Development.* New York: United Nations Development Programme. http://hdr.undp.org/en/reports/global/hdr2009/

United Nations High Commissioner for Refugees (UNHCR). 2009. *2008 Global Trends: Refugees, Asylum-Seekers, Returnees, Internally Displaced and Stateless Persons.* Geneva: UNHCR. http://www.unhcr.org/pages/49c3646c4d6.html

UNHCR. 2010. *Number of Forcibly Displaced Rises to 43.3 Million Last Year, the Highest Level since Mid-1990s.* Geneva: UNHCR. http://www.unhcr.org/4c176c969.html

Vasta, E. 2007. "From Ethnic Minorities to Ethnic Majority Policy: Multiculturalism and the Shift to Assimilationism in the Netherlands." *Ethnic and Racial Studies* 30 (5): 713–740.

Zetter, R. 2009. *Forced Migration in an Era of Global Financial Crisis – What Will Happen to Refugees?* Basingstoke: Palgrave Macmillan.

Faces of globalization and the borders of states: from asylum seekers to citizens

Paul James

Global Cities Institute, RMIT University, Melbourne, Australia

Intensifying processes of globalization have led to a series of tensions around the way in which even the most cosmopolitan democracies now treat people who move across their borders. Non-citizens have become problems. The postcolonial settler nation-states – Australia, Canada, the USA and others – were 'founded' by immigrants and refugees who moved globally to become citizens in these 'new lands'. Such countries were made by migrants displacing indigenous others. However, in a conflict-ridden world in which the displacement of persons has become endemic – and in a media-connected world where the possibility of finding a better place to live has become increasingly imaginable and desired – these countries are now attempting to manage that global flow of people by stringent homeland security measures that are becoming increasingly problematic. While they are constituted through the modern imaginary of liberal democratic norms, human rights and rule of law, in each country over the last few years, rules have been bent, breached or bolstered in order to keep people out. The essay argues that given the globalization of people movement, the nation-state has reached the limits of responding though unilateral or even regional multilateral arrangements.

1. Introduction

Intensifying processes of globalization have led to a series of tensions around the way in which even the most cosmopolitan democracies now treat non-citizens who move across their borders. The postcolonial settler nation-states – Australia, Canada, the USA and others – were 'founded' by immigrants and refugees who moved globally to become citizens in these 'new lands'. Such countries were made by migrants displacing indigenous others. However, in a conflict-ridden world in which the displacement of persons has become endemic – and in a media-connected world where the possibility of finding a better place to live has become increasingly imaginable and desired – these countries are now attempting to manage that global flow of non-citizens by stringent homeland security measures that are becoming increasingly problematic.

Historically, as these communities-polities formed as nation-states, they moved away from the ideology of blood as the basis of citizenship (*jus sanguinis*) to espouse a counter-ideology – territorial placement as the basis of national political rights (*jus soli*). The enacted practice of *jus soli* was never straightforward. Having a white face or at least being European continued to have a legalized or implicit predominance in the settler states, at least for the first half of the twentieth century. For example, Australia had an explicit

'White Australia' policy up until the middle of the twentieth century. It was implicitly based on race and blood, and particularly concerned to keep out the Chinese, even if its explicit expression was a literacy test. Across the second half of the twentieth century, these states indeed endeavoured to become more cosmopolitan. However, more recently, as significant numbers of migrants and refugees have come actively to seek relocation and citizenship, Australia, Canada and USA have by various means hardened their border protection against particular categories of such placements. The debates have been ferocious. These countries may be concerned to play a humanitarian role in the world; however, they have struggled to maintain this role in relation to refugees. They are constituted through the modern imaginary of liberal democratic norms, human rights and rule of law; however, in each country, over the last few years, rules have been bent, breached or bolstered in order to keep out those people who either do not come in an accepted way or do not fit the accepted criteria for enhancing the national interest.

In Australia, the Howard government in 2001, for example, established a tortuous legal precedent that continues to apply in the present. The government effectively defined certain Australian islands as non-Australian territory for the purpose of those applying for visas or seeking refugee status. Simply put, those islands that allow easier access to Australia for refugees coming by boat from countries were excised and denationalized as 'off-shore places'. From these excised places, outsiders who arrive cannot apply for visas in the same way as other refugees – read: 'cannot be afforded refugee status except after extraordinary processing and extended incarceration'. For all other purposes the islands are fundamentally part of the nation-state. Apart from its practical significance, this excision goes against the historical nature of national territoriality, namely that nation-states neither treat their territory as fading off at its edges nor define different parts of that territory as having variable ontological status. Weasel words have been developed to confirm that these islands remain Australian territory. Under the Act, to 'enter Australia' is carefully defined to mean 'to enter the migration zone', and given that these islands remain part of the migration zone they legally remain part of Australia.[1] But whatever the final adjudication on the sovereignty question, the political-legal twists and turns are indicative of the complexity that boundary-crossing holds for Australians and the lengths that the Australian state is prepared to go to deter border-crossers *of a certain kind* – a group of non-citizens who have now been formally named as 'asylum seekers'.

In the USA, the funding of their border patrol has increased significantly with radars, sensors, robotic aerial vehicles and newly constructed fence lines constructed along the borders. This was part of a new and very expensive plan called the Secure Border Initiative. The budget for border control doubled over the five years from $1700 million in 2005 to $3600 million in 2010. Campaigns such as *Operation Hold-the-Line* in the El Paso area and *Operation Gatekeeper* in San Diego resulted in increasing numbers of 'deportable aliens' being located, but overall the operations have been of mixed success. The flawed SBI*net* virtual fence-line initiative was finally cancelled in 2011 (Koslowski 2011). This does not mean, however, that the issue of border control has diminished nor that a liberal globally oriented president is changing the mode of operation. In 2010, President Barack Obama signed the *Southwest Border Security Act* into law. This appropriation of $600 million supplemented the deployment a month earlier of 1200 National Guard troops to the Mexican borderlands.

In Canada, laws on movements across the border have significantly tightened. Unlike Australia, Canada has not until recently had a mandatory detention system for asylum seekers, but in 2010 the state passed Bill C-49 into law. That legislation creates a new class of aliens, 'designated foreign nationals'. Such foreign nationals have to be placed in detention upon arrival. Such a designated foreigner is defined as any non-citizen arriving in Canada in relation to whom the Minister declares either that their claim to stay cannot be processed 'in a timely manner' or that they may have been assisted in their passage by a person who may have profited by the boundary-crossing. Under this new regime, in 2010, the number of applications for asylum decreased by 30%. Overall, increasingly restrictive rules and regulations have come to be presented as the natural order of things. Intriguingly, by a clever technocratic definition, the government website presents the rules of immigration *as if* they are primordial. In the following passage, note the shift from the first sentence to the second set of sentences:

> Canadian immigration is the set of rules, regulations, directives, policies and the Act of Parliament that regulates the entry of each person in to Canada. Immigration, the entrance of people into a country for the purpose of settling there, has always played a central role in Canadian history. It was as much a feature of ancient times, when the ancestors of Canada's native peoples migrated from Asia by land via Beringia or by sea via the Japanese current, as it is of the present day, when immigrants from around the world come to this country in the thousands.[2]

This is the context. While the rhetoric differs, the borders of liberal-democratic nation-states are increasingly hardening, at least for certain categories of non-citizens.

2. The faces of the other

I begin with these contextualizing examples not simply as critique, but in the first instance to note that the practices and projections have become more vexatious and contradictory, both for those who move and those who administer their moving. Whatever the intentions or national ethos of the countries in question, their treatment of asylum seekers as a *category* has become simultaneously more abstract, more ugly and more concerned to project an image of the state as being a 'good international citizen'[3] – a fascinating metaphor in this instance that extends the concept of 'citizen' beyond the homeland or polis. In the second instance, developed further into the essay, the same examples will be used to argue that given the globalization of people movement the nation-state has reached the limits of responding though unilateral or even regional multilateral arrangements (á la Prime Minister Julia Gillard's 'Malaysia Solution'). Without having a way of adequately responding to the contemporary movement of people, the settler states are caught between humanitarian self-projection and bureaucratized self-protection. That is, for all of their humanitarian concern – some of which is deeply believed in relation to actual individuals who are seen to suffer – when it comes to *categories of persons*, the countries of the USA, Canada and Australia have become caught up in an instrumentally rational process of desperately defending their borders against certain kinds of embodied movement. Border control is now given effect by a mode of organization framed by instrumental rationality, even as the vision of engagement is projected by a rhetoric of humanitarian concern and good policing.[4] The effect is brutal; the affect is intended to be comforting – at least to those citizens already at home inside the borders.

Underlying that theme about the framing dominance of a more abstract mode of organization is a further theme. In the context of this tightening of rules in the settler nation-states, the present essay begins to open up an exploration of the relationship between what might be called *embodied globalization* and the different ways in which the various categories of people who move across borders are represented symbolically, photographically, textually and practically. Here the context is important to understanding the tensions between the various forms of representation. Why is it in the cases of Australia, Canada and the USA that, while intimate photographs of those who stand as exemplary figures of the nation are everywhere in the media and on websites, the faces of asylum seekers are relatively absent in contemporary state projections?

Facial images of citizens are everywhere. In the public spheres of the USA, Canada and Australia, national imagining predominantly takes the form of images of landmarks or photo-mosaics of faces that signify the historical, multicultural or melting-pot nation. There are regular state-projected events and national day celebrations for those migrants accepted as national citizens. The cameras are invited in. By contrast, with rare exceptions, there are no state-organized public ceremonies to welcome refugees to the country.

For their citizens – or for *legal* border-crossers – passport photographs, face scans, identity documentation, *vox populi* and street surveillance have become naturalized as either virtues or necessities. The US program US-VISIT, for example, collected biometric scans of the faces of 113 million people crossing its borders between 2004 and 2008. Photography of faces for security reasons is now almost as naturalized as the requirement that 'aliens' go through a naturalization process to become citizens. By comparison, the depiction of the faces of asylum seekers has, at least across the last three decades, become much more ambiguous. It is now the stuff of contention. Counter-journalists seek to expose the truth of pain by showing the faces of those who suffer. Alternatively, increasing numbers of politicians and critics of reception policies dehumanize such persons with talk of queue jumpers (Australia and Canada), boat people (Australia and the USA) and illegals (the USA and Canada), none of which, it is claimed, should get special treatment.[5] Indeed, in the case of Australia, the government has developed legal statute and human-rights rhetoric to argue that exposing the identity of refugees through photographic images is a breach of their privacy.

Given that it is not uncommon to project photographs of refugees who are *not* seeking asylum – that is, refugees who are safely located away from the possibility of seeking homeland entry in 'our' country – the effacement of asylum seekers cannot be just because of concern for the privacy of strangers in danger. For example, there are numerous contemporary photographs of refugees on the US Defence Information Directorate website, even close-ups of young children or refugees being airlifted across other national borders – but there are few images of asylum seekers that might come to the USA. The only exceptions over the last couple of decades are photos of some Kurdish children in 1997 and a couple of Soviet defectors in 1989, Anatoly Kachenko and Alexander Kendr.[6] These exceptions are instances with very direct political implications.

The evidence that asylum seekers are being effaced remains necessarily circumstantial. It is much harder to explore an absence than a given pattern of representation. Nevertheless, the evidence here, and as further developed below, suggests that governments would prefer that asylum seekers are effaced and turned into abstract Others. For the most part, asylum seekers who are being processed are detained away from public areas in places where their faces cannot be readily seen. They tend to be out of sight and, therefore (by design or otherwise), out of mind, except for moments of individualized embodied sympathy.

The next section of the discussion responds to the question as to why it is important to talk about faces in the context of globalization. The argument here is that faces of those who move are an important *subjective* part of the process of embodied globalization, and that this remains crucial to understanding the contemporary human condition despite the emphasis in the literature on global flows as financial and trade-based. Following on from that, the essay examines transformations in the way in which those who move – refugees and other entrants (usually citizens of another state) – are constituted and managed. Here the underlying argument is first that there is a split between the subjective meanings afforded asylum seekers (they are constituted as a risk or intrusion) and the objective processes of their management (they are constituted as an in-between category to be regulated). Second, it is suggested that those objective processes of state management of the movement across the borders of liberal democracies can neither be described adequately as open to a global flow (akin to open markets) nor as bounded by a set of restrictive enclaves (constituting closed nations). In one important sense, the process that I have begun to describe brings together both features at the same time. That is, linking the two points together, the pattern is clear. Liberal democracies, for all their proclamations to being receptive, humane and welcoming 'open societies', are most receptive to those who move in ways that support the market or contribute to the national interest, and least receptive to those who are a risk. As a way of responding critically to these developments, the last section of the essay suggests the need for a global covenant on the movement of peoples (Held 2004). It argues for a negotiated global governance process responding to the question of asylum seekers.

3.   Why is it important to talk about faces and actual bodies?

The embodied movement of people is the oldest form of globalization. If globalization is understood as the extension of social relations across world-space, then, despite the tendency in much of the literature to emphasize extensions of relations in the abstracted realms of financial exchange and disembodied communication technologies, it remains the case that embodied globalization is a continuing and fundamental feature of the present.

While there are many ways of delineating different forms of globalization – the classic delineation being by domain: economic, ecological, political and cultural – different forms of globalization can usefully be distinguished for our purposes through an emphasis on levels of integration/differentiation: from embodied globalization through to agency-extended globalization, object-extended globalization and most abstractly to disembodied globalization. Embodied globalization, meaning simply the movement of bodies across world-space, was a dominant characteristic of *traditional* extensions globally. Since the time of the early empires and population upheavals, people carried their stories, sensibilities and practices of community over vast distances. This intersected with other forms of globalization. Agency-extended globalization refers to the way in which agents of polities, corporations, religious sodalities and other organizations became central carriers of processes of global extension. Object extension refers to the way in which objects such as commodities, traded goods, museum artefacts and icons moved across the world also carrying social relations. Finally, disembodied extension refers to processes of interchange where the actual bodies of persons become irrelevant to the dominant mode of integration/differentiation, at least at one level. This approach allows us to understand what is happening to the borders of nation-states. Contra all those arguments about a borderless world, global flows and a flat earth, the global movement of people is differentiated and complex (Bude and Durrschmidt 2010).

In any one situation today we tend to send a complex intersection of all these forms of globalization, even if disembodied globalization has become the organizing form. Nevertheless, while embodied globalization has today been overlaid by other far more powerful modalities of global extension – commodity exchange, the transmission of electronic symbols of capital or satellite-connected communication of culture – the *objective* movement of people remains an important global phenomenon. It is both a global phenomenon *and* a process to which broader processes of globalization contribute locally. The manifold processes of globalization contribute to unsettling existing local life-worlds, accentuating past and present cleavages of identity politics, intensifying the communicative bases for making economic and cultural comparisons, increasing the objective divisions of wealth or disrupting older authority structures, and putting pressure on modern state operations, particularly postcolonial states. These are factors that induce people to move. And, in turn, the staccato and hyper-regulated movements (not flows) of refugees and migrants are crucial to making new communities in new places and to challenging nation-states with basic questions of who is to be allowed to cross their borders and in what manner. Embodied globalization may not be able to generate more than negative expressions of political power in this world, but it affects the way states manage their borders. And as those states – the USA, Canada and Australia included – change their policies and subjective projections into the world, so too do the people who move change the way in which they respond.

The embodied dimension of globalization also continues to have an important *subjective* dimension. It is evidenced in artistic expressions, photographs and other visual representations, going back most prominently to Edward Steichen's 'Family of Man' exhibition in 1955, which toured the world for nearly a decade (object extension supported by institutional agency extension). While photos and advertising renditions of planet earth have over the past few decades come to be the predominant visual coding for the global, images of faces have become the most intriguing, ironically now carried predominantly by disembodied extension through the mass media and Internet. National Geographic's composite image of 'the world's most typical person' was created from combining 190,000 photographs of faces is one version. The face is quite particular – a 28-year-old Han Chinese man – but it is also global-generic, computer-generated and highly pixelated. More typically found in advertisements, the global face often takes the form of an androgynous Eurasian with an enigmatic Mona-Lisa-like expression representing the diversity of the global community. The face of Benetton generated in 2000, for example, was made up of a sociologically calculated Eurasian mix of the world's population to form an Every Woman. In parallel, the global 'Face of Tomorrow' comes in male and female, and looks Euro-South Asian.[7] The other figure who reinforces the condensation of meaning around faces is the veiled female face. As a legal insider, she is the other side of the effacing argument. In states such as France, which also tends to efface its Others, she is forced to reveal her face to show that she is part of the Republic.

Arthus-Bertrand's '6 Billion Others' Project goes back to the Family-of-Man approach to photograph actual persons from around the globe, including veiled faces: 'Flying over the planet to make the book *Earth from Above*', he says, 'I often wondered what I could learn about the men and women that I saw beneath me'. In the romantic words of an abstract outsider, he dreams of 'being able to hear their words and comprehend what it is that unites us'. Hence, he publishes a book of portraits and voices. However, in the same paragraph Arthus-Bertrand's sentiments express a reverse but analogous tension to that described in this essay: 'But as soon as I returned to the ground, the problems began. I found myself faced by bureaucratic rigidity in each country and, above all, by the rigidity of the borders' (Arthus-Bertrand 2009, 5).

This links to the argument of this essay. It is not an argument against borders (quite the opposite), but it is a plea for being reflexive *and* ethical about how we manage those borders and the movement of non-citizens. Here the concept of *the queue* returns in an intriguing way. We have all become so concerned about the practice (or political invention) of *queue jumping*, arguing for or against the notion, that we sometimes forget that the queuing itself, like the categories of people that it describes, has been split objectively and subjectively. *Objectively*, it has become a taken-for-granted (increasing disembodied) practice of linear abstract justice that has as its main objective the slowing down of actual bodies. Queuing thus maintains real connections to questions of fairness, but it has increasingly become part of an abstract calculus of minimal compliance with rules of justice. At the very same time, *subjectively*, we feel sorry for those people who wait. The concept recalls lines of tired individuals, sagging at the knees, standing, waiting their turn. It is a concept which came into common use in mid-twentieth-century England, referring to hungry people waiting on post-war rationing handouts. However, for all the subjectively framed images in our mind of poor people standing in queues, such pictures now mask a massive apparatus of abstracted adjudication that deploys rules and 'point systems' to mediate or defer the intense difficulty of making ethical judgements. As Fuller (2005) writes:

> Queues are a form of control. They are material abstractions that structure relations between one and the many. They are both 'stateless', inasmuch as that they can form anywhere and that each server request is considered independently (this is certain true technically for TCP/IP, but also 'in principle' true for embodied lines – although queues in both contexts are not without affective residues, the most visible being server burnout and queue-rage). They are also 'state' structures, in the way they produced 'territory', marking out the borders between the orderly queue and unruly and unpredictable mob, and in the way they reproduce across all levels of social interaction – limiting potential into algorithms of probability.

Queues, used in the context of the movement of non-citizens, are material abstractions. This is the key to understanding their dominant contemporary nature. It is no coincidence then that the different faces/bodies of globalization queue to cross borders in different ways according to specified and codified (abstracted) differences of risk and financial cost or return. *The Citizen* – now the globally taken-for-granted base condition of political normalcy in the world – is allowed to cross the borders of their own nation-state in a prioritized or facilitated fashion. This goes back to the eighteenth-century European notion of 'the people' as the body of citizenry. To be a citizen is to have state-recognized membership in a corporate body, and it is from this notion of an abstract body politic that states claim the right to facilitate the passage of some bodies without counting the cost –citizens – and to regulate or close their borders against others. *The Migrant* or *The Tourist*, a documented citizen from somewhere else, has regulated rights. But like the national citizen, as long as each individual has the required documentation that proves that she or he will enhance the national interest, they move across alien nation-state borders in a facilitated state-sanctioned way. This is based on a person-by-person assessment of what state they come from, whether they will bring money or skills with them, and whether they will draw on public resources for more than a brief period.

However, after that it gets more difficult. *The Irregular Migrant* is a person who finds him- or herself with a structurally changing, legally defined status in relation to border-crossing. Such a person becomes irregular because something else happens to make them irregular. Sometimes it is because, as a non-citizen who once crossed the state border legally, the individual now remains within the state territory for too long and without the explicit and continuing sanction of the host state. For example, persons who overstayed their visas in Arizona have since 2004 become subject to harsher and harsher laws, including the Legal Arizona Workers Act and S.B. 1070. In some cases, the irregular migrant is a person who was once welcomed and now is not wanted, simply because a state changed their rules of residency (McNevin 2011). For example, the annulling of automatically renewable 10-year residency permits in France rendered many migrants as illegal *sans-papiers* – and, even more problematically, their children as stateless until they are legally called otherwise (thus qualifying historical principle of *jus soli* upon which French citizenship has been formed).

The Asylum Seeker is a stateless person seeking asylum but not yet accepted by another nation-state as a 'refugee'. This is an in-between position that makes meaningful such bizarre designations as a person having no status in excised offshore places. By comparison, *The Refugee* is a displaced person who is outside their original state of citizenry, is a forced migrant *and* is recognized as such. She or he is a person who now has a legally recognized place in a new state, or at least a right to have such a status. In legal terms they have a new place to reside, however constrained or appalling that place might be, while in colloquial terms they are people at a distance for whom we should feel sympathy. Of those many faces of globalization – and here we are talking of embodied faces rather than the disembodied faces of *Facebook* and the mass media – it is then the irregular migrant and the asylum seeker who are the most contentious, and of central concern to this essay.

4. What has happened in the shift towards the dominance of disembodied globalization?

The intensification of globalization and, in particular, the increasing dominance of disembodied globalization has, in association with the ideology of neoliberal or market globalism (Steger 2004, 2008), thrown basic questions of political identity and nation-state-based belonging into turmoil. In this context, writers who suggest that the turmoil can be understood in terms of continuing dominant ideologies of sedentarism, a bias towards staying in place rather than moving, or deep ambivalence towards mobility, have simply got the wrong end of the stick (Malkki 1992; Papastergiadis 2010). The undercurrent of their analysis reveals more about their own postmodern biases towards mobility as a good thing. More pointedly, they have missed the dominant changes in global sensibility over the past two decades, which has gone the same way to extol the virtues of movement. Most conceptions of mobility now carry a positive valency. Just compare the imperative of words such as 'mobility' and 'interconnectivity' to the mixed meanings of other words including 'rooted', 'stagnating', 'parochial' and 'static' to get a sense of how in the Global North we now value the freedom to move. Currently, for example, between 5% and 6% of people in the USA move their residence across a municipal boundary. Less than one-third of the population of the USA live in the same area in which they were born (Molloy, Smith, and Wozniak 2011). The people we want to slow down or restrict are those who move ambiguously and require resources from us – specifically, asylum seekers and irregular migrants. It is they who are at the centre of this turmoil, while financial capital and electronic communications move in relatively unregulated ways, and business people, tourists and assimilating (good) migrants are beckoned to our shores. Over the course of the twentieth century into the present, the relation between the citizen and the refugee has become increasingly vexatious, but it is specifically asylum seekers and irregular (bad) migrants whom we have come to fear.

A second misapprehension is that this xenophobia is coming back into contention because more people are moving across borders. In fact, since the early 1990s, increasing state regulation, which makes it harder for certain categories of people to cross borders, has meant that the number of those defined technically as refugees has gone down by at least a third. This is all the more dramatic because the numbers counted include people whom the United Nations High Commissioner for Refugees (UNHCR) has found it necessary after 2007 to call 'people in refugee-like situations'. It also includes refugees who have been living in camps for more than a generation. According to UNHCR data, the numbers of asylum seekers have also been diminishing significantly. Across the last decade, applications globally for asylum have gone down by about 40%.[8] The reason for this is not readily apparent, but it seems to be in part simply because the process of applying has become harder. In more technical terms, we can say that because the standing of different categories of persons has become increasingly rationalized, objectified and codified, states can present to themselves data which suggest that the numbers of refugees (the numbers of deserving people in need) are not going up. At the same time, however, those individuals called 'internally displaced persons' or IDPs – that is, those who are displaced but do not cross a national border – have been increasing (Birkeland, Halff, and Jennings 2010), as have been the number of irregular migrants. In summary, the number of displaced persons is going up while the numbers of persons who cross borders is going down.

Since states began to define the limits of their citizenry, the insider (the citizen) and the outsider (the refugee, the stranger) have long been constituted in relation to each other – and they continue to be mutually defining – but the tension between them is becoming increasingly acute. However, with that intensifying tension, new terms of identification have been interposed to name those people who do not quite fit – again it is the asylum seeker and irregular migrant. 'We' cannot blame refugees or exclude them from the blessings of our citizenship, but 'we' can exclude or remove undeserving boundary-crossers from our homelands. And, in this view, asylum seekers and irregular migrants are potentially and probably those who are most acutely part of the categories of 'the undeserving' or 'the queue jumping'.

In summary, there have been a series of political transformations that have been part of this process of global change. First, the movement of persons across borders (whether it be tourists, migrants or refugees) is more intensely managed than ever before. There has been a globalization of the process of managing the movement of people with different nation-states, including the USA, Canada and Australia, learning from each and employing common techniques. Second, the definition of refugees has been lifted out of the human sense of strangers-in-need to become technically framed. In Australia the technical term 'asylum seekers' and the colloquial term 'boat people' have become linked together as objects of risk. Responses to them have become increasingly rationalized (in both senses of the word). Third, the status of persons inside borders – both citizens and irregular migrants – is more intensely managed that ever before. There has been a refinement of naturalization processes, and the legal standing of persons (complicated by dual citizenry in a globalizing world) is more contingent. We are seeing instances of denationalization, deporting and the revocation of citizenship including the singling out of previously naturalized or dual citizens. In some countries we are witnessing the redefining of citizenry status, usually in relation to labour migration and so-called guest workers. In the case of the Arizona S.B. 1070 Act (2010) – gently projected as the 'Support Our Law Enforcement and Safe Neighborhoods Act' – this has been extended and deepened, and despite legal challenges it is currently being used as a model in a number of state legislatures across the USA.

Fourth, as I began to argue earlier, asylum seekers are being effaced. This too, of course, is being contested, but a few examples should carry the sense of the pattern of change. It is, for example, possible to find numbers of official Australian and US government photographs from the 1970s and early 1980s of asylum seekers from Vietnam. One photo from 1979 (US National Archives, ARC Identifier 558538/Local Identifier 428-N-1176806) shows a close-up of a family with three small children on the deck of USS Wabash, AOR-5 in the South China Sea. They are now safe 'after twenty-eight boat people were picked up from their wooden boat by a whaleboat from the oiler'. Another shot in 1982 shows the expectant faces of Vietnamese refugees aboard the guided missile cruiser USS FOX (CG-33). Another from 1984 depicts Master at Arms First Class Jose Morillo wearing white gloves and holding a baby, 'one of 35 Vietnamese refugees rescued by the amphibious command ship USS BLUE RIDGE (LCC 19) 350 miles northeast of Cam Ranh Bay, Vietnam. They had spent eight days at sea in a 35 foot fishing boat'.[9] There is no embarrassment here, no sense that we are infringing on their right to anonymity, no sense that children deserve protection from being used for state propaganda about its bounteous mercy. The only contemporary examples from that same archive which depict refugees moving across borders show individuals from the 2011 Tunisian airlift: these refugees were being airlifted from Djerba to Cairo under a standing request with the Egyptian government.[10] There is no chance of those individuals crossing into the US homeland. From my exploration, there are no recent photos on the website by US military personnel of any non-citizen crossing into US territory.

Australia provides us with a shameful example of a period of (possibly intentional) effacement of asylum seekers. It was the time of the Border Protection Bill discussed at the beginning of my essay. At the centre of the controversy was a verbal image that the Immigration Minister used for broadcasting on 7 October 2001, describing anonymous asylum seekers as throwing their children overboard in an attempt to get the Australian navy to rescue them. There were photographs, he said: 'I have not seen it myself and apparently the quality is not very good and it's infra-red or something but I am told that someone had looked at it and it is an absolute fact, children were thrown overboard' (Reith quoted in Weller 2002, 2). According to evidence presented to a later Senate Enquiry, within hours this was known at high levels to be untrue, but it became the centrepiece of an election campaign a month later which the government used to sweep back into power. The year significantly was 2001. It was two months after the attack on the twin towers, and the Australian government sought to suggest that groups of asylum seekers might possibly provide a cover for terrorists to enter the country. In the background was another event called the Tampa Crisis. In August of the same year, the government had refused landing rights in Australia for a Norwegian freighter carrying 438 rescued Afghan asylum seekers. The Australian government sent a Special Air Services elite force to make sure that it did not land, and part of the role of that contingent was to make sure that journalists did not get any photographs of the faces of the Afghan men, women and children. The evidence is not conclusive, but my argument that the basis of this effacement was instrumentally political rather than human rights concerns is strongly supported by circumstantial evidence. Leach (2001, 29–30) describes the situation thus:

In a positively Orwellian twist, the level of government agency and intent was revealed in the Senate inquiry. Under cross examination, the director of defence communication strategies, Brian Humphreys, told the hearing that Ross Hampton had directly instructed defence photographers not take pictures of asylum seekers. The Navy was apparently given explicit guidelines to ensure 'no personalising or humanising images' were to be taken. Defence officials said Mr Reith's staff did not want to allow photographs to create sympathy for asylum seekers. Subsequently, defence media liaison director Tim Bloomfield described Government restrictions preventing any military comment on asylum seekers operations as 'a form of censorship'. Similarly, Department of Immigration, Multiculturalism and Indigenous Affairs (DIMIA) restrictions on journalists prevent them from interviewing any person detained under Australian immigration law. This effective gag on the press requires that '[a]n Immigration Officer will accompany journalists at all times', and further that '[r]epresentatives of the Department will view the photographs/film for use with the resulting report/s'. Ostensibly, these provisions are meant to ensure that staff or people detained are not identifiable. Effectively, they also ensure that the Australian press cannot respond to pleas to be heard.

Taking photographs of the faces of asylum seekers is certainly complicated. The Charter of Rome, launched in 2008 by the National Council of the Journalists' Association (Consiglio Nazionale dell'Ordine dei Giornalisti) and the Italian National Press Federation (Federazione Nazionale della Stampa Italiana) presents the human rights concerns well. It aims to

> Safeguard those asylum seekers, refugees, victims of trafficking and migrants who choose to speak with the media by adopting solutions as regards their identity and image so as to ensure that they are not identifiable. Asylum seekers, refugees, victims of trafficking and migrants who are identifiable – as well as the latter's relatives – may face reprisals on the part of the authorities in their country of origin, of non-state entities or of criminal organisations. Moreover, individuals who belong to a different socio-cultural context, where the press plays a limited role, may not be aware of global media dynamics and may thus not be able to foresee all the consequences of their decision to appear in the media.[11]

However, most human rights advocates argue alternatively that refugees and asylum seekers should have the right to choose whether or not they are photographed. This takes us to the heart of the human rights theme.

5. In this context what has happened to the definition of a refugee?

The penultimate step in my argument is to now reverse the point of focus and turn the spotlight on the 1951 Convention Relating to the Status of Refugees as a core example of the limits to liberal human rights. If I can show that even in this important area of humanitarian concern – in the very source of the current definition of what is a refugee – that processes of codification and rationalization have come to efface the meaning of being a stranger in need of asylum, then the comprehensiveness of the process can be fully seen.

There is no doubt that the apparently simple concept of 'refugees' needs clarifying. This has become particularly necessary in the context of the dogmatic legalizing of terms such as 'asylum seekers' or the modern narrowing of the term 'refugee' to only refer to political refugees. Refugees, in the way that I have been using the term, are *forced migrants* who seek refuge in another place. They are people who feel compelled by threatening cultural, economic, political or ecological reasons to leave the place that they call home and feel the need to find refuge elsewhere. The related term 'asylum seeker' simply refers to those who by one means or another communicate a desire for that refuge. Being an asylum seeker in this definition does not require actually arriving at the border of a nation-state as the legalized definition of asylum seeker would have it. The terrible perversities that have been visited on asylum seekers to Australia over the last decade have been in the name of a legal definition. Similarly, being a refugee in this definition is not contingent upon the crossing of national borders. This is consistent with the original use of the term *refugié*, from the Old French term *refuge*, used to describe the thousands of Huguenots who in 1685 migrated after the revocation of the Edict of Nantes.

The definition used in this essay is thus significantly simpler and much broader than spelt out in the most influential definition of a refugee, the Convention Relating to the Status of Refugees. According to the source document from 1951:

the term 'refugee' shall apply to any person who:

(1) Has been considered a refugee under the Arrangements of 12 May 1926 and 30 June 1928 or under the Conventions of 28 October 1933 and 10 February 1938, the Protocol of 14 September 1939 or the Constitution of the International Refugee Organization;

> Decisions of non-eligibility taken by the International Refugee Organization during the period of its activities shall not prevent the status of refugee being accorded to persons who fulfil the conditions of paragraph 2 of this section;
> (2) As a result of events occurring before 1 January 1951 and owing to well-founded fear of being persecuted for reasons of race, religion, nationality, membership of a particular social group or political opinion, is outside the country of his nationality and is unable, or owing to such fear, is unwilling to avail himself of the protection of that country; or who, not having a nationality and being outside the country of his former habitual residence as a result of such events, is unable or, owing to such fear, is unwilling to return to it.[12]

Most of the writings on refugees today extract a neat, potted and misleading summary from this passage to say that the term 'refugee' refers to a person who 'owing to well-founded fear of being persecuted for reasons of race, religion, nationality, membership of a particular social group or political opinion, is outside the country of his [or her] nationality and is unable, or owing to such fear, is unwilling to avail himself of the protection of that country'. It sounds impressive and precise, but this rendition is self-serving. It props up the politics of those who framed the Convention and were scared of the potential consequences of the world on the move. What the potted definition misses out on is first that refugees have been defined in terms of those moving across nation-state borders, as if national identity excludes all other displacements of equal consequence (Gibney 2004, 5–9). Thus, refugees were defined by the emerging dominance of the nation-state, and, conversely, national responses to refugees began to define what kind of community a nation-state was becoming. More tenuously, refugees were defined as having certain nationalities. The first formal definition of a refugee, the 12 May 1926 Arrangement, for example, defined a refugee as 'Any person of Russian origin who does not enjoy or who no longer enjoys the protection of the Government of the Union of Soviet Socialist Republics and who has not acquired another nationality'.[13] It is very narrow, to say the least. Second, the neat definition of Article 1 glides over the fine print a little further down the page that allows state signatories to choose to restrict the definition of refugees to only those who have come from Europe, and during a very particular time-period. Some of the signatories to the Convention were fearful that the masses from the Global South might turn up on their doorsteps demanding a different kind of refuge. They were very careful to demarcate who was a legal refugee and what events counted in causing such status. In this process, World War II was treated as a massive aberration in the history of the displacement, not to be repeated or supplanted by other forces of human disruption:

> For the purposes of this Convention, the words 'events occurring before 1 January 1951' in article 1, section A, shall be understood to mean either (a) 'events occurring in Europe before 1 January 1951'; or (b) 'events occurring in Europe or elsewhere before 1 January 1951'; and each Contracting State shall make a declaration at the time of signature, ratification or accession, specifying which of these meanings it applies for the purpose of its obligations under this Convention.[14]

Third, it gives credence to the notion that *personal* individualized 'fear of being persecuted' is the core reason for needing support. War, upheaval, famine and pestilence do not in the conventional definition make for refugee status. It does not matter that civilian deaths as a proportion of deaths in war escalated to 10% in World War I, and to more than 90% of the 40 million killed since 1945. It only matters that persons fear the persecution of their state. Article 1 of the 1967 Protocol Relating to the Status of Refugees took away the geographical delimitation of the 1951 definition,[15] however, it does not respond to this problem. Over the last few decades, the UNHCR has *in practice* broadened this definition to include generalized military upheaval, but it has met with considerable opposition from Global North nation-states and it has been unable to formalize this broadening of its mandate. In effect, the legal definitions still carry all the baggage of the past.

Fourth, the definition misses out on the emerging dominance of *legal rationalism* in defining who is in need. This overt and dominating form of legalism, where legal rationality comes to be pursued for its own sake, grew up with the modern bureaucratic state and became one of its lines of defence. The legalese of the 1951 Convention and the 1967 Protocol turns flesh-and-blood people, individuals in need, into abstracted persons bound by a single moment is history. The Convention was written in response to a moment that forced the generosity of all – World War II – but it left out the generalizing insecurity that was dealt to an increasing number of populations outside the immediate theatre of war.

Fifth, the definition does not allow itself to be extended in time. The phrase 'As a result of events occurring before 1 January 1951' restricts the definition of refugee status to known events and times. Certainly, the 1967 Protocol Relating to the Status of Refugees took away the temporal limitations of the 1951 definition, but the point remains. For all their concern, nation-states could not anticipate handling the question of people in need without considerable legalized delimitation. Those five points explain how, although official Australian policy was strongly against the granting of asylum becoming a human right, Australia was able to become a signatory to the Convention, all the while maintaining the White Australia policy (Brennan 2007, Chap. 1). Then, and now, the legally enshrined right of the sovereign nation-state to say 'no' preceded the rights of those in need. The Australia that says 'no' has again become an ugly feature of our time.

6. Towards a new global covenant?

The current global/state-based approach to asylum seekers, refugees and irregular migrants is not working. Within constrained political boundaries and limited framing of what is possible, and despite a significant erosion of its power and influence, the UNHCR is doing a laudable job in enjoining states to act, documenting the problems of refugees and supporting people in camps (Loescher and Milner 2011). However, for all of this we have reached an impasse where a crisis of negative politics prevails. Taken together, the numbers of refugees, people in refugee-like situations, IDPs, asylum seekers and irregular migrants have increased dramatically over the course of the last century and into this one, and all that we seem able to do in response is to barricade our borders against more arrivals and to distribute aid to those stuck in camps. The negative politics ironically has not even worked to keep people from continuing to come. A complex mix of globalizing communications and intensifying global tensions compounding problems at the local level are providing the reasons, the motivations and the possibilities for increasing numbers of people to attempt to move across borders.

It is not viable in the long run that states are becoming less likely to engage productively and positively with global bodies such as the UNHCR. An extensive process called the Global Consultations on International Protection begun in 2000 did no more in reality than confirm the 1951 Convention. In concluding this essay, I want to join with the many advocates of the need for an enhanced positive regime of global governance in the area of the movement and displacement of persons. We have what Stephen Castles in this special issue calls 'a global governance deficit'. However, the problem is not simply the lack of institutionalized arrangements – a reconstituted and empowered UNHCR would provide an adequate institutional home for a changed regime. At the core of the problem is how responses are socially framed.

Among the many problems here is the nature of the ethical framing of the problem. Because currently the problem is countered under a one-dimensional, modern, rights-based discourse, then like the Millennium Goals, the issue gets reduced to metrics and competing claims. For example, it means that the counter-claim from states that they have a right to decide who comes across their borders and who stays is given an equal ethical standing with the needs of strangers. Within the current reductive regime of modern rights this is an ornery but comfortably abstract philosophical position to hold. However, without suggesting how an ethics of rights can be grounded at two deeper levels – (1) an ethics of care through which fundamental questions of difference/identity, inclusion/exclusion and mobility/belonging are negotiated; and (2) an ethics of foundations through which questions about being human on this planet are brought into contention – then we will stay with a negative politics of contesting claims (see James 2006, Chap. 12). Some writers have attempted to elaborate an ethics of care through the ambivalent notion of hospitality (cf. Friese 2010; Wilson 2010). This needs to be placed in a larger context of dialogue and policy.

A global covenant and a negotiated governance process would provide such a context. Australia, the USA and Canada as major receiving countries of the global movement of people could take a major lead in such a process. In the case of Australia, it would mean a moderated and graduated but fundamental rethinking of its refugee and immigration policy. First, without changing any other policies in the first instance, the government could, instead of effacing asylum seekers, begin by simply acknowledging the humanity of those who move and the importance of responding to the needs of strangers at a distance. As part of this it could, for example, after expedited due legal diligence in relation to those who arrive, negotiate national and local welcome-to-country and welcome-to-community ceremonies for those who have been accepted to stay. At the global level this would signal a change of rhetorical stance. Second, the Australian government could annul the legal contortions over excised offshore places.

Third, instead of engaging in deeply instrumental and flawed negotiations over regional and off-shore processing centres (Australia),[16] mandatory detention (Australia and Canada) or fences versus more border guards (the USA), the governments of Australia, Canada and the USA could call for and begin a global process of negotiating how asylum seekers and refugees in general can be handled regionally. This would entail global negotiation over how across the world we might equitably share the burden of the movement of people in various states of need. In this context, regional processing centres might work as the delegated centres of a global governance scheme rather than as instrumentally oriented places to slow down the movement of asylum seekers across borders. In this context, mandatory detention would become a brief stay in a processing centre rather than a means of deterring people smugglers. Refugees would enter these delegated processing centres, located in all signatory countries, knowing that they would be treated fairly, but not knowing in which country of the many in the regional pact they would end up being placed. Given the range of countries in any one regional pact – rich and poor – this would deter economic migrants from using refugee status as a way of bypassing immigration laws without requiring that refugees spend up to five years in detention to slow down the rate of asylum seeking.

Fourth, within the country, governments could initiate a long-term *deliberated* debate over who we will welcome to our country. Will it be predominantly skilled or wealthy migrants that add to the national interest as is currently the case, or might the balance be shifted substantially to those in need for whom we have a responsibility? For all the initial insecurity that it would engender in those who are vulnerable to fear-mongering, it would be the first time for the Australian, Canadian or US people that this question was debated democratically at length and not treated as an ethics to be deferred and handled by self-serving metrics. It would, if handled well, institute a long-term positive politics. And if governments working with civil society were able to do some of these things, then nation-states could again talk of being good international citizens.

Notes

1. *Migration Amendment (Excision from Migration Zone) Act No 127. 2001.* See the Australian Department of Immigration and Citizenship website, http://www.immi.gov.au/legislation/amendments/2005/050722/lc22072005.htm (accessed July 4, 2013). Amendment No. 128 allowed that 'An officer may take an offshore entry person from Australia to a country in respect of which a declaration is in force under subsection (3)'. In other words, asylum seekers could be 'deported' without the embarrassment of breaching the refoulement provision under the United Nations 1951 Refugees Convention and the 1967 Protocol. For a history of the relationship of Christmas Island, one of the excised places, see Chambers (2011).
2. From the Canadian immigration website, http://www.canadaimmigrationvisa.com/visatype.html (accessed March 19, 2013).
3. See Linklater (2007), Chap. 4, 'What is a Good International Citizen?' The central figure to use this term in Australian politics was Gareth Evans. It was removed as an objective of Australian foreign policy by the Liberal National Coalition in the late 1990s.
4. The term comes from Habermas (1987), although the methodological framing comes from James (2006).
5. According to the *Vancouver Sun*, 'The Harper government laid out a series of reforms on Thursday that it said would go after "ruthless profiteers" who coordinate illegal people-smuggling operations and asylum seekers who "jump the immigration queue"', October 22, 2010. The significance of this language is considerable. It takes on the rhetoric of Australia's Howard government from many years earlier.
6. From http://www.defenseimagery.mil/index.html (accessed April 14, 2011).
7. It can be visited by going to the online world 'Second Life' and its version of the Contemporary Art Museum Saint Gery.
8. UNHCR Statistical Online Population Database, http://www.unhcr.org/pages/4a013eb06.html (accessed July 4, 2013).
9. US Defence Information Directorate website, http://www.defenseimagery.mil/index.html (accessed April 14, 2011).
10. US Department of Defence website, http://www.defense.gov/news/newsarticle.aspx?id=63133 (accessed April 14, 2013).
11. http://ethicaljournalisminitiative.org/en/contents/charter-of-rome (accessed April 10, 2013).
12. Chapter 1, Article 1 of the Convention relating to the Status of Refugees Convention relating to the Status of Refugees, Office of the High Commissioner for Human Rights, adopted on 28 July 1951 by the United Nations Conference of Plenipotentiaries on the Status of Refugees and Stateless Persons convened under General Assembly resolution 429 (V) of 14 December 1950.
13. League of Nations, Arrangement Relating to the Issue of Identify Certificates to Russian and Armenian Refugees, 12 May 1926, League of Nations, Treaty Series Vol. LXXXIX, No. 2004, available at: http://www.unhcr.org/refworld/docid/3dd8b5802.html (accessed April 14, 2013).
14. Chapter 1, Article 1, subsection B.1.
15. It reads: 'For the purpose of the present Protocol, the term "refugee" shall, except as regards the application of paragraph 3 of this article, mean any person within the definition of article I of the Convention as if the words "As a result of events occurring before 1 January 1951 and … " and the words " … as a result of such events", in article 1 A (2) were omitted'.
16. The irony of the recent Australian High Court decision is that the offshore option may be off the table, and the government might be forced into this position for the wrong reason.

References

Arthus-Bertrand, Y., ed. 2009. *6 Billion Others: Portraits of Humanity from Around the World.* New York: Abrams.

Birkeland, N. M., K. Halff, and E. Jennings, eds. 2010. *Internal Displacement: Global Overview of Trends and Developments in 2009.* Geneva: Internal Displacement Monitoring Centre and the Norwegian Refugee Council.

Brennan, F. 2007. *Tampering with Asylum: A Universal Humanitarian Problem.* 2nd ed. Brisbane: University of Queensland Press.

Bude, H., and J. Durrschmidt. 2010. "What Is Wrong with Globalization? Contra 'Flow Speak' – Towards and Existential Turn in the Theory of Globalization." *European Journal of Social Theory* 13 (4): 481–500.

Chambers, P. 2011. "Society Has Been Defended: Following the Shifting Shape of the State Through Australia's Christmas Island." *International Political Sociology* 5 (1): 18–34.

Friese, H. 2010. "The Limits of Hospitality: Political Philosophy Undocumented Migration and the Local Arena." *European Journal of Social Theory* 13 (3): 323–341.

Fuller, G. 2005. "The Queue: Network Topologies and Motion Capture." Conference Proceedings for Capturing the Moving Mind: Management and Movement in the Age of Permanently Temporary War, September 11–20.

Gibney, M. J. 2004. *The Ethics and Politics of Asylum: Liberal Democracy and the Response to Refugees.* Cambridge: Cambridge University Press.

Habermas, J. 1987. *The Theory of Communicative Action, Volume Two: Lifeworld and System.* Cambridge: Polity Press.

Held, D. 2004. *Global Covenant: The Social Democratic Alternative to the Washington Consensus.* Cambridge: Polity Press.

James, P. 2006. *Globalism, Nationalism, Tribalism.* London: Sage.

Koslowski, R. 2011. *The Evolution of Border Controls as a Mechanism to Prevent Illegal Migration.* Washington, DC: Migration Policy Institute.

Leach, M. 2001. "Disturbing Practices': Dehumanizing Asylum Seekers in the 'Refugee Crisis in Australia, 2001–2002." *Refuge* 21 (3): 29–30.

Linklater, A. 2007. *Critical Theory and World Politics: Citizenship, Sovereignty and Humanity.* Abingdon: Routledge.

Loescher, G., and J. Milner. 2011. "UNHCR and the Global Governance of Refugees." In *Global Migration Governance*, edited by A. Betts, 189–209. Oxford: Oxford University Press.

Malkki, L. 1992. "National Geographic: The Rooting of Peoples and the Territorialization of National Identity Among Scholars and Refugees." *Cultural Anthropology* 7 (1): 24–44.

McNevin, A. 2011. *Contesting Citizenship: Irregular Migrants and New Frontiers of the Political.* New York: Columbia University Press.

Molloy, R., C. L. Smith, and A. Wozniak. 2011. *Internal Migration in the United States.* Washington, DC: Finance and Economics Discussion Series, Divisions of Research & Statistics and Monetary Affairs, Federal Reserve Board.

Papastergiadis, N. 2010. "Wars of Mobility." *European Journal of Social Theory* 13 (3): 343–361.

Steger, M. B., ed. 2004. *Rethinking Globalism.* Lanham, MD: Rowman and Littlefield.

Steger, M. B. 2008. *The Rise of the Global Imaginary.* Oxford: Oxford University Press.

Weller, P. 2002. *Don't Tell the Prime Minister.* Melbourne: Scribe.

Wilson, E. K. 2010. "Protecting the Unprotected: Reconceptualizing Refugee Protection Through the Notion of Hospitality." *Local-Global* 8: 100–122.

The ideology of temporary labour migration in the post-global era

Catherine Dauvergne and Sarah Marsden

Faculty of Law, University of British Columbia, Vancouver, British Columbia, Canada

Temporary labour migration is becoming intellectually topical once again. Following renewed government interest in temporary labour migration on a global level, migration scholars are now also showing renewed interest in the area. In this essay, we seek to explore the potential of these two movements, by states and by scholars, to yield different outcomes than earlier dialogues surrounding guest-worker programmes in the 1970s and 1980s. By looking at key ideological elements of temporary labour migration, we assess the potential for an alternative trajectory for understanding and reframing the discussion in terms that are capable of responding in a more emancipatory way to the lived experiences of migrant workers. We identify three concepts central to most analyses of temporary migration policies and programmes: temporariness, the labour market and rights. Our central contention is that these concepts function ideologically, and as such they constrain innovation with regard to temporary migrant labour programmes. We draw on Hannah Arendt's work in *The Human Condition* to work towards an alternative conception of what is at stake in temporary migration programmes.

1. Introduction

Temporary labour migration has become intellectually topical once again. Slightly behind renewed government interest in temporary labour migration on a global level, migration scholars are now showing renewed interest in the area (e.g. Castles 2006, 741; Martin 2006; Vetrovec 2007; Carens 2010; Rosewarne 2010; Zapata-Barrero, Faúndez García, and Sánchez-Montijano 2012). In this essay, we explore the potential of these two movements, by states and by scholars, to yield different outcomes than earlier dialogues surrounding European guest-worker programmes in the 1970s and 1980s. By looking at key ideological elements of temporary labour migration, we assess the potential for an alternative trajectory for understanding and reframing the discussion in terms that are capable of responding in a more emancipatory way to the lived experiences of migrant workers.

We are drawn to an analysis of the ideology of temporary labour migration because we are interested in interrogating the common premises underlying current conversations about temporary labour migration. We aim for an understanding of the function of certain concepts that form the core of the central questions about temporary labour migration programmes, regardless of one's position about whether these programmes work well. We have identified three concepts central to most analyses of temporary migration policies and programmes: temporariness, the labour market and rights. Our central contention is that these concepts function ideologically, and as such they constrain innovation with regard to temporary migrant labour programmes. We draw on Hannah Arendt's *The Human Condition* to work towards an alternative conception of what is at stake in temporary migration programmes.

Our aim is to build on earlier waves of scholarship regarding European guest-worker programmes (for example, Martin and Miller 1980; Castles 1986; Rudolph 1996). Accordingly, we take as known quantities those insights of this guest-worker scholarship that have been so well established that they appear almost as trope in contemporary conversation. Primary among these are that once temporary migrant labourers arrive, it is difficult to ensure their departure, and the longer they remain, the harder it is to develop a theoretical argument for their exclusion from the polity and the territory. Similarly, we seek to build upon the insight that while workers may be invited, it is human beings who arrive. These touchstones are vital to understanding the linkage between temporary labour migration and illegal migration, and the policy trade-offs between the two categories that underpin state policy but which, for fairly obvious reasons, are rarely articulated by policy-makers (Dauvergne 2008). We situate our analysis in what we call the 'post-global' era because a key difference from earlier guest-worker programmes is the backdrop of advancing globalization. No matter how one defines globalization, its pervasive effects are now standard features of migration policy-making (Held et al. 1999). Drawing on this older scholarship, and the resurgence of temporary labour migration initiatives in the post-global era, we have identified three elements that feature in all analysis of these programmes: temporariness, labour markets and rights. This article demonstrates that these three elements converge into an ideology of temporary labour migration.

Arendt's acute formulation of citizenship as 'the right to have rights' has become a touchstone of migration analyses (Arendt [1951] 1958). But her work has far greater and more complex reach in this area. We draw on Arendt's perspicacious treatment of the human condition (Arendt [1958] 1998) to help envision a way through the ideology of temporary labour migration. Arendt's rich treatise could be read in almost its entirety as a study of labour under conditions of globalization. In this essay, we draw out potential Arendtian responses to the key ideological elements of temporary labour migration. We also invoke the spirit of *The Human Condition* in two ways. A great admirer of Marx, Arendt was also a limning critic, believing that his account of labour and of its relation to ideology was insufficiently complex and sometimes simply wrong. She honours Marx's contributions with a deep respect, and we hope that some trace of this respect will be found in our engagement with the concept of ideology and the notion of rights for migrant workers. Arendt was also an inveterate optimist. The underlying structure of *The Human Condition* relies on a succession of redemptive movements. Man is saved: an enormous moment in her trenchant engagement with technology, knowledge and postmodernity. Arendt's optimism builds directly from her understanding of forgiveness as a fundamental distinction of humanity, which allows us to amend the unchangeable consequences of our actions. Arendt's optimism is compelling, and we draw on it unabashedly as we seek to imagine a way out of what has become a political and legal gridlock.

Following a brief discussion of ideology as a framing concept, we describe current temporary labour migration trends, paying attention to what is 'new' at present and to points of convergence between the states we take as examples (Canada, Australia, the USA and the UK). This sketch grounds our consideration of the notion of temporariness and the aims and interests it serves. The subsequent section considers the representation of national labour markets within temporary labour migration programmes. Following this, we turn to the possibilities and impossibilities of rights remedies for temporary workers. In concluding, we draw on Arendt's insight that labour is a vital aspect of the human condition in order to consider new ways of conceptualizing temporary migrant labour programmes.

2. Ideology

In electing to use the concept of ideology, we draw on its intellectual tradition, and in particular, upon its acute focus on social relations of domination and how such relations are replicated without resort to violence. This perspective is particularly useful for discussing temporary migrant labour because it is common to hear how these programmes can be rendered 'beneficial' to both the parties to an employment relationship – the employer and the migrant worker – and the shadow parties to the relationship – the host state and the state of origin (e.g. Ruhs 2005; IOM 2008), despite profound inequalities that underpin these relationships. What we reject of ideology's intellectual freight, in the company of much contemporary post-Marxist work, is the notion of ideology as false consciousness. This particular shorthand goes further than is necessary and opens the way for an irresolvable debate about the nature of truth.

What is most compelling and appropriate about the concept of ideology for our analysis is what Purvis and Hunt have termed its 'directionality'. In their words, '... ideology always works to favour some and to disadvantage others' (Purvis and Hunt 1993, 478). In this sense, ideology has a sharper edge than other concepts we might have chosen, such as 'discourse', or even 'theory' or 'theoretical framework'. As Purvis and Hunt (1993, 478) elaborate:

> ... the critical project of a theory of ideology is concerned to explain how the forms of consciousness generated by the lived experience of subordinate classes and social groups facilitate the reproduction of existing social relations and thus impede such classes and groups from developing forms of consciousness that reveal the nature of their subordination. *In its simplest and most pervasive form ideology presents the existing social relations as both natural and inevitable; particular interests come to be disassociated from their specific location and come to appear as universal and neutral.* (emphasis added)

This edge works well for our analysis, because while we are engaged in advocating for better legal protections for migrant workers, we are also reticent about the promises of rights remedies as permanent solutions to the barriers and difficulties facing migrant workers. Our analysis derives in large part from our desire to express this tension underlying advocacy efforts.

The ideology of temporary labour migration involves the interdependent concepts of temporariness, labour markets and rights. Temporariness is presented as a neutral policy objective, valuable because it facilitates the import of just enough labour to meet particular labour market gaps (GCIM 2005, 12). The framing of people as 'labour' opens the way for rights abuses and exploitation, and thus creates the need to protect the rights of temporary migrant workers. Accordingly, a labour market analysis and a rights analysis are not alternative perspectives; they occupy the same ideological terrain. Our objective is to interrogate these concepts and analyse how they function ideologically to reproduce social relations of domination and to make those relations appear natural and inevitable, and in the case of temporary migrant labour, mutually beneficial. Arendt's imaginative work elucidates the limits of rights-based analysis by identifying both labour and work as aspects of the human condition. This is a strong distinction from current rights discourse, where critical focus is on how human dignity has been subordinated to labour.

3. Temporariness

We are primarily interested in the recent increase in temporary labour migration to industrialized, rich Western nations and how this increase is presented politically.

We begin by looking briefly at four examples: the USA, Canada, Australia and the UK. These examples reflect in part that this work originated as part of a conference about immigrant democracies. We sought to examine whether these programmes that have ramped up over the past five years differed from the continental European programmes that had been the focus of much scholarly critique in the 1980s (for example, Martin and Miller 1980; Castles 1986; Brubaker 1989; Rudolph 1996; Ruhs 2005). We analyse the data in greater detail in a companion article (Marsden and Dauvergne, 2013). Here, we present these numbers briefly to ground our discussion of temporariness.

According to the Organization for Economic Cooperation and Development (OECD), approximately 2.5 million temporary labour migrants entered its member states in 2006, about three times the number of permanent migrants to the same countries that year (OECD 2008). This figure is based on a definition of temporary that includes mandatory return to country of origin as a condition of entry into the receiving country, and thus includes intra-company transferees, working holiday visa holders and 'free circulation' migrants. The International Organization for Migration (IOM) indicates that there has been a 'significant growth in temporary labour migration' in most developed countries since 1990, and again since 2000 (IOM 2008, 32). The IOM describes the potential of temporary migration programmes, and particularly low-skilled labour migration programmes, as a 'win-win-win' situation. The first two ostensible 'wins' are for the migrants and the labour economies of receiving countries. The third 'win' of temporary labour migration, as described by the IOM, is to the economy of the sending nation, which improves through remittances, job creation and ongoing connection of the migrants to their home country (IOM 2008, 92).

In the USA, temporary migrant worker entries have consistently exceeded both the total number of permanent residents from all categories (including economic, family, refugee, etc.) and the total number of employment-based permanent resident entries over the past decade, as illustrated by Figure 1.

These data show only a modest increase in temporary migrant admissions, and also confirm that temporary worker admissions have consistently outnumbered permanent worker admissions to the USA. At this level, no recent shift is apparent; however, within

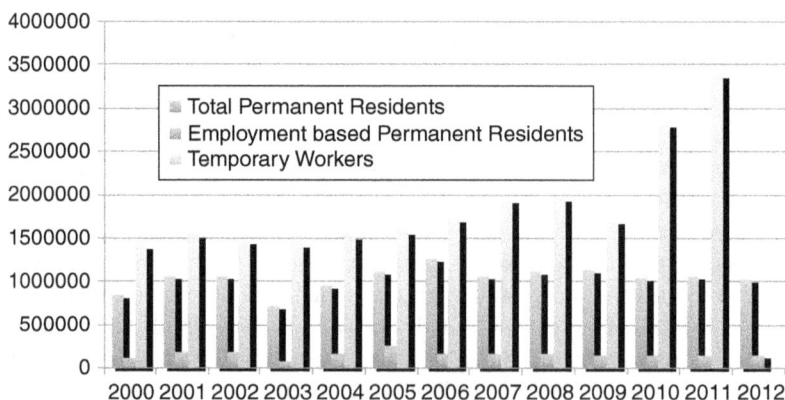

Figure 1. Permanent and temporary migration to the USA (admissions, including family members). Note: The data represented in the tables here have been compiled from publicly available government data in each country. We have arranged the graphs ourselves and have regrouped some figures to improve the comparability between countries.

the temporary worker category, there has been a shift towards admissions of temporary workers categorized as having lower skill levels (Figure 2). Viewing the two sets of data together, an increase in low-skilled worker admissions is evident in both raw numbers and proportionally. While temporary migrants to the USA can theoretically obtain permanent residence, the path is arduous and is much more difficult for those in lower skill classifications. The data also suggest a cut in temporary admissions concurrent to the economic downturn in the USA, which is not evident in the permanent admissions numbers. Interestingly, the flow of illegal entry also appears to have decreased in the past five years (Passel and Cohn, 2010).

In Canada, temporary foreign worker entries have been on a gradual increase in terms of pure numbers since 2003. The number of temporary foreign workers entering Canada exceeded the number of economic-class permanent residents entering Canada for the first time in 2006, and this pattern has continued since that time (Figure 3).

As in the USA, work classified as low skilled is on the increase by pure numbers and as a proportion of migrant labour as well (Figure 4). Unfortunately, the large number of 'level not stated' entries in government data decreases the transparency of this information.[1] By way of legal regulation, migrant workers in low-skilled categories are more likely to be separated from family, have few renewals options and have limited access to permanent residence as compared to those classified as high-skilled workers.

Australia has also participated in the trend towards admitting more temporary migrant workers in lower skill classifications, in a somewhat more oblique manner.

The government data regarding temporary migrant workers focus on the 457 visa class, which is based on an employer's specific labour need, and the vast majority are professionals, managers and skilled tradespersons or other high-skilled positions (Figure 5). The Working Holiday programme is available to applicants between the ages of 18 and 30 from a specified list of other rich, highly industrialized nations and is designed 'to be particularly helpful to regional employers in providing short term casual employment to industries such as hospitality and rural industries' (Australian Bureau of Statistics 2010). Cumulatively, these two temporary labour-based categories now far exceed the number of permanent skill-based entries per year. In addition, Australia has seen significant growth in student visas since 2006, with which foreign students are allowed to work up to 20 hours per week; in 2008, the work permit became automatically issued alongside the study permit (Department of Immigration and Citizenship 2010). It would appear, therefore, that the appetite for temporary workers

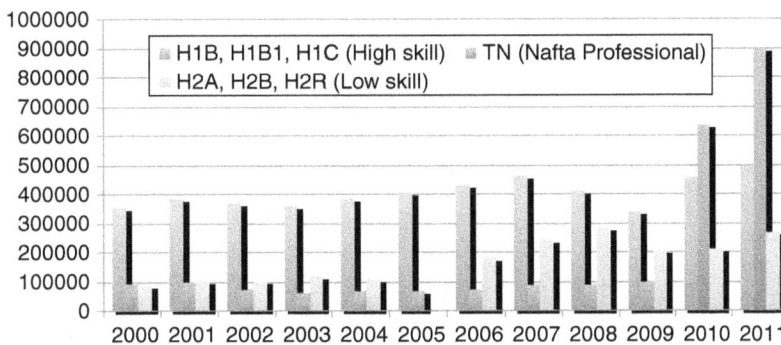

Figure 2. Temporary labour migration to the USA by skill classification (admissions, not including family members).

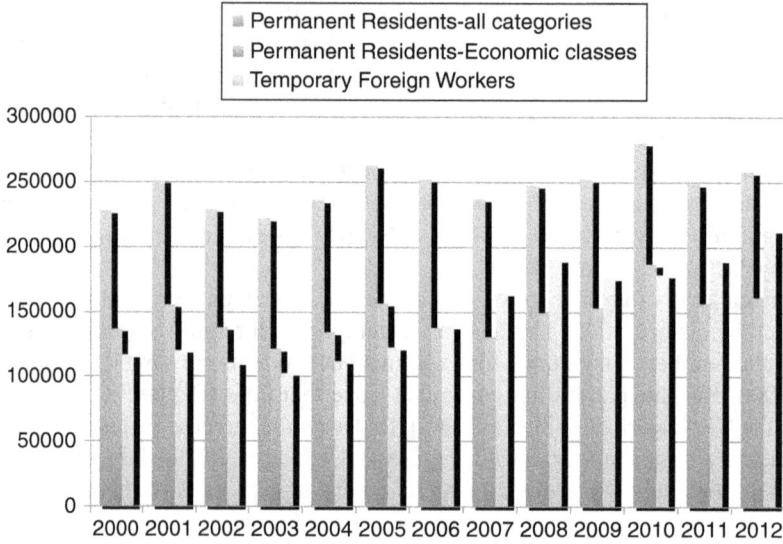

Figure 3.   Permanent and temporary migration to Canada (admissions) (CIC 2013a).

with limited entitlements is being absorbed in two visa categories that mask the labour being undertaken and that in large part do not lead to permanent residence. At the same time, the Minister of Immigration has posted a stated goal of reducing temporary work permits by 50% by 2012, revealing a surprising level of doublespeak (Minister for Immigration and Citizenship 2010). In addition to these trends, in 2008, the Australian government started a Pacific Seasonal Workers programme to bring in a maximum of 2500 workers annually from various poorer Pacific nations to work in low-skilled agricultural positions (DEEWR 2010).

In the UK, 2004 and 2007 expansions of the European Union (EU) have led to dramatic changes in immigration patterns (Figure 6).

In 2004, the UK implemented the Worker Registration Scheme, in which nationals of newly acceded nations were required to register in order to work in the UK. This was followed in 2008 with a dramatic reduction in the categories of temporary migration, and further changes to its migration system in mid-2010 that will reduce entry of non-UK nationals (Home Office 2010). The registration scheme ended in 2011. Given the policy

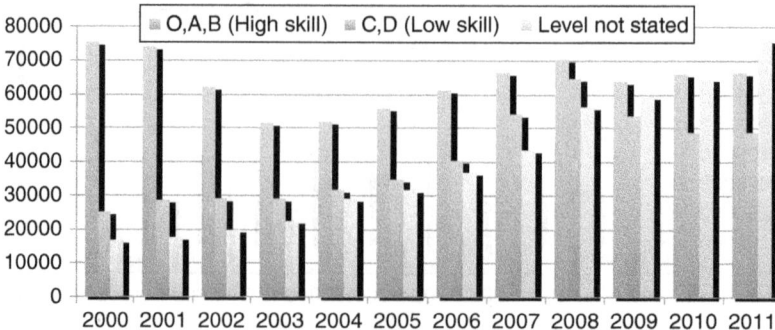

Figure 4.   Temporary labour migration to Canada by skill level (CIC 2013a).

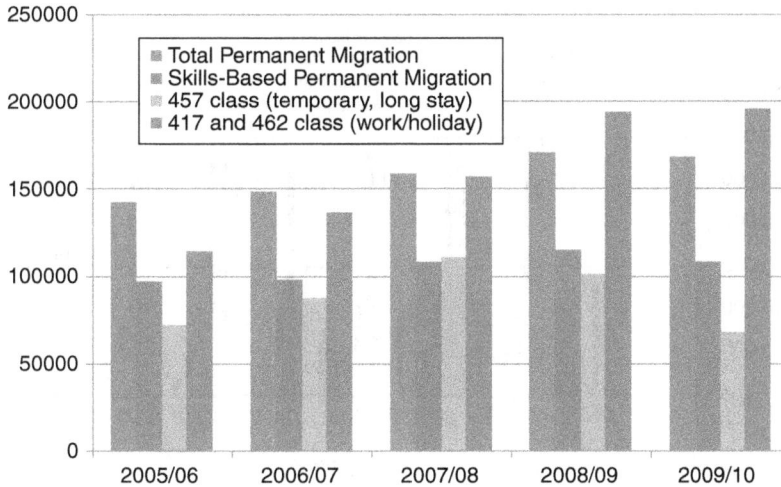

Figure 5.   Temporary and permanent migration to Australia.

shifts of the past five years, the focus of British labour migration policy appears to be the entry of accession country migrants for low-skilled positions, with high-skilled and specific programme temporary migration available to non-EU nationals on an increasingly limited basis.

While it is being achieved in different ways in each of these four states, the overall trend is for increased entry of workers classified as low-skilled. In the USA, this shift is marginal within an overall system where temporary migration has long outstripped permanent migration, and has traditionally been a route – however narrow and circuitous – to permanent status. In Canada, the predominance of the temporary as an explicit category is new, and dovetails with an increase in the proportion of temporary workers in low-skilled categories. In Australia, it appears that temporary labour migration is being significantly masked by working holidaymaker and foreign student visa categories. In Britain, an influx of low-skilled workers from the 2004 and 2007 EU expansions has eclipsed the purported need to admit temporary foreign workers from other countries. Through the use of registration rather than migration per se, this programme functions to submerge and make invisible the requirements and restrictions which distinguish this group of workers from citizen workers in the UK. In the first three cases, temporariness is emphasized as the low-skill numbers grow. Britain's policy is distinct from that in the states with a longer and more explicit immigration tradition, and thus provides an important counterpoint for testing our argument.

Against this backdrop, we can begin to explore how temporariness functions ideologically. At the most basic level, the label is illusory. While permission to stay may be time limited, many migrants who arrive on a temporary basis remain permanently with or without permission (Batalova 2006; Legomsky 2009, 148; Papademetriou et al. 2009). This insight is not new, and indeed close attention to it is at the core of much guest-worker scholarship and is embedded in many regulatory structures. Furthermore, it is increasingly true that the jobs filled by temporary migrant labour programmes are also not temporary (Fudge and MacPhail 2009). Immigration policy in each of the countries we examine acknowledges this and, rather than precluding a conversion of temporary status to permanent status, seeks to distinguish who will be able to make that

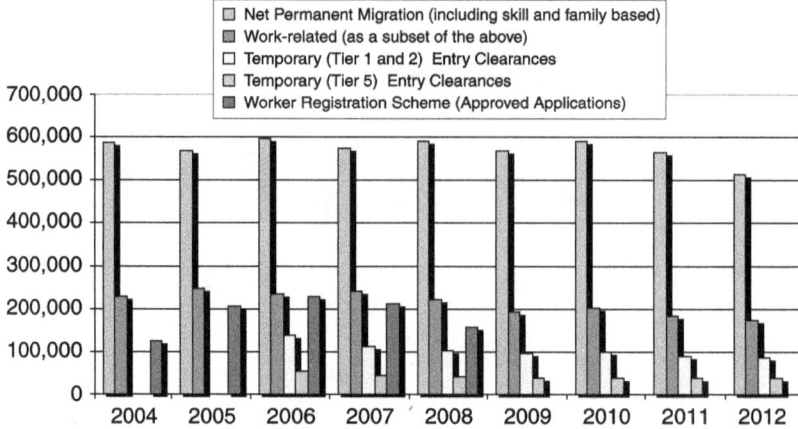

Figure 6. Temporary and permanent migration to the UK.
Note: Net permanent migration and work related:
http://www.ons.gov.uk/ons/rel/migration1/migration-statistics-quarterly-report/february-2013/msqr-feb13.html
http://www.ons.gov.uk/ons/dcp171778_300382.pdf (used chart xls, for 'inflow' as of June for each year, Figure 2.12, excluding 'British Citizens').
Tier-based data from table ho-tcm77-300438.xls, linked from http://www.ons.gov.uk/ons/dcp 171778_300382.pdf, Figure 3.12.
Worker Registration Scheme, 2009 and 2010, taken from Migration Statistics Quarterly Report: November 2010, estimated from graphic table provided at p. 15. http://www.ons.gov.uk/ons/rel/migration1/migration-statistics-quarterly-report/november-2010/index.html
Note: this category closed in 2011. See UK Border Agency, Home Office 2011 'Worker Registration Scheme.' Accessed April 23, 2013. http://www.ukba.homeoffice.gov.uk/workingintheuk/eea/wrs/
Long-term (net permanent) migration figures taken from charts, excluding British citizens. As described in the definitions accompanying these charts, long-term migration is determined using the UN definition of one year or more, and while this does not represent naturalization directly, other studies use these data to represent some degree of permanence, with an exception in the case of students: http://www.migrationobservatory.ox.ac.uk/britains-70-million-debate/3-net-migration-and-immigration-overview-0

shift. Understanding this as an ideological function means accepting that temporariness, rather than leading to a 'win-win-win', embeds and normalizes a directionality in which workers' rights are limited and states' rights (to expel, to control) are expanded. A second ideological function of temporariness is that it distracts attention from inequality between regulatory regimes applied to 'high-skilled' versus 'low-skilled' workers. That is, a focus on appropriate rights restrictions to ensure that workers will in fact depart at the end of their permitted period masks the fact that the current surge is primarily about giving those with lower skills fewer rights. Attention to 'temporariness' makes it seem natural and inevitable (to return to Purvis and Hunt's phrasing) that these workers will have restricted rights. However, given the overt inaccuracy of the 'temporary' label, the contemporary rise in both numbers and popularity of these programmes (Ruhs 2005) facilitates curbing entitlements for those categorized as low-skilled because rights restrictions are the only way to ensure actual temporary stays. This equation is the essence of Ruhs and Martin's persuasive 'numbers vs. rights' argument (Ruhs and Martin 2008; Marsden and Dauvergne, 2013).

Temporariness is but one of the three components of the ideology of temporary labour migration, but focusing on this criterion alone has explanatory power in analysing the *divergence* in contemporary programmes between our example states. In the USA, where migrant rights have the longest and most sophisticated history of political contestation and where illegal migration is vastly higher than in the other three states, temporariness predominated long before the current surge (Durand, Massey, and Parrado 1999). Illegal migration provides a pool of workers with even fewer rights protections than temporary workers. In Australia, the surge in low-skilled temporary work is almost completely hidden, reflecting the long-standing (and atypical for Western democracies) consensual approach to migration management that marks Australian party politics. In Canada, relative transparency about rights restrictions based on skill level has attracted the most intense scholarly critique of these three countries (Preibisch 2007; Carens 2008; Fudge and MacPhail 2009). Finally, in the UK, where EU expansion has fractured the linkage between temporariness and low-skilled admissions, the immigration system has undergone a full-scale overhaul, with responses ranging from High Court review of permanent migration caps to crisis rhetoric (Casciani 2010; *Guardian [UK] 2010*).

We can begin here to see the acuity of Arendt's lens. Two points are directly linked to temporariness. The first is the very broad point that labour is but one of the three aspects of the human condition. It is impossible to separate it from the others (work and action). Arendt builds this argument in part by drawing on Marx's introduction of the vital idea of 'surplus', asserting that labour's productivity

> ... does not lie in any of labour's products, but in the human 'power' whose strength is not exhausted when it has produced the means of its own subsistence and survival but is capable of producing a surplus beyond what is necessary for its own 'reproduction'. (Arendt [1958] 1998, 88)

The fact that labour is never self-contained, but is always productive of something more than itself, *and* is an aspect of being human, goes a great deal of the way to explaining why it is impossible for states to simply 'import labour'.

The second Arendtian insight at this point is her suspicion of the distinction between skilled and unskilled labour. 'Every activity requires a certain amount of skill, the activity of cleaning and cooking no less than the writing of a book or the building of a house', ' ... unskilled work is a contradiction in terms' (Arendt [1958] 1998, 90). Arendt makes this point in part to emphasize the distinction between her conceptions of work and labour, but it is useful beyond that objective: within the current division of labour, all requirement for skill is eliminated by labour fragmentation. As such, skilled/unskilled labels communicate social valuations rather than inherent truths. With these insights in mind, we turn to consider the second element of the ideology of temporary labour migration, the labour market.

4. The labour market

In post-global conditions, migration is analysed and understood almost exclusively in economic terms (Dauvergne 2008, 29–49). One consequence of the discourses of globalization is that we are remarkably unselfconscious about a reductive economic analysis. The insistence on economic paradigms is at its most acute when talking of temporary labour migration because the insistence on temporariness attempts to turn people into 'pure' economic inputs who will depart when their labour is no longer necessary. Temporary labour migration programmes are driven by employer demand and mediated by state policy, which matches migrants to defined gaps in the national labour market. This objective rests on a number of assumptions: that labour shortages can be identified with a high degree of specificity; that training is globally transferable and that migration programmes can be tailored to provide a kind of 'just-in-time' delivery of workers.

As temporary migrant labour schemes come under increasing scrutiny, the labour market analysis tends to become increasingly focused. Typically, checks are introduced to ensure, at least ostensibly, that citizen workers are genuinely unavailable and to ensure that the labour market is a level playing field by ensuring that temporary workers are not simply more desirable because they are being paid less or otherwise exploited. For example, in Canada, prospective employers of temporary workers are required to obtain a 'labour market opinion' documenting demand for a specific position (CIC 2013c); in the USA, the law requires a similar process of 'labour certification' (USCIS 2010). In Australia, the new Pacific Seasonal Worker programme requires employer to be approved in advance of recruiting foreign workers (DEEWR 2010).

The presumption behind these policies is that a better understanding of the labour market, and regulations based on this knowledge, will produce better temporary migrant worker programmes. To summarize simplistically, the improvements will be tripartite. From the perspective of industry, the right workers will be made available at the right time. From the state perspective, production will rise as quickly as possible and the temporary nature of the programme will ensure that in slow times unemployment is exported and thus non-existent. There ought even to be benefits from the perspective of the worker through wage parity with citizen workers and close matching of skills with vacancies.

This sounds quite straightforward, and not particularly novel, which is telling. We gain insight into why labour market proposals are front and centre to improving temporary migrant worker programmes from a state point of view, yet meet with limited success, through attention to how labour markets function ideologically. All workers rely on remunerative work to support themselves; migrant workers also rely on the endorsement and approval of employers to obtain basic status, and contingent membership, in the states where they work or seek to work. Thus, the basic condition of any migrant worker is marked by an in inherent degree of subordination that identifies the labour market analysis as a directional ideological terrain. In the 'win-win-win' analysis, this subordination is justified by the presumption that the migrant worker is better off under these conditions than she would be at home. The fact that this may well be the case reinforces the ideological function of the discourse.

In this terrain, the idea of a 'market' is presented as natural and politically neutral, an arena where employers and workers engage in free exchange, which is regulated primarily to protect the interests of workers. Adam Smith's depiction of the free market was a thought experiment devised in a time of horrendous abuse and exploitation of workers. What remains firmly embedded in the policy talk is the assumption that labour markets are naturally occurring. For example, the Global Commission on International Migration's analysis of migration and work laments that market reforms have not been able to fundamentally transform labour markets in developing countries (GCIM 2005, 12). Ruhs writes that policy actors have now generally accepted a persistent 'demand' for migrants in the labour markets of high-income countries (Ruhs 2005). The Canadian government's circular on how to hire temporary foreign workers begins with the statement:

> Short-term labour shortages are a common occurrence in many sectors of Canada's economy. They can affect workplaces that need employees with highly specialized skills, seasonal businesses such as tourism and agriculture, or entire regions during periods of rapid economic

expansion, like the pre-Olympics construction boom in British Columbia or the development of the oil and gas sector in Alberta. (CIC 2013b)

In varying ways, each of these policy analyses presents the labour market as a terrain that governments can observe and possibly act in, but that develop independently of state action, and that state action may fail to influence at all. The labour market seems here to exist independently of the state, of workers and of industrial actors.

But the labour market is an analytical and theoretical tool. It is made up of layer upon layer of assumption, regulation, absence of regulation, choice, and agency by individuals and collective actors such as firms and states. The prevalence of economic discourse in immigration policy means that the labour market is pervasively employed to justify regulatory strategy with little recognition that it is construction and not a force of nature. The aspiration to tailor temporary migration programmes more and more closely to the labour market simply cannot be fully achieved because the labour market remains theoretical, while people are not. In addition, labour market analysis within migration policy occurs at the national scale. It thus ignores globalization and the increasingly international function of labour supply and demand, but because the labour market is built on a national premise, this feature becomes understood as an assumption of the model rather than a flaw.

One of the ideological functions of the labour market construct is, therefore, to make this device seem natural and inevitable, masking the ongoing efforts by many actors to ensure its continued existence and function. The labour market also embeds the characteristic of directionality, especially in the case of temporary migrant workers. Because temporary migrant workers depend on employers for their very 'existence', they are much more vulnerable within the market than the other actors in the triple 'win' equation. The vulnerability of all workers, countered to a degree by the organization of labour, is magnified in the case of migrant workers, and efforts to organize migrant labour are in their infancy (Russo 2012).

Arendt argued that the contemporary world was marked by the ascendancy of labour over both 'work' and 'active life'. One consequence of this reversal of the hierarchy of the ancient world is that the 'public' realm has been largely replaced by the 'social' and by the concomitant rise of social sciences. These transformations in human life account for the impaired political life of postmodernity as well as the hegemonic rise of technological knowledge. Unpacking this transformation assists in analysing how the idea of the labour market works in discourses about temporary labour migration.

Arendt traces the rise of labour from the time of Locke's 'discovery' that labour is the source of all property (Arendt [1958] 1998, 101). This led in a relatively short time to '... the new social realm [that] transformed all modern communities into societies of labourers and jobholders; in other words, they became at once centred around the one activity necessary to sustain life'. This does not mean that all members of society are labourers, or even workers, '... but only that all members consider whatever they do primarily as a way to sustain their own lives and those of their families' (Arendt [1958] 1998, 46). Under these conditions, and supported by the division of labour, labouring activity moves from the private into the new and ever expanding 'social' realm – neither completely private nor completely public. Arendt ([1958] 1998, 40) remarks that 'the striking coincidence of the rise of society with the decline of the family indicates clearly that what actually took place was the absorption of the family unit into corresponding social groups'. Within the social realm, labour grows 'unnaturally', leading to a constant acceleration in the productivity of labour (Arendt [1958] 1998, 47).

This constant acceleration in productivity maps precisely onto the economic assumption of infinite growth as the mark of a healthy economy. It is, thus, no surprise that Arendt reserves particular disdain for economics:

> Economics – until the modern age a not too important part of ethics and politics and based on the assumption that men act with respect to their economic activities as they act in every other respect – could achieve a scientific character only when men had become social beings and unanimously followed certain patterns of behavior, so that those who did not keep the rules could be considered to be asocial or abnormal. ([1958] 1998, 42)

The reliance of economic analysis on statistics (notably, much of current economics, half a century after Arendt's work, is completely absorbed in mathematic modelling) drew particular concern from Arendt. Statistics, which she called 'the mathematical treatment of reality', denote an era of conformism, behaviourism and automatism in human affairs. The harm of this view of the world is that it transforms our way of knowing and experiencing reality:

> statistical uniformity is by no means a harmless scientific ideal; it is the no longer secret political ideal of a society which, entirely submerged in the routine of everyday living, is at peace with the scientific outlook inherent in its very existence. (Arendt [1958] 1998, 43)

This sharp critique could have been aimed directly at the idea of a labour market: a mathematically based economic fiction. All efforts to improve temporary labour migration programmes, by improving our understanding of labour markets, rely on having better statistics. Arendt's insights help us understand the harms of this formula for improvement: if the labour market is a representation, not a 'reality', a clearer understanding of it offers little for improving circumstances of individual human beings. Arendt's insights, besides simply raising a general scepticism, locate this concern with the shift through which labour has come to predominate over other aspects of the human condition. This returns us to a central problem in recrafting temporary labour migration programmes: they reduce people to labour alone. Arendt's understanding of the social realm as an impoverished setting for human interaction is also predictive of key pitfalls in migrant labour programmes because a diminishing of family rights and a loss of privacy often parallel the exclusive focus on labour and skill levels.

Arendt's critique of the social realm also suggests some insights into the dilemma of equality rights as a corrective tool, an issue that falls within both our discussion of the labour market and our following section on rights. The idea of a labour market assumes equal parties striking a mutually beneficial bargain. Law's only way of formulating equality is to assess it in rights terms. This is the classic win-win, on which win-win-win riffs. Few inroads have been made into correcting inequalities within the labour market, despite the triteness of this observation. One avenue to rethinking this can be drawn from Arendt's observation that equality in the social realm is based on conformity – much impoverished in comparison with the Greek concept of political equality: '... the victory of equality in the modern world is on the political and legal recognition of the fact that society has conquered the public realm, and that distinction and difference have become private matters for the individual' (Arendt [1958] 1998, 41). Arendt laments the loss of distinction that results from a turn towards social life rather than political life, and the way this shift channels equality into legal discourse. This observation turns us towards the law, which has claimed equality as its own, and in which rights are the key modus operandi.

5. Rights

It is not surprising that in response to the expansion of temporary migrant worker programmes legal scholars are increasingly concerned with the rights of temporary migrant workers. Temporary labour migration programmes are generally premised on temporary workers having fewer labour, association and mobility rights than permanent migrants or citizens. At the very least, permission to remain in a host country is time limited. In highly structured examples, employment may be restricted to a particular employer or economic sector (such the direct employer requirement of Australian 457 visas), accommodation may be restricted (such as domestic and some agricultural workers in the USA) and family life may be restricted (such as the mandatory separation from family members within Canada's low-skilled migration scheme). The question is whether rights-based understandings and advocacy can adequately address these problems. Through his thought-provoking consideration of the ethics of temporary labour migration, Reilly (2011) concludes that temporary labour migration schemes may not be able to meet the ethical parameters of liberalism. Yet, liberal states are increasingly and actively recruiting temporary migrant workers or otherwise filling the so-called low-skilled labour market demands through classes of migrant workers, whether overt or obscured.

Advances *within* a domestic rights framework are certainly possible. As Martin Ruhs and Philip Martin argue, structuring programmes to better protect workers' rights can assist in avoiding some of the pitfalls of earlier guest-worker programmes (Ruhs and Martin 2008), and the counter-hegemonic potential of rights work at the grass roots has a role (Basok 2009). In general terms, two paths towards significant rights advances can be observed. In Canada, a number of legislative and policy initiatives have emerged aimed at protecting temporary workers' rights. These include some innovative and creative measures such as foreign worker hotlines and proactive worker protection procedures, such as site visits in Alberta, and foreign worker protection legislation and registration in Manitoba (Fudge and MacPhail 2009). The alternative (though not mutually exclusive) path is for temporary migrant workers to receive protections through the support of labour unions. This strategy has had some high-profile successes in the USA (Bacon 2008).

On the whole, however, rights protections for temporary foreign workers have not been as successful in practice as their rhetoric promises. Although successful in concrete gains in working conditions and thus beneficial for workers, even in the best possible outcomes, rights protections have not challenged the underlying social relations that are entrenched in and supported by migrant worker programmes. Furthermore, all rights entitlements require resources, advocacy and initiative to bring them to fruition. These barriers are exacerbated in the case of temporary migrant workers by virtue of their compromised membership status in the receiving nation, particularly low-wage workers who would most benefit from enhanced legal protections. Both individual complaints and test-case litigation may be deterred by the very fact of temporary status, given the time it takes to see a legal complaint through. In addition, non-citizen workers cannot advocate for their own rights through representative democratic processes. For all these reasons, although rights may exist on paper, their enforcement is less likely to be monitored in the case of temporary non-citizens. Two recent studies in the Canadian context have focused close attention on the rights of temporary migrant workers. Nakache and Kinoshita (2010) have comprehensively described the rights gap for foreign workers in the Canadian province of Alberta. Fudge and MacPhail (2009) have analysed a series of attempts to address rights gaps, and have concluded that none are likely to be successful. In Australia, the Pacific Seasonal Workers programme was carefully structured with the rights of workers in mind. Ironically, the programme appears underused in its first stages, undoubtedly in part because the programme cannot address the identified labour market need with such robust rights protections in place (MacDermott and Opeskin 2010, 288).

On an international level, the saga of the *Convention on the Rights of All Migrant Workers and Members of Their Families* illustrates the failed promise of rights protections for temporary migrant workers. The Convention certainly contains some significant advances for migrant workers with legal status, such as to right to unionize, and parity with citizens in terms of social security benefits. Nevertheless, the overall story of the *Convention* is not optimistic. Opened for ratification in 1990, it took 13 years to receive the 20 ratifications required to bring the Convention into force in July 2003. As of April 2013, there were only 46 states party to it, none of which are predominantly migrant receiving countries. In addition, the *Convention* has the effect of drawing a stark demarcation between documented and undocumented workers, thus re-emphasizing the paucity of rights entitlements for those working outside the parameters of migration law. For all of these reasons, the *Convention* stands as a beacon of what has not been achieved in the realm of rights (Pecoud and Guchteneire 2006; Dauvergne 2008, 19–28).

The inability to fully specify a constellation of rights that would alleviate the conditions of temporary migrant workers points us to the ideological elements of the rights discussion. Rights solutions can only ever be partially successful because the condition of temporary migrant work is anchored in a fundamental subordination. This subordination is partially expressed in Alexander Reilly's work, in that he queries whether an ethical outcome is possible in the absence of secure and equitable membership status (Reilly 2011). Casting concern about the condition of temporary migrant workers in the language of rights is valuable because it can lead to improvements in those rights, and to incremental change in conditions of living and working. It is impossible, however, within rights discourse, to erase the underlying subordination of temporary migrant workers. Talking in rights terms, inevitably calls up the 'right' of the state to exclude non-members as an aspect of sovereignty. This exclusion power undermines attempts to articulate rights claims for those with any type of temporary status, and reinforces a fundamental inequality between citizens and non-citizens.

Rights talk about temporary migrant workers is, therefore, imbued with what Purvis and Hunt termed the 'directionality' of ideology. It advantages some (the state, the nationals, national industry) over others (the temporary, the migrants). It cannot do otherwise without undoing the basic parameters of the conversation. The state right to exclude non-citizens is paramount; indeed, it is the cornerstone of all legal analysis of migration (*Canada (M.E.I.)* v. *Chiarelli* [1992] 1 S.C.R. 711). Similarly, the right of citizens to enter and remain in the territory of their nationality is almost the sole exception at international law to the right of states to close their borders. While migrant workers do acquire rights within their state of employment, they must first seek permission to simply 'be' there, at the most basic level. The fundamental condition of temporary migrant work is that this permission will expire.

Furthermore, and vitally, rights talk, with its underlying values of equality and legality, presents the subordinate position of the temporary migrant worker as (again in Purvis and Hunt's language) 'natural and inevitable'. In other words, it is perilously easy to assert that temporary migrant workers *should* have fewer rights than permanent workers or than citizens. Indeed, temporary migrant worker programmes begin from this supposition. While the idea that rights have limits is a familiar one within rights discourses, the tendency remains to assume the fairness of rights. This is particularly true with citizenship rights, and is the nub of Arendt's casting of citizenship as the 'right to have rights' (Arendt [1951] 1958) and of Shachar's (2009) playful casting of citizenship as the prize in the 'birthright lottery'. The debate about rights protections for temporary migrant workers cannot reach around itself to address its underlying premises. National rights debates provide an important and worthwhile challenge with which to engage. However, rights victories will be partial and contingent and will bump up against strong states' rights claims in this arena. Focusing *exclusively* on rights arguments, therefore, will detract from other work that addresses the question of subordination.

The ideological nature of rights for temporary migrant workers is especially vexed for advocates. Rights arguments are the principal tool within Western legal systems in fashioning arguments for individuals. In the international sphere, human rights have been the hallmark of emancipation. It is important to emphasize, therefore, that we are not asserting that rights arguments are bad for temporary migrant workers. Quite the contrary, they are important tools that we will keep using. Rights are neither false consciousness, nor a twenty-first century opiate for the masses. But even in their most idealized form and with perfect effectiveness, they can only ever offer up partial remedies for temporary migrant workers. Without a fundamental reconceptualization of temporary migrant work, they are the best political tool available. This hegemonic sway of rights discourse means that one of its further ideological functions is to distract from the underlying subordination of temporary migrant work. Because there are essential goals that can be achieved within rights frameworks, and because the argument beyond rights is so difficult, and so politically challenging, most advocacy goes no further than rights. This is already hard enough.

Arendt's analysis of the human condition offers insights that surpass her axiomatic right to have rights. With characteristic conceptual force, she contrasts citizenship not with non-citizenship, but with slavery. Her conceptualization could have been tailored to the condition of the temporary migrant worker. She states:

> The chief difference between slave labour and modern, free labour is not that the labourer possesses personal freedom – freedom of movement, economic activity, and personal inviolability – but that he is admitted to the political realm and full emancipated as a citizen.

Arendt's form of expression clearly locates rights – of movement, association and economic – as being of a different order than citizenship, and her reason for this ordering is because of the location of labour, within society, within history and within the human condition. Arendt continues in this same passage to equate free labourers in antiquity with 'resident aliens', arguing that ' ... the turning point in the history of labour came with the abolition of property qualifications for the right to vote' (Arendt [1958] 1998, 217).

Arendt's analysis of the consequences of the 'emancipation of the laboring classes' further develops a view of the ideological function of rights talk. Arendt contends that

> ... the emancipation of the laboring classes from oppression and exploitation certainly meant progress in the direction of non-violence. It is much less certain that it was also progress in the direction of freedom. No man-exerted violence, except the violence used in torture, can match the natural force which necessity itself compels. ([1958] 1998, 129)

Similarly, the rights struggle may serve to lessen specific instances of oppression and exploitation, but insofar as the main proxy for membership is the formulation of the worker as labour in a free market through an employment relationship, categorical inequality for the migrant worker is implied in the basic terms of the relationship. If we consider the likely factors determining a worker's departure to a foreign nation, we can readily substitute the Arendtian term 'necessity' for the term 'economic benefit' as a critical approach to unpacking the dominant ideology of temporary labour migration. If we see necessity as what drives the worker's choice to migrate, using Arendt's logic, existing social relations are reconstituted and entrenched under the auspices of a 'natural force' without recourse to violence or coercion. This is the essence of ideology's work.

6. Beyond ideology: lessons from Hannah Arendt

Current debate about how to expand temporary labour migration while avoiding the pitfall of the guest-worker programmes of the 1970s and 1980s is dominated by the concepts of temporariness, labour markets and workers' rights. The ideological function of these concepts limits challenge to the paradigm of temporary labour, and decreases the potential for avoiding past mistakes. In looking for a way forward, we can, paradoxically, turn back again to Arendt.

Perhaps the most significant change in the landscape for current temporary migrant labour programmes, in contrast to those of the recent past, is the progress of globalization. This too was foreseeable to Arendt in 1958, and, focusing precisely on what is unresolvable about temporary migrant worker programmes, she identified the failure of citizenship to move into a global realm as the most serious problem of globalization for the human condition:

> The decline of the European nation-state system; the economic and geographic shrinkage of the earth, so that prosperity and depression tend to become world-wide phenomena; the transformation of mankind, which until our own time was an abstract notion or a guiding principle for humanists only, into a really existing entity whose members at the most distant points of the globe need less time to meet than the members of a nation needed a generation ago – these mark the beginnings of the last state in this development. Just as the family and its property were replaced by class membership and national territory, so mankind now begins to nationally bound societies and the earth replaces the limited state territory. But whatever the future may bring, the process of world alienation, started by expropriation and characterized by an ever-increasing progress in wealth, can only assume even more radical proportions if it is permitted to follow its own inherent law. For men cannot become citizens of the world as they are citizens of their countries, and social men cannot own collectively as family and household men own their private property. (Arendt [1958] 1998, 257)

The evolution of temporary labour programmes in the half century since Arendt's analysis confirms her prescience.

The best example of the inability of citizenship to successfully 'migrate' to the global stage is seen in the expansion of the EU, and, in our work, in the labour migration consequences for the UK. While there is much talk, and some legal structure, behind the idea of European citizenship, what is in fact provided for in contemporary Europe is labour mobility. Workers and work seekers are free to move, others are not. The effect of this is the complete transformation of 'citizenship' into 'labour citizenship'. This has all the deleterious consequences Arendt foresaw: political participation is severed from citizenship; inequalities that limit labouring (for example, disability, racism, language skills) are removed from the realm of citizenship, impoverishing our understandings of equality; labour 'skill' is not only reified, but also becomes the basis of mobility and thus citizenship itself. The predominance of labour that Arendt railed against is perfected in this transformation: one's *existence* as citizen is contingent upon one's value as labourer. This equation hollows the idea of citizenship and deprives it of meaning. In the post-global UK, conditions of inequality and exploitation are expanding rather than contracting as the (comparative) expansion of borders for labour has facilitated the expansion of exploitive labour practices.

One can hardly conclude that globalization must be 'stopped' or 'wound back' and it is scarcely more realistic to suggest that temporary labour migration programmes be halted. What else might an inveterate optimist offer? Arendt's optimism is grounded in the human capacity both to permanently alter the world and to make the future different from the past. In temporary labour migration, we can begin this by recognizing that temporariness brings with it a fundamental inequality. Better policy pays attention to this, and seeks to make amends for it, rather than seeking simply to make it disappear, which is impossible. Unmasking inequality created through temporariness and through the tight focus on national labour markets is the place to begin remedying. Rights advocacy can continue to blunt the edges of exploitation, but is also vital to remember that this is all it can achieve. An increase in temporary labour migration is an increase in inequality. We should advocate to roll this back: to ensure trajectories to permanence are available to those confined to the least 'skilled' categories. It is probably the case that states themselves incur a liability to those who remain in a temporary status for too long; this is an appropriate corollary to the massive power to deport and exclude. Economic modelling of labour 'costs' can be made to cost the loss of rights to privacy, family, accommodation and association. That temporary labour migration can be made to look like a 'win-win-win' is a consequence of profound global inequalities. Our human capacity to both forgive and amend depends upon acknowledging responsibilities and shouldering them. Arendt saw this capacity as redemptive for the human condition. Her lesson bears repeating.

Note

1. We have made inquires about the 'level not stated' category but have not received a clear answer. It is most likely that these numbers represent work permits issued to people who are entitled to them because a family member, most likely their partner, has a work permit that is specifically classified.

References

Arendt, H. [1951] 1958. *The Origins of Totalitarianism*. New York: Meridian.

Arendt, H. [1958] 1998. *The Human Condition*. Chicago, IL: University of Chicago Press.

Australian Bureau of Statistics. 2010. "3416.0 – Perspectives on Migrants, 2009." Accessed May 4, 2010. http://www.abs.gov.au/AUSSTATS/abs@.nsf/Previousproducts/3416.0Main%20 Features52009?opendocument&tabname=Summary&prodno = 3416.0&issue = 2009&num = &view =

Bacon, D. 2008. *Illegal People: How Globalization Creates Migration and Criminalizes Immigrants*. Boston, MA: Beacon Press.

Basok, T. 2009. "Counter-Hegemonic Human Rights Discourses and Migrant Rights Activism in the U.S. and Canada." *International Journal of Comparative Sociology* 50 (2): 179–201.

Batalova, J. 2006. "The Growing Connection Between Temporary and Permanent Immigration Systems." *Migration Policy Institute Task Force Insight*, No. 14.

Brubaker, W. R., ed. 1989. *Immigration and the Politics of Citizenship in Europe and North America*. Lanham, MD: University Press of America.

Carens, J. 2008. "Live-in Domestics, Seasonal Workers, and Others Hard to Locate on the Map of Democracy." Special issue: Philosophy, Politics and Society. *Journal of Political Philosophy* 16 (4): 419–445.

Carens, J. 2010. *Immigrants and the Right to Stay*. Cambridge, MA: MIT Press.

Casciani, D. 2010. "Q&A: UK Immigration Cap." *BBC Online*. Accessed January 29, 2013. http://www.bbc.co.uk/news/10436228

Castles, S. 1986. "The Guest-Worker in Western Europe – An Obituary." *International Migration Review* 20: 761–778.

Castles, S. 2006. "Guestworkers in Europe: A Resurrection?" *International Migration Review* 40 (4): 741–766.

CIC (Citizenship and Immigration Canada). 2013a. "Facts and Figures 2012 – Immigration Overview: Permanent and Temporary Residents." Accessed February 17, 2014. http://www.cic.gc.ca/english/resources/statistics/facts2011/index.asp

CIC. 2013b. "Hiring Temporary Foreign Workers." http://www.cic.gc.ca/english/department/media/articles/tfw.asp

CIC. 2013c. "Labour Market Opinion Basics." Accessed May 29. http://www.cic.gc.ca/english/work/employers/lmo-basics.asp

Dauvergne, C. 2008. *Making People Illegal: What Globalization Means for Migration and Law.* Cambridge: Cambridge University Press.

DEEWR (Department of Education, Employment and Workplace Relations). 2010. "Approved Employers." Accessed January 29, 2011. http://www.deewr.gov.au/Employment/Programs/PSWPS/Pages/ApprovedEmployers.aspx

Department of Immigration and Citizenship. 2010. "New Permission to Work Arrangement for Student Visa Holders." Accessed January 29, 2010. http://www.immi.gov.au/students/_pdf/permission-to-work-students.pdf

Durand, J., Douglas S. Massey, and Emilio A. Parrado. 1999. "The New Era of Mexican Migration to the United States." Special issue: Rethinking History and the Nation-State: Mexico and the United States as a Case Study. *Journal of American History* 86 (2): 518–536.

Fudge, J., and F. MacPhail. 2009. "The Temporary Foreign Worker Program in Canada: Low-Skilled Workers as an Extreme Form of Flexible Labour." *Comparative Labor Law and Policy Journal* 31: 101–113.

GCIM (Global Commission on International Migration). 2005. *Migration in an Interconnected World: New Directions for Action.* Geneva: Global Commission on International Migration.

Guardian [UK]. 2010. "Migration: Cap Hope." Editorial and commentary. Accessed January 29, 2011. http://www.guardian.co.uk/commentisfree/2010/nov/24/immigration-cap-editorial

Held, D., A. McGrew, D. Goldblatt, and J. Perraton. 1999. *Global Transformations: Politics, Economics and Culture.* Cambridge: Polity Press.

Home Office. 2010. "Limit on Non-EU Workers." Accessed June 28, 2010. http://www.homeoffice.gov.uk/media-centre/news/immigration-limit11

IOM (International Organization of Migration). 2008. *World Migration 2008: Managing Labour Mobility in the Evolving Global Economy.* Geneva: International Organization of Migration.

Legomsky, S. 2009. "Portraits of the Undocumented Immigrant: A Dialogue." *Georgia Law Review* 44 (65): 65–160.

MacDermott, T., and B. Opeskin. 2010. "Pacific Seasonal Labour in Australia: Exploiting Opportunities or Exploiting Workers?" *Pacific Affairs* 83 (2): 283–305.

Marsden, S., and C. Dauvergne. 2013. "Beyond Numbers versus Rights: Shifting the Parameters of Debate on Temporary Labour Migration." *Journal of International Migration and Integration,* 1–12.

Martin, P. 2006. *Managing Labor Migration in the 21st Century.* New Haven, CT: Yale University Press.

Martin, P. L., and M. J. Miller. 1980. "Guestworkers: Lessons from Western Europe." *Industrial and Labor Relations Review* 33 (3): 315–330.

Minister for Immigration and Citizenship. 2010. "A Simpler Visa System." Accessed June 4, 2010. http://web.archive.org/web/20100813123147/http://www.minister.immi.gov.au/media/media-releases/2010/ce10046.htm

Nakache, D., and P. Kinoshita. 2010. *The Canadian Temporary Foreign Worker Program: Do Short-Term Economic Needs Prevail Over Human Rights Concerns?* Montreal: Institute for Research on Public Policy.

OECD (Organization for Economic Cooperation and Development). 2008. *Temporary Labour Migration: An Illusory Promise?* Paris: OECD.

Papademetriou, D., Doris Meissner, Marc R. Rosenblum, and Madeleine Sumption. 2009. *Aligning Temporary Immigration Visas with US Labor Market Needs: The Case for a New System of Provisional Visas.* Washington, DC: Migration Policy Institute.

Passel, J., and D. Cohn. 2010. "U.S. Unauthorized Immigration Flows are Down Sharply Since Mid-Decade." Accessed September 1. http://www.pewhispanic.org/2010/09/01/us-unauthorized-immigration-flows-are-down-sharply-since-mid-decade/

Pecoud, A., and P. Guchteneire. 2006. "Migration, Human Rights and the United Nations: An Investigation into the Obstacles to the UN Convention on Migrant Workers' Rights." *Windsor Yearbook of Access to Justice* 24: 241–266.

Preibisch, K. 2007. "Local Produce, Foreign Labor: Labor Mobility Programs and Global Trade Competitiveness in Canada." *Rural Sociology* 72 (3): 418–445.

Purvis, T., and A. Hunt. 1993. "Discourse, Ideology, Discourse, Ideology, Discourse, Ideology . . . ." *British Journal of Sociology* 44 (3): 473–499.

Reilly, A. 2011. "The Ethics of Seasonal Labour Migration." *Griffith Law Review* 20 (1): 127–152.

Rosewarne, S. 2010. "Globalisation and Commodification of Labour: Temporary Labour Migration." *Economic and Labour Relations Review* 20 (2): 99–110.

Rudolph, H. 1996. "The New Gastarbeiter System in Germany." *Journal of Ethnic and Migration Studies* 22 (2): 287–300.

Ruhs, M. 2005. "The Potential of Temporary Migration Programmes in Future International Migration Policy." Paper prepared for the Policy Analysis and Research Programme of the Global Commission on International Migration, Global Commission on International Migration, Geneva, September.

Ruhs, M., and Philip Martin. 2008. "Number vs. Rights: Trade-Offs and Migrant Worker Programs." *International Migration Review* 42 (1): 249–265.

Russo, R. 2012. "Solidarity Forever Canadians Never: SAWP Workers in Canada." PhD diss., University of British Columbia.

Shachar, A. 2009. *The Birthright Lottery: Citizenship and Global Inequality*. Cambridge, MA: Harvard University Press.

USCIS (United States Citizenship and Immigration Service). 2010. "Employer Information." Accessed August 8, 2010. http://www.uscis.gov/portal/site/uscis/menuitem.eb1d4c2a3e5b9ac 89243c6a7543f6d1a/?vgnextoid=ff1d83453d4a3210VgnVCM100000b92ca60aRCRD&vgnext channel = ff1d83453d4a3210VgnVCM100000b92ca60aRCRD

Vetrovec, S. 2007. "Circular Migration: The Way Forward in Global Policy." International Migration Institute (IMI) Working Papers, WP-07-04.

Zapata-Barrero, R., R. Faúndez Garcıa, and E. Sánchez-Montijano. 2012. "Circular Temporary Labour Migration: Reassessing Established Public Policies." *International Journal of Population Research* 2012: 1–13.

Index

For Product Safety Concerns and Information please contact our EU
representative GPSR@taylorandfrancis.com
Taylor & Francis Verlag GmbH, Kaufingerstraße 24, 80331 München, Germany

www.ingramcontent.com/pod-product-compliance
Lightning Source LLC
Chambersburg PA
CBHW081436270326
41932CB00019B/3222

* 9 7 8 1 1 3 8 0 5 7 9 8 2 *